Glimpses of Traditional Indian Life

Other Publications from Bhakti Vikas Trust

Books by His Holiness Bhakti Vikāsa Swami

A Beginner's Guide to Kṛṣṇa Consciousness

A Message to the Youth of India

Brahmacarya in Kṛṣṇa Consciousness

Jaya Śrīla Prabhupāda!

Lekha-mālā

Mothers and Masters

My Memories of Śrīla Prabhupāda

On Pilgrimage in Holy India

On Speaking Strongly in Śrīla Prabhupāda's Service

Patropadeśa (two volumes)

Rāmāyaṇa

Śrī Bhaktisiddhānta Vaibhava (three volumes)

Śrī Caitanya Mahāprabhu

Śrī Vaṁśīdāsa Bābājī

The Story of Rasikānanda

Gauḍīya Vaiṣṇava Padyāvalī (Bengali)

Vaiṣṇava Śikhā o Sādhana (Bengali)

Books by Other Authors

Śrī Cāṇakya-nīti (Patita Pāvana Dāsa Adhikārī)

Rethinking Darwin (Lalitānātha Dāsa)

Who is Supreme? (Gokula Candra Dāsa)

Viveka-śatakam (by Prabodhānanda Sarasvatī)

Glimpses of Traditional Indian Life

by

Bhakti Vikāsa Swami
and others

ISBN 978-93-82109-10-5

Previous Printings: 12,000 copies

Fourth Printing (2022): 40,000 copies

books.bvks.com

books@bvks.com

WhatsApp# +(91)-7016811202

The words *Conversation, Lecture, Letter,* and *purport* indicate quotations taken from published editions by or involving Śrīla Prabhupāda. *Conversation* subsumes all types of discussions with Śrīla Prabhupāda, variously classified by the Bhaktivedanta Archives as Morning Walks, Press Conferences, Room Conversations, etc. All such quotations are copyrighted by The Bhaktivedanta Book Trust International, Inc.

Published by Bhakti Vikas Trust, Surat, India

Printed in India

Dedicated

to those devotees
who have taken up
Śrīla Prabhupāda's instruction
to live simply on the land.

Contents

About the Author ix

Other Contributors x

Introduction xii

Village Life in Bangladesh 1

Recollections by Bhakti Vikāsa Swami

Growing Up in the Land of Jagannātha 82

An interview with Braja Hari Dāsa

Lokanātha Swami's Childhood Home 113

Excerpts from morning walks with Mahārāja

Arrows, Monkeys, and Mangoes 118

An interview with Narmadā Swami

Brought up in Devotion 171

An interview with R. Raṅganāthan

Respiritualize or Perish 215

An interview with Rasarāja Dāsa

The Procession: A Reminiscence 261

by Rasarāja Dāsa

Appendix 1: Relevant Quotes from Śrīla Prabhupāda 266

Appendix 2: A letter to TIME 282

Appendix 3: World Happiness Survey 283

Glossary 285

Sanskrit/Bengali Pronunciation Guide 295

The Author

Born in Britain in 1957, the author joined ISKCON (International Society for Krishna Consciousness) in London in 1975 and was initiated that year, with the name Ilāpati dāsa by the founder-*ācārya*, His Divine Grace A. C. Bhaktivedanta Swami Prabhupāda.

From 1977 to 1979 Ilāpati dāsa was based in India, mostly traveling in West Bengal distributing Śrīla Prabhupāda's books. He spent the following ten years helping to pioneer ISKCON's preaching in Bangladesh, Burma, Thailand, and Malaysia.

In 1989 he was granted the order of sannyāsa, receiving the name Bhakti Vikāsa Swami, and again made his base in India. Since then he has preached Kṛṣṇa consciousness throughout the subcontinent, lecturing in English, Hindi, and Bengali. He also spends a few months each year preaching in the West. His television lectures in Hindi have reached millions worldwide.

Bhakti Vikāsa Swami writes extensively on Kṛṣṇa conscious topics. His books have been translated into over twenty languages, with more than one million in print.

Additionally, he is involved in developing several *gurukulas* and also Vedic rural projects based on simple living and high thinking.

Other Contributors

Braja Hari Dāsa left home and joined ISKCON in 1984. For several years he led ISKCON Mumbai's outstanding book distribution department, before becoming involved in temple management. Since 1995 he has been managing ISKCON's famous temple at Juhu in Mumbai and is known for his dutifulness, humility, and calm manner of dealing with even the most difficult situations.

Lokanātha Swami needs no introduction to members of ISKCON. One of the first Indian devotees to remain steady within our society, Lokanātha Swami became globally known for initiating Pādayātras (walking festivals) in over 100 countries, and for organizing preparations for the Śrīla Prabhupāda Centennial. Lokanātha Swami continues to travel, preach, write, and lead the joyful *kīrtanas* he is famous for.

Narmadā Swami left his automobile business and grown-up family in 1976 at the age of 48 in search for the purpose of life. He joined ISKCON in 1981 and accepted *sannyāsa* in 1985. After many years of managerial service with the Bhaktivedanta Book Trust in Mumbai, he passed away in Kārtika 2006 in the sacred land of Vṛndāvana.

R. Raṅganāthan is from a traditional Śrī Vaiṣṇava family in South India and is now based in Dubai. In 1998, along with his wife and eldest daughter, he received Gauḍīya Vaiṣṇava initiation from Bhakti Vikāsa Swami and was named Raṅganātha Dāsa.

Rasarāja Dāsa (Ravi Gomatam, Ph.D.) is also of South Indian Vaiṣṇava lineage. After earning his M.E. in 1974 from the Birla Institute of Technology and Science in Rajasthan, he worked for Air India in Mumbai. In 1977 he emigrated to America and developed systems software for General Motors, Ford, and other major companies. After a short and superficial period of attraction to American life, Rasarāja became inspired by Śrīla Prabhupāda's books and joined ISKCON in 1980, rejecting an opportunity for a major career advancement. At present he is the international secretary of the Bhaktivedanta Institute, the academic and educational wing of ISKCON.

For his Ph.D. he did important work in the foundations of quantum mechanics, integrating the views of Einstein and Bohr. And in collaboration with the Birla Institute of Technology and Science, he initiated the world's first M.S./Ph.D. program in Consciousness Studies — a new, interdisciplinary area of study in modern science, involving such fields as neuroscience, artificial intelligence, quantum physics, molecular biology, and cognitive philosophy. Among his many publications is a co-edited volume of essays on science and religion, to which many eminent scholars, including six Nobel Laureates, have contributed. He has lectured across the globe on the spiritual teachings of the *Vedas* and topics connecting them to modern science.

Introduction

Sometime in 1993 in Dubai, while driving me back from an evening lecture program, my good friend Raṅganāthan started to tell me about his childhood in a traditional Śrī Vaiṣṇava village in South India.[1] Encouraged by my interest he went on talking even after we reached my apartment; and it was well after midnight when I finally got out of the car. I lay down to rest thinking about the pleasing life he had led, and how even now people could again live like that if they would simply agree to.

My memory wandered over the years I had spent in India and Bangladesh. In the course of preaching Kṛṣṇa consciousness, I had traveled throughout the Indian subcontinent and experienced the varieties of Hindu culture prominent in each area. Having stayed in the homes of many pious and cultured Hindus, I had gradually come to learn something about real culture. I thought of the many cultured persons I knew throughout the Indian subcontinent, living representatives of a dying way of life. I resolved to compose a book based on interviews with such people, to try to convey a feeling of what life in the old India was like, and what it could and should be like even now. I began contemplating how man had gone wrong in his quest for technological development, what traditional societies had possessed but we now lack, and what the actual criteria of civilization should be.

A principal goal of an enlightened culture is to elevate its members to their ultimate capacity. A truly advanced society

1. Śrī Vaiṣṇava — adherent of the bona fide Vaiṣṇava *sampradāya* that worships Kṛṣṇa in His majestic form as Nārāyaṇa.

strives not simply for the ephemeral requirements of eating, sleeping, mating, and defending, for even animals do that. Real human civilization begins with philosophical inquiry into the nature of God, the universe, and the ontological position of living beings. Therefore spiritually oriented civilizations throughout the world's history had practiced a realistic approach to life that catered to all aspects of the individual — physical, mental, intellectual, and spiritual — while stressing his responsibility to society at large. And as man has to live with and by nature's mercy, traditional land-based cultures stressed respect for all life and cooperation with her. The people of such cultures sought to extract from the earth only as much as needed, and to give back proportionately.

In traditional societies man fulfilled his needs in a simple and eco-friendly way. Material requirements were met without undue struggle. There were no industrial complexes producing endless varieties of unnecessary accessories to an artificial way of life; nor were there huge shopping plazas for touting unwanted goods; nor was there an advertising industry goading the masses to buy such things. The economic system was based on need, not greed. Trade was limited and mostly by barter — "I give you something you need, you give me something I need." There were no stocks, shares, market crashes, currency speculation, budget balancing, inflation, mass unemployment, or strikes.

Life's basic necessities — food, clothing, housing materials, and fuel — were available from the land. Cotton was spun at home. Every village would have a potter to make vessels for cooking. In larger villages a blacksmith would forge simple farming and cooking utensils, razors (one razor would last a lifetime), and other such items, using either non-locally produced or recycled metal. Rope and string were made locally from fibers of plants such as coconut, jute, and flax. Water was available from rivers, wells, and ponds. There was no need for waterworks, sewage systems, lavatories, or taps. Nor was there need of electricity, for people were accustomed to living without complex machines. Lamps burning home-produced vegetable oil supplied light. The heat of summer would be tolerated, with bamboo hand fans giving a little relief; winter would be met with extra blankets and wood fires. Medicines, cosmetics, and dyes were made at home from plants, rocks, and other natural ingredients. Furniture was not required, for people would sit, eat, cook, study, and sleep on the floor.

Those leading such pristine lives tended to be innocent and unpretentious. They didn't have strong negative emotions. Bitterness, depression, and the like were practically unknown. People tended to be satisfied with what they had, and considered advancement not in terms of surrounding oneself with material possessions, but in becoming detached from such objects. Life based on these values was simple, sensible, and pleasing, and tended to foster laudable qualities such as honesty, respect for others, and kindness.

Of course, rural living does not automatically bring peace of mind and spiritual wisdom. Some villagers are little more spiritually enlightened than the dogs and buffaloes that they live among. And city dwellers who try to "get away from it all" by moving to the country often merely bring their passion and problems with them. This material world being intrinsically miserable, true happiness lies in God realization, which transcends both the excessive sensuality of city life and the complacent tranquility of the country. For either in town or village, human life without endeavor for God consciousness is little better than that of the animals. Nevertheless, simple agrarian life is more conducive to God realization than the complex urban society of today. For those with eyes to see it, everything in nature speaks of God. Therefore sages traditionally preferred to live far from the hubbub of urban life. Breathing fresh air and drinking pure water, they could peacefully meditate upon God as the cause and upholder of nature.

Unfortunately, industrialized man has strayed far from such innocent existence. Modern city life is highly artificial, being far removed from its source of sustenance. Even if of theistic bent, city dwellers tend to have very little knowledge of the relationship between God, nature, and man. They think that food comes from a shop, light from a switch, and health from a pill. Multinational corporations rape Mother Earth, exploit her resources, entice people to hellish factories, and sell all kinds of junk to them. Industrialization and consumerism engender selfishness, ignorance, and gross materialism. Secular education teaches man to consider himself master of his own destiny, and nature a beast to be hacked and tortured into submission as an adjunct to "progress."

For all their advancement and economic development, modern townsfolk cannot get even fresh food, what to speak of peace and contentment. The millionaire living in his posh apartment with all modern amenities cannot get even fresh vegetables, a staple of the poor villager. In modern cities potable water must be purchased because the tap water is repeatedly recycled sewage mixed with chemicals; nor does bottled mineral water have vigor or taste comparable to that of fresh river or well water.

People in big cities drive out to the country on weekends just to breathe some fresh air, whereas in the village *air* means fresh air. What a nasty civilization — that crowds people into unhealthy, crime-ridden cities, has them work in horrible conditions, and provides them poisonous air and food.

Because city dwellers don't have to walk very much, carry water, or labor in fields, they tend to look down upon villagers as backward and primitive. But for all their modern conveniences, city folk must exercise artificially or else develop conditions like diabetes, hypertension, heart disease, arthritis, constipation, and so on.

Such artificial living makes for artificial people, who may smile superficially but are hollow within. The modern city dweller is constantly over-stimulated with a bombardment of information, advertisements, and so-called entertainment. But his heart remains spiritually and emotionally empty. Although modern man can hardly envisage life without cars, computers, television, and innumerable other diversions, this plethora of gadgets is a meager substitute for peace of mind.

Most villagers in the Third World still rise early, work the land, and hardly ever travel far from home. Despite their apparent poverty, they are often more content than those who have more money than necessary. Villagers tend to be better mentally balanced than those who live life "in the fast lane," divorced from the simple pleasures of stable family life and mutual sharing.

But village life throughout the world is under threat of extinction, as the demands of consumer society are fast standardizing the planet into one vast urbanized megacomplex. Traditional cultures and values are being destroyed and people being reduced to screws in a massive economic machine. The charm has even been extracted from agriculture — now it is "agribusiness." Sanity has all but been civilized out of existence.

Modern life is a ridiculously over-hyped grovel for sense gratification. Although the mindless pursuit of wealth, luxury, power, and sex have never brought satisfaction to anyone, nonetheless lust and greed are promoted as desirable — indeed indispensable — to modern man. There is constant pressure to adopt the foolish ideals imposed by the entertainment and advertising industries. Consciously or unconsciously people try to cut profiles shaped in movie studios. Too busy trying to be someone else, they remain ignorant of their own identity. Anxious to "get ahead" by any means, they nonetheless have no knowledge of what really lies ahead.

In *Bhagavad-gītā* Lord Kṛṣṇa describes lust, anger, and greed as gateways to hell. Of course modern men don't like to believe in hell, despite busily creating it on earth. Their habits are unregulated, imbalanced, unhealthy, and sinful;

their bellies filled with junk food and animal corpses; their values perverted. They cannot trust even their spouses, children, or parents. They're proud of their big buildings, big highways, big economy, and big universities, but their minds are so agitated that they cannot sleep without the aid of a sleeping pill. The "advancement" of which they are so proud is simply a ploy to make them work like beasts for the sake of sense enjoyment. Gorging on flesh, becoming intoxicated, living in a fantasy world of sex, violence, and myriad nonsensical diversions — all this is considered normal to modern "civilized" man. Psychosis, neurosis, crime, violence, divorce, homosexuality, threat of nuclear holocaust — are all part of everyday life.

Genuine spiritual culture, or the search for God, is almost completely absent in modern society. The materialistic worldview is so deeply embedded that cultivation of transcendental knowledge is not only not encouraged but is hardly even thought about, not even by leading intellectuals. The slaughter of millions of animals is considered so normal and acceptable that it continues year after year without protest. Governments not only sanction but support divorce, contraception, abortion, and homosexuality. Our godless society is so fallen in every aspect that many books could be written describing its moral decrepitude. But one word succinctly describes it all: *insanity*.

As noted by Sir Arnold Toynbee, the late British historian: "The cause of [the world's malady] is spiritual. We are suffering from having sold our souls to the pursuit of an objective which is both spiritually wrong and practically unattainable. We have to reconsider our objective and change it, and until we do this, we shall not have peace either amongst ourselves or within each of us."[2]

Much has been discussed about the harm man has inflicted upon himself and other living beings in the name of progress. The more enlightened victims-cum-participants in this catastrophe are looking for solutions to the enormous mess man has landed himself and the planet in. Traditional societies and values, once rejected as primitive and useless, are again being reexamined, at least by some.

People talk of going back to nature, not knowing that most of the world never left it. For instance, if someone were to drive a bullock cart into a city or town in America, he would undoubtedly be featured in the local newspaper; and he would almost certainly need police permission to bring bulls into an urban area. Yet in most parts of India bull-power is still as common as that nasty, noisy, only-seemingly-better replacement called the tractor.

The original culture of India is based on Vedic wisdom, subsuming a vast body of knowledge covering all manner of subjects from astronomy and mathematics to architecture, economics, and even the enlightened application of warfare and sex. Vedic culture is based on profound metaphysical philosophy, its essence being the quest for freedom from birth and death, culminating in highly developed love of God. In India religion was never compartmentalized as merely one aspect of life. It was life. And everything within life was ultimately directed toward a transcendental goal. Although other parts of the world are not without religious

2. From an article that appeared in the London *Observer,* October 1972.

ethos, the degree to which it has been developed in India is outstanding.

Unfortunately, over the past few centuries the Vedic legacy has been infiltrated by many non-Vedic ideas. Gradually the original Vedic culture has been modified, diluted, and contaminated in various ways, to become what is now known as Hinduism.

Still, whatever real culture remains in India is valuable and worth learning from. For even today bits and pieces of traditional India still survive. Behold the Saurashtrian cowherd leaning on his elaborately carved stick, his feet adorned with curled-up, ornately designed shoes, his face with a similarly curling mustache, and his head covered with fifty meters of ribboned white cloth, intricately wrapped as a huge turban.[3] And see his son calling each cow of his herd by name and playing a flute to gather them. Meet a small band of pilgrims on perhaps a thousand-kilometer journey to visit places of God, singing *bhajanas* as they walk, taking provisions from pious people along the way, and stopping at midday to cook chapatis on a fire made from twigs and leaves. Note groups of village women walking several kilometers to the nearest well or river — their brass water pots stacked one atop another on their heads, their colorful clothing reflecting the early morning sun, their thick silver anklets just visible under their *sārīs* and their bracelets jostling as they march along singing to Kṛṣṇa with childish simplicity.

---

3. Saurashtra — an area of Gujarat where many members of an ancient cowherd community still adhere to their traditions.

Yet the essence of Indian culture goes far deeper even than these charming external manifestations. It is based on a subtle spiritual philosophy impenetrable by those not prepared to enter into its intricacies. And the difficulty in comprehension is compounded by negative propaganda inflicted for over two hundred years by Western scholars upon Indian culture and religion.[4]

Europeans attempted to justify their forceful domination of India, which they dubbed "civilizing the natives," by labeling her great heritage as superstition. An example is found in *Hindu Manners, Customs, and Ceremonies,* by Abbe Dubois, a French missionary who lived in South India in the late eighteenth and early nineteenth centuries. Dubois minutely observed and recorded the intricacies of life in India, and his 770-page volume is so interesting that it is still in print. However, Dubois was a bigot who saw only with the eye and not the heart. Although he mixed intimately with the local inhabitants, inwardly he held them in utter disdain and considered that the sole hope for their improvement lay not merely in conversion to Christianity but in wholesale Westernization and rejection of their tradition.

Stalwart Christian that he was, Dubois hardly could have foreseen Western man's becoming more heathen than the pagans he sought to civilize. Yet Western man is no less enthusiastic to benevolently impose upon the uncivilized peoples his latest fetish: science and technology.

---

4. For a summary of the British attitude, see "The First Indologists," a chapter of *Elements of Vedic Thought and Culture,* by Satsvarūpa dāsa Gosvāmī.

Until recently it was widely believed that scientific progress would usher in paradise. A book published in 1965 by the United States Information Service declared: "In the short space since she won independence, India has taken huge strides toward assuring the blessings of modern life for her citizens. In health, education, industry, and development, India is forging ahead. The changes are coming and will come to India's villages too — not to destroy the peace and dignity of rural life, but to enhance it with more security, more of the good things of the world. Change is beginning to come. In the villages, hope shines through."

But nowadays at least some in the West are realizing the mistake of foisting their economy and values on the so-called underdeveloped world. As man gropes for alternatives to soul-killing "civilization," the significance of Indian culture is emerging from under the very muck which the West sought to bury it in, for Westerners themselves are taking leading roles in promoting this oldest of human civilizations.

Śrīla A. C. Bhaktivedanta Swami Prabhupāda, the founder-*ācārya* of ISKCON and the greatest exponent of Vedic culture in the modern age, was keenly aware of discrepancies in human society and strove to establish Vedic culture as a blueprint for reviving spiritual values throughout the world:

> Vedic culture is perfect for human society, perfect culture. You have to adopt it. Then you become happy. The whole human society becomes happy, never mind where it is. It is a science, how to live just like human beings, not like cats and dogs. That is Vedic culture.

Everyone is happy. Still, those who are following Vedic principles, they are more happy than others.

Because it is the society of *śūdras* everywhere, there is confusion. No brain. Simply want, want, want, want, want. And in brahminical culture, you will find even a very poor *brāhmaṇa* — no source of income, no fixation of foodstuff even — he is happy. He is happy by his knowledge. He'll satisfy himself. If he does not get his food, then he will think that, "This day Kṛṣṇa desired that I should not have my food. Oh, it is Kṛṣṇa's pleasure. It is Kṛṣṇa's mercy."[5]

We are just trying to introduce the real civilization. Actually there is no civilization at the present moment. They are simply cats and dogs fighting one another. This is not civilization. Atheists and demons are predominating. And because they have got big, big skyscraper buildings and many motorcars, India has become victimized: "Oh, without this motorcar and without this skyscraper building, we are condemned." So they are trying to imitate. They have forgotten their own culture, the best culture, Vedic culture. So this is the first time that we are trying to conquer over the demonic culture with this Vedic culture. This is the first time. So it is very pleasing that you have joined this movement. If you want to make the human society happy, give them this culture of Kṛṣṇa consciousness.[6]

---

5. From a conversation with Śrīla Prabhupāda, 21 September 1973.

6. From a *Śrīmad-Bhāgavatam* lecture by Śrīla Prabhupāda, 28 February 1976.

During my travels in India I was often amazed at the naturally aristocratic deportment of many families I stayed with. Having been raised an uncouth *mleccha,* I sometimes felt embarrassed to be among such elevated people, especially since they respected and served us as sādhus. They were unaffectedly well-behaved and cultured, yet humble, without artificial sophistication or snobbishness. Their family life was ordered and content to a degree I had never seen in the West. For example, Indian children obeyed their parents without question. I have several times been the guest of prosperous businessmen whose adult children were unhesitatingly and ungrudgingly obedient to them.

Occasionally I would visit a Sanskrit professor who had mentored thousands of students during his long career. Although widely known and highly respected throughout Orissa, he would insist on bowing down before me, despite my attempts to stop him. And he would try to stop me from returning his obeisances, although he was clearly pleased that I had imbibed the impulse to do so. My family background and previous activities were low class and abominable, especially compared to his. I could speak but a few words of Sanskrit and was young enough to be his son, yet he saw the positive: "Whatever his past may be, he is a *sannyāsī* and therefore worshipable. He has renounced all prospects of material enjoyment to serve Śrī Hari. For all my learning, I am a householder bound within the material world. I must bow down."

Moving among such people gave me an inside perspective on Indian civilization and brought it to life for me. Indian culture was no longer merely theoretical — quaint and antiquated customs to be read in a book meant only for anthropologists or the wistful. I came to develop an appreciation for the value of true human culture, and to understand that without it even the high philosophical ideals I was professing and practicing were incomplete.

The glimpses presented herein are of life as it was not so long ago, in the India before modernization. We find a more or less contented populace with no serious social or psychological problems. Life was conducted basically as it had been for thousands of years previously. And most importantly, at the base of its moral codes, family ideals, and educational values, we find a society with knowledge of God and the soul.

This book is meant to share experiences and realizations of Indian culture, especially with persons who have little opportunity to familiarize themselves with it first-hand. *Glimpses of Traditional Indian Life* is not an attempt to comprehensively analyze Indian cultural life, nor to suggest how it could be revived in the much-changed circumstances of today. It is meant to give an impression of life as it was, with the hope that it may help to inspire a revival of Vedic culture in a milieu dangerously devoid of values. Although writing about Vedic lifestyle is a significantly lesser task than implementing it throughout the world, it is nevertheless an important first step toward creating awareness of it.

Śrīla Prabhupāda often stressed that all necessities of life can be procured from the land. He wanted ideal farming communities established across the globe. Such communities would have Kṛṣṇa consciousness as their basis; dependence on land, cows, and Kṛṣṇa as their sustenance; simple living and high thinking as their motto; and Vedic culture as their way of life. *Glimpses of Traditional Indian Life* may give vision and direction to the founding fathers of such communities. And to those searching amidst the kaleidoscope of alternative lifestyles, it may provide orientation toward a way of life that has endured through time.

Furthermore it is hoped that this work will enlighten its Indian readers as to the value and depth of their own culture and inspire them to return to its roots rather than foolishly aping the West. Yet *Glimpses* may also appeal to sociologists, anthropologists, or anyone interested in broadening his knowledge of humankind.

The first section of *Glimpses* is based on personal recollections of the several years I spent in West Bengal and Bangladesh; the rest is comprised of interviews with initiated members of ISKCON who were brought up in traditional ways in different parts of India. A picture emerges of a rich and deeply religious culture with many features common throughout the subcontinent yet also with abundant regional variations. And while some points are repeated, each narrative reflects the interviewee's unique vision and realization.

Although several terms and concepts discussed herein will be unfamiliar to some readers, I have not endeavored to explain each and every point in detail. For instance, an attempt to define "Śrī Vaiṣṇava" could be the subject of a doctoral thesis. As anthropologists concur, to really understand a culture one must live within it. Nonetheless readers of this book should be able to get some feeling of what life was like in traditional India.

Many words from Indian culture used herein have now entered the English language and are listed in standard dictionaries; non-English and technical terms are explained in the Glossary. Some words from Sanskrit and vernacular Indian languages have been rendered with diacritical marks, a guide to which is provided at the end of the book. To retain their original flavor, conversations conducted in that curious dialect known as "Indian English" are mostly left unedited.

I plan to follow this publication with *Vaiṣṇava Culture, Etiquette, and Behavior* — a large work giving extensive guidance to devotees; and other books, such as *Family Life in Kṛṣṇa Consciousness,* that will similarly combine Śrīla Prabhupāda's directions with practical observations of Vedic culture at work. I pray to the Supreme Lord Śrī Kṛṣṇa Caitanya Mahāprabhu to guide my thoughts, and to all Vaiṣṇavas present and future that they may appreciate this endeavor and find it helpful in their lives.[7]

Thanks are due to Nanda Kumāra Dāsa and Śobha Rādhikā Dāsī for transcription of interviews, to the interviewees for offering their time and realizations, to Jagat Puruṣa Dāsa for

7. Śrī Kṛṣṇa Caitanya Mahāprabhu — the form of Kṛṣṇa who descended 500 years ago to distribute the highest love of God by the process of chanting His holy names.

editing, and to the many devotees whose collective financial contributions went toward the publication of this book.

Many thanks also to Guru-kṛṣṇa Dāsa for editing this revised edition, as also to Gaṅgā Devī Dāsī for proofreading and further editing suggestions and to Rasika Śekhara Dāsa for the new cover design.

Village Life in Bangladesh

A Personal Recollection

Bhakti Vikāsa Swami shares his memories of rural Bangladesh. He describes a way of life close to the original Vedic culture. This sublime culture, being inherently religious and in harmony with nature, helps the villagers to live happily despite their many hardships.

Prologue

I first went to Bangladesh in 1979 as a member of the ISKCON worldwide preaching mission. I stayed there, at first continuously and then intermittently, for about seven years and traveled extensively throughout the country. While preaching there I endured physical hardships and repeated sickness. But even more difficult for me was adjusting to a culture quite different to that in which I was raised.

My British forefathers had sailed forth to India to "civilize" the natives and bathe them in the blood of Jesus. The British conquered, ruled, and ultimately retreated. And now I was coming, having been conquered by Indian culture — specifically Gauḍīya Vaiṣṇavism, the religion of the Bengalis.[8] But although I had adopted the practices and philosophy of Kṛṣṇa consciousness, my outlook on life was still very British. I considered "my own" culture the best, not recognizing that other people have different values that also may be valid. It took me some time to accept that my ethnocentricity was simply a form of false pride. The process of adjustment was sometimes painful. I had to reevaluate my conceptions of right and wrong and of proper and improper behavior. Ultimately I came to accept that the way Bengali people act and think is not inferior or wrong just because it is different.

Quoting the renowned Bengali poet Michael Madhusūdana Datta, Śrīla Prabhupāda once told Prabhāviṣṇu Swami, under whom I served in Bangladesh, that he should preach in Bangladesh with the courage of an Englishman and

---

8. Although the names Bengal/Bangladesh and Bengali/Bangladeshi have been used almost interchangeably in this essay, the distinction should be understood. Bengal is now politically divided into West Bengal, a state of India; and Bangladesh, East Bengal, now an independent nation. Thus all Bangladeshis, except a few minorities, are Bengalis, but not all Bengalis are Bangladeshis.

Gauḍīya Vaiṣṇavism is the sect of Vaiṣṇavism founded by Caitanya Mahāprabhu and now spread all over the world in the form of the Hare Kṛṣṇa movement.

The culture of the Gauḍīya Vaiṣṇavas in Bangladesh and West Bengal is practically identical. But one major difference is that Gauḍīya Vaiṣṇavism is the predominating culture of Bangladeshi Hindus, whereas in West Bengal the same culture is prominent but not predominating.

the heart of a Bengali mother.[9] I found the part about being like a Bengali mother difficult. With Anglo-Saxon brusqueness, I considered Bengalis to be overly sentimental, inefficient, and devious in their dealings. A plethora of customs and rituals, and what I perceived as superstitions and fetishes, seemed to govern every aspect of their lives. This apparent foolishness was repulsive to the mundane rationalist deep-seated in my psyche, who I didn't even know was there. Only gradually did I stop seeing apparent faults and come to understand what a great culture I was living in. By closely associating with Bangladeshis for several years, I came to appreciate that their outward poverty and lack of sophistication belies an inner richness that cannot be acquired by any amount of modern conveniences or university degrees.

As I came to understand the meaning and utility of Bengali ways, I accepted and embraced them wholeheartedly. Considering that the Kṛṣṇa consciousness movement is endeavoring to spread Gauḍīya Vaiṣṇava culture throughout the world, I realized how fortunate I was to be one of the few Western devotees to learn about it firsthand.

I have visited many holy places and met many cultured, learned, and saintly individuals, but as a people, Bangladeshi Hindus are closest to the original Vaiṣṇava culture. And they observe the customs and etiquette of Vaiṣṇavism not with ritualistic drudgery, but with joy and verve. Bengalis take pleasure in receiving guests, offering obeisances to

9. From a conversation with Śrīla Prabhupāda, 10 August 1977.

superiors, and so on.[10] Such pleasing behavior, combined with genuine affection for others, is at the heart of Gauḍīya Vaiṣṇavism. Indeed, when this synthesis of proper conduct and natural love is focused on Kṛṣṇa, that is the perfection of life.

Bengal is especially significant because Śrī Caitanya Mahāprabhu, the founder of the Hare Kṛṣṇa movement, appeared there 500 years ago and naturally spoke and preached in the native language and acted mostly according to local customs. Thus Caitanya Mahāprabhu's branch of Vaiṣṇavism is an intrinsic part of Bengali culture, and much of the literature of the Gauḍīya Vaiṣṇavas is in Bengali. Indeed practically all great Gauḍīya Vaiṣṇava *ācāryas* appeared in Bengal, the most recent and prominent being the founder-*ācārya* of the International Society for Kṛṣṇa Consciousness, His Divine Grace A. C. Bhaktivedanta Swami Prabhupāda.

Of course not all Bangladeshis are highly advanced Vaiṣṇavas; most are Muslims. Yet even Muslim culture is strongly influenced by Gauḍīya Vaiṣṇavism. Although Vaiṣṇavism in Bengal is much influenced by *sahajiyā*-ism and other misleading doctrines, the basic Vaiṣṇava way of life is still intact.[11] Therefore, although I appreciated

10. In Vaiṣṇava culture, obeisances are offered either by kneeling and touching the head to the floor, or (indicative of even more respect) prostrating the whole body, head down, on the floor.

11. *Sahajiyā*-ism refers both to a specific deviatory branch of Vaiṣṇavism and to the many sub-cults similar to it (*Sahaja* — easy). *Sahajiyās* advocate that the path of spiritual realization is so easy that rigid scriptural rules are not necessary. *Sahajiyā*-ism is typified by esoteric emotional expression, and perversion of basic

A group of Śrī Vaiṣṇavas with their guru (circa 1900).

A potter bringing his wares to market (Bengal).

A public ferry on the Gaṅgā at Navadvip, West Bengal.

Working a handloom (Bengal).

A village woman taking the stones out of *dāl* on the veranda of her thatched mud home. Note the cow dung patties in the foreground (Orissa).

A pukur (pond) and thatched house typical of Bengali villages.

In the bazaar (Bengal).

A group of Bengali villagers.

Cooking rice outdoors on a mud stove (Bengal).

Manipuri devotees performing *kīrtana*.

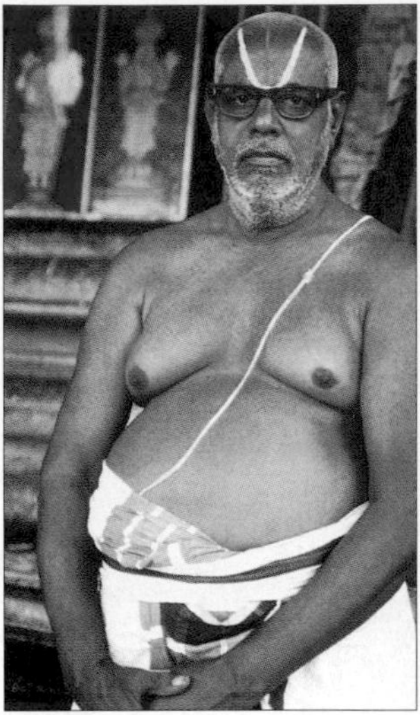

A Śrī Vaiṣṇava *brāhmaṇa*.

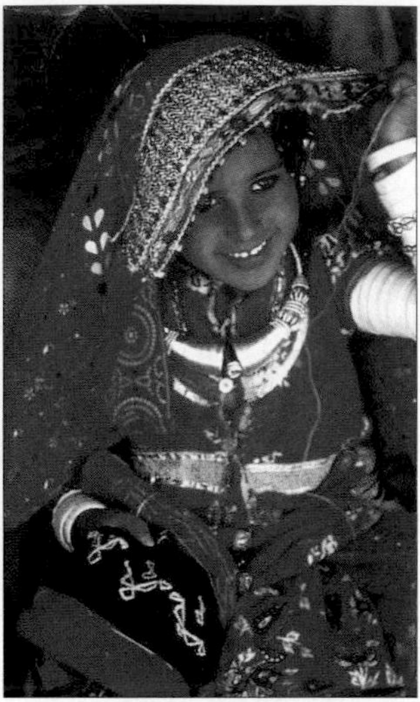

A young girl from the Kutch district of Gujarat.

Fetching water (Gujarat).

Building a bamboo bridge (Bengal).

Ploughing fields in the monsoon. In the background, rice is transplanted under the shelter of bamboo capes (South India).

whatever culture remains in other parts of the subcontinent, I concluded that Bangladesh is the best place to get direct experience of traditional Gauḍīya Vaiṣṇavism.

Nevertheless life in Bengal is difficult; thus eventually I felt an urge to move on. But in hindsight I realize how much I learned during my years in Bengal about life, people, and culture. Living in Bangladesh changed my outlook on life almost as deeply as did my initial coming to Kṛṣṇa consciousness. My experiences in Bangladesh took me to a new phase of awareness, that Kṛṣṇa consciousness is more than a philosophy, belief, or even a religion — but a complete way of life.

Foreigners in the Villages

When we first went to Bangladesh, the Hindus there were influenced by propaganda that Hinduism is a dying religion and the world is converting to Islam. Bengalis are naturally open-hearted, extroverted, and excitable people. So wherever our Western devotees went in Bangladesh, local Hindus would accord ecstatic receptions for these foreigners who had adopted the practice of Vaiṣṇavism.

Often an entire village would turn out to greet us with a *kīrtana* procession and a profusion of flowers. They would smear sandalwood paste on our foreheads — a sign of respect offered to honorable persons — decorate us with flower garlands, and throw flowers at our feet or over our

scriptural truths. For instance, the scriptural injunction that one should serve the guru has been distorted by a class of men claiming guru-ship on the basis of birth alone, and thus living comfortably at the expense of others.

heads. The ladies would reverberate *ulu-ulu* by moving the tongue against the palate to make a loud sound that is considered auspicious.

People expected to have an opportunity to touch our feet and take dust from our soles, to touch to their heads and tongues. We sometimes found ourselves in the midst of a frenzy of people eager to get at us. After every man, woman, and child in the village had touched our feet, a foot-washing ceremony would then be conducted. It was embarrassing because we ourselves were fresh out of *māyā*. We certainly felt unworthy of such worshipful treatment, but there was no way to avoid it. The simple village people were anxious not just to see us, but to venerate us as their honored guests. They considered that we, having given up the opulence of the West to come to remind them of their own culture and religion, must be highly advanced souls. They would tell us that their homes, villages, and very lives had been purified by our presence.

We held festivals in the evenings — long functions of *kīrtanas* and lectures with a movie show and sometimes dramas. The local people would eagerly help to erect a stage with bamboo and wooden planks, from which we would show *Bhagavad-gītā* in English, holding it up for them to see; then *Bhagavad-gītā* in German, French, and Spanish. As we continued showing the Gītā in more than thirty languages, the people would start murmuring in increasing amazement. Last of all we would show the Arabic *Gītā,* which would cause a hubbub because Bangladesh is dominated by Muslims. After the program many people would demand to see the Arabic *Gītā* up close, to verify that it really existed.

Every night we would show the movie of ISKCON activities around the world, and whenever the scene of frying puris in a large pan of ghee came, the crowd would inevitably gasp and murmur. Ghee was a luxury; they could not imagine having gallons of it for deep frying.

The programs would almost invariably start late and often continue throughout the night. In Bangladesh there really is no concept of starting anything on time. When we would ask what time our program should begin, we'd be told, "Toward evening" or "After everyone has come," as if it were obvious. In Bengal the time to begin a function is when everybody has arrived and settled comfortably. However much we tried for a fixed time, the program would begin only when everyone was present and ready. But after everyone had come no one was in a hurry to leave. They quite expected to stay up all night if there was something religious and entertaining going on.

People came to know about our programs by word of mouth. News traveled from village to village, and folks would gradually come after finishing their day's work. Sizable crowds would come, at least a few hundred people every night. Bigger functions that were arranged in advance would draw thousands of people, who would walk up to twenty kilometers to attend. For special occasions like these, women would dress in their best sārīs and ornaments and maybe a little make-up — nothing extravagant. Being simple villagers, they dressed according to their means.

All the village dignitaries would one-by-one express appreciation of the Kṛṣṇa consciousness movement's being spread all over the world. Overriding our protests they would ridiculously overpraise us. Despite my regularly urging him not to, a student of Dhaka University who traveled with me for some time would introduce me as a double Ph.D. from Oxford University even though I never attended any university. The local speakers would refer to us as *paramahaṁsas, mahā-bhāgavatas,* and other exaggerated epithets.[12] They often liked to speak a little philosophy also, which was sometimes good in that most Hindus in Bangladesh have at least rudimentary knowledge of Gauḍīya Vaiṣṇava teachings — for instance, that Caitanya Mahāprabhu came to save the fallen souls of Kali-yuga by spreading the holy name. But not so good was when they would include their own speculative ideas.

For many of the Bangladeshi Hindus, having Western sādhus appear in their tranquil pastoral homes was the most amazing and memorable thing that had ever happened in their lives. No Westerners had ever come to their villages before, but now here they were — as devotees of Kṛṣṇa! We foreigners were chanting Hare Kṛṣṇa, their religion; wearing dhotīs, their dress; eating rice and *dāl,* their food; eating with our hands, as they did; and sitting on the floor with them.

In the mornings many people would be waiting to talk to us individually. They were fascinated to see how we applied *tilaka,* performed *ārati,* chanted the names of Kṛṣṇa on beads, and held classes in which we quoted from

---

12. *Paramahaṁsa* and *mahā-bhāgavata* are terms used to denote topmost devotees.

Sanskrit and Bengali scriptures.[13] We spoke to them in Bengali, exhorting them to preserve their traditions and assuring them that Vaiṣṇavism was better than the affluent decadence of the West. Our hosts were deeply pleased and had no reservations about expressing that to us.

Persons who ate simple foods and could barely afford more would stretch themselves beyond their means to cook a wonderful *prasāda* feast and serve it to us with affection. They would bring out a tiny bottle of homemade ghee (their entire accumulated stock) to sprinkle on the rice and add to the already delicious flavors.

I began to understand what Śrīla Prabhupāda meant by "Bengali mother." The elderly women would encourage us to eat more and more, well beyond our capacity. *Gala parjonto,* they would say: "Up to the neck!" They would keep refilling our plates, just to make sure that there were plenty of remnants left to distribute to the eager villagers.

Sometimes the enthusiasm of our hosts would be overwhelming. All wanted to feed us and have us visit their homes to bless them, and all expected us to engage in personal conversation with them. Indeed they were quite insistent, which put a strain on our lives — and digestion. But that was richly compensated by the natural pleasure and beautiful *kīrtanas* with which people received us, and the joyful mood that prevailed wherever we went. We were getting a glimpse of how it would be if the whole world were Kṛṣṇa conscious.

---

13. Throughout this book, the term *scripture* is used to denote *śāstra,* i.e. the original Vedic scriptures and later derivative scriptures that uphold the same teachings.

East and West Bengal

Bengal has traditionally been divided into East and West. This is partly because East Bengal has always been somewhat isolated and inaccessible, being a land of many rivers and, previously, of many jungles. In *Śrī Caitanya-caritāmṛta* East Bengal is referred to as Baṅga, and West Bengal as Gauḍa. East Bengal is presently Bangladesh, and the western part of Bengal is the state of West Bengal, India.

Although East and West Bengal share the same language and culture, they have always been somewhat different. But that difference was accentuated by Bengal's division into West Bengal and Bangladesh, on the plea that the Muslim populace of East Bengal was sufficient to demand a separate state, although when India was partitioned in 1947 the Muslim population of East Bengal was only slightly greater than that of Hindus. Despite constant migration from East Bengal to India since then, Bangladesh still has a sizable Hindu population, the highest of any nation other than India.

Historically Hindus in West Bengal have been more inclined toward the śākta cult, but in Bangladesh almost all Hindus follow Śrī Caitanya Mahāprabhu's *saṅkīrtana* movement, the Vaiṣṇava religion of worshiping Gaura-Nitāi and Rādhā-Kṛṣṇa with *mṛdaṅgas* and *karatālas*. Traditionally West Bengal has been known for fine culture, East Bengal for folk culture. Although Dhaka, East Bengal's capital, was previously known for high culture, most of the province was considered rustic. In *Caitanya-bhāgavata* it is recorded that in His youth Caitanya Mahāprabhu would joke with His friends about the accent of the East Bengalis and would imitate it. Even today West Bengalis tend to look down on East Bengalis as being somewhat homespun and artless.

Bangladeshis are overall more respectful, hospitable, friendly, and happy than their kinsfolk in West Bengal, as is immediately noticeable when crossing the border. Industrialization and urbanization as well as communism, with its atheistic and rebellious overtones, have done much to change the attitude of West Bengalis and erode their highly developed original culture. Yet in Bangladesh traditional culture is still the way of life. It has not yet been engulfed by the worldwide cultural takeover initiated by Western industries and mass media.

Climate and Seasons

A difficult climate is intrinsic to the ethos of life in Bengal. The year is divided into six seasons, each of which is supposed to begin on the first day of a two-month period; and amazingly, the weather is so regular that the seasons correspond almost exactly to the months. The Bengali calendar is still the most widely used. Its months begin and end in the middle of the months of the Gregorian calendar. Gregorian and Muslim calendars are also followed, but the Bengali calendar is the most suitable for farmers. Its months are divided into two phases, according to the moon's waxing and waning. By necessity, villagers are aware of these phases.

With each night of the waxing moon, fields and pathways gradually become more and more bathed in soft radiance. On nights during the full-moon period, fields are clearly illuminated and a country boat can be plied in a narrow canal without using a lamp. But as the moon wanes, the deepness of night gradually thickens, revealing God's greatness in the fantastic cosmography of stars. On windy monsoon nights the moon appears to dance in and out of the clouds. But on new-moon nights when the clouds are thick, the blackness becomes so dense that it can be difficult to see even one's own hand held before his eyes.

Each of the seasons has its own mood and flavor. There is a sense of achievement at merely having survived the summer and rains, whereas the pleasantness of winter days tends to breed a feeling of contentment.

The seasons change abruptly. One day it is spring, with hot days and pleasantly cool nights, and on the next it becomes summer, with intensely hot days and uncomfortably hot nights. The rains start in mid-June and continue for four months. It is a relief when they stop, but then the heat returns, combined with enervating humidity. Thereupon the countryside looks extraordinarily beautiful and green.

The tail end of the monsoon along with the following season is called *śarat* (autumn), and lasts until mid-October. After that comes *hemanta,* the dewy season, which extends till mid-December. This period is pleasant, with crisp cool nights and warm days, about thirty degrees Celsius. Fruit and vegetables flourish. In the mornings there is mist or occasional light rain. Then comes winter, pleasantly cool in the day but cold at night. Although not Siberian cold, nonetheless people retire for sleep soon after dark, wrapped up against the chill.

By mid-February the days get hot again and there's a sense of passively waiting for the real heat to arrive. By that time there hasn't been much rain for several months, so the land is dry and dusty. As spring progresses it grows hotter and hotter, and when summer comes in mid-April it's almost too hot to do anything.

During summer everything stops at midday. In towns the shops are closed and streets empty. Everyone goes indoors, closes shutters to keep the hot air out, and sleeps until the worst heat has abated. Animals try to find a shady spot near some water to relax, waiting for the swelter to subside. Bees come out of their hives and sit for hours in the shade, fanning themselves with their wings. Birds sit in trees — not singing, just surviving. Not a sound is heard. All is still. Even the leaves don't rustle. Only toward late afternoon does the temperature reduce slightly and things come back to life.

Although the nights are less oppressive, it is still sometimes too hot to sleep. In villages, if there is no all-night drama or *kīrtana* function, people just lie outside on mats, wafting themselves with hand fans, chatting and waiting until late night, when it will be cool enough to snooze. Sometimes we would submerge ourselves in a river or pond to cool off. Taking bath during the day didn't help much because immediately after drying off, one's body would again become wet with sweat.

Occasional slight relief from summer heat comes in the form of *boishaki jhar,* the storm after a long torrid day.[14] The unrelenting heat is suddenly broken by a furious wind, shortly followed by heavy rain. In ten minutes the storm is over, but it can be intense. Banana trees are felled and anything lying around outside gets blown away.

---

14. *Boishaki* — of the month of Boishak, one of the two months of summer; *jhar* — storm.

One afternoon in Boishak while I was sitting in the shade in the courtyard of a family home, there was a slight deep rumble of thunder in the distance. The eldest man of the house said, *bolche ami aschi:* "He says, 'I am coming.'" Immediately all members of the household scrambled to put everything away. There were bed sheets and quilts out in the sun for airing, and *dāl boris* being dried.[15] Everything was completely still and the sky a brilliant, uninterrupted blue. But "He says, 'I am coming,'" and indeed within fifteen minutes the heavens were black, shaking with angry thunder and volleying rain and lightning.

But after Boishak comes another month of summer, with not even temporary relief from the heat; as soon as the sun rises it burns. When there is neither rain nor scope for deep tube-well irrigation, drinking water becomes scarce, leading to diseases of humans and animals. Worse is when crops fail. If, as often happens, drought is followed by floods, suffering is compounded.

Once I was invited to go on a *harināma* party around a village. It had been a particularly long and hot summer, the monsoon was overdue, and all living beings were suffering. We spent the entire morning chanting from house to house, accompanied by a group of children. At each home the residents would throw a precious bucket of water in the courtyard and the youngsters would roll in the slippery mud thus created. I thought this was rather strange (but anyway, there were so many strange things going on). Years later I learned that that particular type of *harināma* procession is traditionally performed to invoke rain.

15. *Dāl bori* — food preparation described below.

As summer wears on, all creation awaits the thick dark monsoon clouds that convert blinding midday into twilight. Then storms come, interspersing semi-darkness with lightning that momentarily and surrealistically illuminates everything. The clouds growl and roar, the first few drops of rain splatter down, and forceful torrents quickly follow. The monsoon always begins spectacularly, never merely drizzling, and the world rejoices.

At the onset of these rains, the dried-out earth suddenly becomes green again. Cows enjoy fresh new grass that springs up everywhere. And frogs also become inspired; at night seemingly thousands of them make a cacophony of croaking so loud that it's difficult to sleep.

But the rains aren't welcome for long, for they become even more trying than summer's heat. Sometimes it pours almost constantly, with few intermissions, for days on end. Everything gets sticky and wet. Clothes cannot be dried properly and homes reek of rotting cloth. The earth that was baked hard and cracked now becomes dangerously slippery in some places, and in others turns into sloughs of clinging mud so thick that if one steps into it he gets stuck. The monsoon is a time of ill health. The densely humid atmosphere, regular exposure to rain, and frequent change of temperature and humidity occasioned by stopping and starting rains, cause digestive and stomach disorders. Contaminated drinking water is often a problem, as it is impossible to keep mud and sewage from mixing with rivers and ponds. The mosquito population vastly increases. They constantly bite and harass and sometimes form buzzing clouds. In some areas malaria becomes endemic.

Skin rashes, widespread during summer, are universal in monsoon. The combination of heat, humidity, and perspiration assure that everyone is itching. Young children are especially prone to becoming covered with sores. All in all it is a greatly trying season. Still, Bangladeshis tolerate it; what else can they do? Yet the monsoon also has its appeal. There's a charm in sitting indoors and looking out at a storm. There are even traditional musical ragas that specifically complement the atmosphere during rains.

Many severe storms brew in the Bay of Bengal, and Bangladesh, West Bengal, and Orissa get the worst of most of them. Bangladesh in particular has always been heavily hit. Although they mostly occur during rainy season, cyclones can come at any time of the year; and it is not unusual for tens of thousands of people to die in any given storm. During the past two hundred years there has been an average of more than one severe cyclone every year, several of which have killed hundreds of thousands of people and innumerable domestic animals, and have devastated vast areas of crops and countless houses and buildings.[16]

Rivers and Floods

Most of Bangladesh lies in the delta of the Gaṅgā (Ganges), where that mighty current splits into innumerable rivers

16. Two of the most devastating storms in recent history occurred in November 1970 and December 1971, in which 500,000 and 140,000 people, respectively, were estimated to have died. The latter storm is also said to have destroyed 80% of the nation's livestock. By the very nature of calamities, such estimates cannot be considered very accurate. Indeed, firsthand experience leads many to suspect that official disaster figures tend toward underestimation.

and sub-streams. Here Gaṅgā is known as Padmā and is joined by the Brahmaputra and several other zealous rivers that force their way through the flat terrain toward the Bay of Bengal. There are numerous ferries where roads and rivers intersect, although gradually more bridges are being built. The rivers themselves serve as roads, for there are almost as many miles of navigable waterways as there are of roads. People go on three-, five-, twelve-, or even twenty-hour journeys by launches and steamers. When they get to a main ferry ghat, they may get a smaller boat to their village, or walk.

Bangladesh is quite unlike dry parts of the subcontinent, such as Rajasthan. Although parts of Bengal become arid and dusty during summer, most of the country is lush and green. Almost all the land is barely above sea level and exceedingly flat. In the rainy season all the great rivers swell and rush down from the Himalayas, through north and northeast India and also Bangladesh, on their way to the sea. This onslaught, coupled with the profuse rainfall in Bangladesh itself, ensures that every year most of the country is seriously flooded and that nearly all of it is at least partially inundated.

When flying over Bangladesh during the rainy season, the entire country appears like a huge lake, with clumps of trees and villages here or there. Villages are built on whatever high land is available. If there is no high ground in a given locale, villagers come together to raise up some earth and construct houses there. A less common alternative is to build houses of bamboo or wood, on bamboo platforms. But such flimsy structures cannot long withstand strong currents. Mud embankments are also erected along rivers to defend villages, towns, and fields. Although this affords some protection, no human effort can control the fury of nature. When rivers in spate break their banks, huge areas of crops and houses and sometimes even larger towns may be devastated.

Once during the monsoon I was traveling in the Sylhet district of northeast Bangladesh. Sylhet has the most extreme climate in Bangladesh — hottest in summer, coldest in winter, wettest in the rains. Because the dirt-track road was an impassable quagmire, we were going by boat to Sachna. The town stood like an island in the ocean, surrounded by inundated fields as far as the eye could see. Large waves washed into the streets at the edge of town, as if to devour it. Tremendous rain was still falling. That day we did *kīrtana,* sitting in the temple before rustic-looking Deities of Jagannātha, Baladeva, and Subhadrā. We had brought a big trunk full of books, somehow or other keeping them dry in spite of incessant downpour. One by one people came, braving the rain, to see the sādhus who had come in the deluge. By the end of the day we had sold all the books.

In the rainy season new rivulets spring up. Many temporary or previously small rivers become big enough for regular boat services, while numerous roads turn into muddy bogs or become overflooded. Some seasonal rivers too small for motorboats may yet be traversed by rowboat. Or if a rivulet is too narrow even for using oars, a boatman may propel his craft by standing at the back and repeatedly thrusting a bamboo pole into the shallow water and against the river bed.

A journey along one of these monsoon streams once took my companions and I through several kilometers of jungle. We were sheltered from the scorching sun by a dim tunnel of foliage interspersed with brilliant shafts of light. The boatman negotiated the many twists and turns of the brook as the rest of us pushed aside leaves and branches of overhanging trees.

Traveling by boat may be a pretty scene, especially just after the rains, when the green is intense, the sky clear, and high rivers afford a good view of the rich panorama. On wide rivers, many types of vessels can be seen — tiny country boats, larger yachts with tattered but pretty sails, small motor launches, and occasionally big steamers.

Small country boats often have an inverted u-shaped cane covering, open at both ends to protect passengers from sun and rain. When the boatman's work is finished, he can also take advantage of its shelter.

Less fortunate are they who have to pull sailboats upstream on windless days. Strong sinewy men on the shore path grasp long ropes attached to the boats. Bending forward under the cruel sun — their eyes fixed on the path ahead, bodies blackened and wet with perspiration, and their breathing hard and deep — they tortuously haul the vessel ahead.

Since Bengal is a land of many people and limited resources, overcrowding and overuse of facilities is normal. As are buses and trucks on land, passenger and freight boats are likewise usually overloaded. Sometimes a load is bigger than the vessel itself, so that the boat, pressed deep into the water, can hardly be seen beneath. This is especially so with cargoes of jute fibers, huge bundles of which are somehow or other fastened onto boats much smaller than they. Not surprisingly, overloading often leads to disasters. Especially in the rainy season hardly a day passes without loss of life on the waters; it is not uncommon for dozens or even hundreds of people to die in such accidents.

I was once on a river journey during rainy season. Upon boarding the launch it appeared solid, but in the middle of a wide choppy river, under fierce bombardment by rain, it seemed tiny and frail. As the storm intensified, the crew was apparently losing control. The captain then negotiated the boat toward the riverbank, where the current was less strong, and put down anchor. One gentleman with a typical Muslim beard turned to his companion and with sparkling eyes said, "Just see Allah's *māyā*." That was a revelation for me: how a person from an apparently less developed religious tradition had unquestioning axiomatic belief in God and saw His hand in everything.

On another occasion, when traveling during the rainy season in Sylhet district, we were taking a flimsy country boat upstream against a strong current, which was intensifying as rain poured increasingly harder. Despite struggling, eventually the boatman couldn't go any farther, and upon seeing a dead body coming the other way, we knew it was time to stop. So we pulled in at the nearest village — a mere patch of high ground with a few houses on it. But as the water level rose, the land was gradually disappearing. That evening we fell asleep not knowing if we would be washed away during the night. Fortunately we awoke next morning to find the rain had stopped. Seeing the water gradually receding, we continued our journey.

Simple Living

Bangladesh means village life. And village life is suitable for cultivating the mode of goodness and thus preferable to life in cities, which for all their comforts are dominated by lower modes.[17] Although by far the world's most densely populated country — 120 million people in an area little more than half the size of Britain — the great majority live in villages.[18] There people have little access to modern ways, which is one reason that the original Bengali culture has not fully broken down.

Village life in Bengal is still in many ways unchanged since time immemorial. Most roads are dirt tracks. People generally live many miles from the nearest paved roads and are accustomed to walking or cycling long distances. The air is pure. There aren't many factory-produced goods. Most houses are made of mud with grass thatch. Coconut, palm, banana, and betel nut trees abound. The blue sky, broad rivers, and water-traffic lifestyle pervade the atmosphere. It's easy to imagine Lord Caitanya's *saṅkīrtana* party emerging from behind the trees.

Throughout the time that I spent in Bangladesh, most villages did not have electricity. And in those with electric lines, the power would come for only an hour or two per day and at low voltage.

---

17. As described in *Bhagavad-gītā*, the mode of goodness, the highest mode, is represented by peacefulness, self-control, and spiritual understanding. The lower modes are those of passion and ignorance.

18. Some microstates, like Singapore, are more densely populated than Bangladesh.

Since Bangladeshis cannot avail themselves of most conveniences offered by modern technology, they are protected from much of its degrading influence. The claws of mass media have yet to penetrate Bangladeshi villages, and most people reside too far away from a cinema to go to one. Furthermore, films shown in Bangladesh are not as degraded as the gross sex-and-violence-ridden movies which have polluted the minds of Indians. Tighter censorship is because of the influence of Islam, which despite so much denigration levied against it, exerts beneficial restraints.[19]

Many of the villages are so remote that people know little about what is happening beyond them. Local goings-on and gossip are the all-important news. Listening to relatively innocuous Bengali programs on battery-run transistor radios is common, by which people may hear of affairs of mighty nations. But to most villagers a more important news item would be a dispute over a goat having strayed into a neighbor's field.

One writer has described that during celebrations following India's independence an elderly villager was accosted for working his fields instead of observing the holiday. "Why aren't you celebrating?" he was asked. "Celebrating what?" came the reply. "Today the British are being driven out!" "The who?" the old man asked. He had never heard of the British.

I would catch up on world news after returning to Dhaka from the villages. Summit meetings, a dollar crisis, missile-

19. Since the first edition of this book was published, electricity and television have become standard accessories in Bangladeshi village homes, and Indian movies standard fare therein — with inevitable degrading effect.

test protests, German election, soccer violence — it all seemed unreal, like fragments of a dream once vivid but now almost forgotten, voices from a world so far away as to be irrelevant.

Being so isolated from modern technological society, Bangladeshi village life is in almost total contrast to that of the industrialized West. Villagers don't know what it means to have attached bathrooms, automobiles, or other innumerable "necessities" of modern civilization. It seems that as long as no one tells them about such things, they're quite happy to live without them. They've never heard of washing machines, toilet paper, sponges for washing plates, air fresheners, canned or frozen food, or even knives and forks.

Being attracted by our *kīrtana,* some young village boys once followed us back to the rented house in Dhaka which we had transformed into an *āśrama*. That house had all modern amenities, as much as can be expected in Bangladesh: doors with handles, municipal water from taps, electric lights, and so on. The boys opened and closed the doors again and again, fascinated to see the latch system, and repeatedly turned the lights on and off. They would also turn on the tap and then walk away leaving the water running. Apparently they thought it was like a river flowing naturally.

Another time in Dhaka, I asked a village boy to make a photocopy but he hadn't the slightest clue what that was. When I tried to explain it to him, he couldn't even begin to comprehend it. City slickers may consider such ignorance to be backward, but then such townsfolk are themselves ignorant of country lore. They don't have the slightest idea how to plow a field or husk rice, nor the names of different crops, trees, insects, and birds. Bangladeshis would talk to us about different rice strains, assuming that we fully understood. But we knew nothing about varieties and qualities of rice or when they should be planted, or about health and hygiene of cattle. Village people might not be able to jive their way through the rat race of a concrete jungle, but streetwise city slickers have no idea how to relate to the goings-on of village life.

An Australian devotee traveling with me for a short time in Bangladesh marveled at how I, a Westerner, was living such an austere life — staying in villages with no proper roads or electric supply, bathing at tube wells, and so on. But I didn't find it particularly austere. It's no great feat to bathe by simply walking over to a tube well, pumping water into a bucket, and throwing it over oneself. And what's the difference between sleeping in a palatial building in a big city or in a mud hut in a village? Millions of people live like that, thinking nothing of it, so why can't we also? Even if there is some austerity, it's fun. It's actually a great adventure for a young man to leave the stereotyped West to wander and preach in distant lands.

Eco-friendly Life

The so-called austerity of village life is for the most part a matter of perception. Lack of modern conveniences is more than compensated for by absence of various miseries that attend them. At least the air is safe to breathe. Pollution is minimal and life is eco-friendly, although few villagers are aware of such a concept.

Many people eat from leaf plates and clay cups, which are used once then thrown away and naturally become reabsorbed into the ecosystem. Cooking pots and reusable plates are washed with earth and grass or coconut husk. Using earth or sand is a simple, natural, effective, and costless way to remove grease and stains, and to shine metal utensils. There is no need of a massive industry to make washing liquids and pollute the environment. Water comes not from taps but directly from rivers, lakes, ponds, or wells. Eating by hand obviates the need for knives and forks.

Villagers use practically no factory-produced items. They know how to utilize nature's resources to produce all requirements for simple living. For instance, they use every part of the coconut tree. Brushes are made from the stiff stems of coconut leaves; string from coconut husks and from jute; and half-coconut shells with a wooden handle attached to them can be used as ladles. Coconut flesh is a most nutritious food that adds unique flavor and nourishment to innumerable sweet and salty preparations. Oil extracted from coconut pulp is rubbed onto the head to add sheen to hair and cool the scalp.

Several dozen varieties of banana are cultivated in Bangladesh. Most are sweet and shorter than those familiar in the West, some growing no more than three centimeters long; but some are sour, or being full of seeds are not very pleasant to eat. Others are best cut before they ripen, to be cooked as a vegetable, excellent for the stomach and liver. Apart from the fruit, banana trees also supply other useful products. The leaves are considered the most high-class type of plate. Hot food placed on a banana leaf causes a substance to emerge that aids digestion. Let the atheists try to explain that! The inside of the tree stem makes a tasty and nutritious vegetable dish, and the flowers of certain varieties of banana tree make an incomparably delicious curry. Banana trees can even be made into paper.

Bamboo also is integral to Bengali life. Multifarious varieties grow everywhere, especially in southern coastal areas. Young bamboo is bent and made into simple furniture, baskets — such as the type carried on a stick, one on each side of the shoulder — and big farmers' hats to shelter from sun and rain. Older bamboo, rigid and strong, is used for making fences and temporary structures, for constructing bridges over the many rivulets of Bangladesh, and as scaffolding. Hand fans for dispelling summer heat are also made from bamboo.

Nowadays few people in Bangladesh make their clothing at home. But in West Bengal, commercial production of cloth by handloom is still a major home industry. And until only recently, most villages throughout Bengal had a blacksmith making agricultural tools, buckets, cooking pots and utensils, and so on. Now mass-produced items from factories are gradually taking over.

The terrible culture of waste — yet another aberration of modern society — simply does not exist in Bengali villages. Everything is used. For instance, old clothes aren't thrown away, but are ripped and used as rags or tampons, or to make the patchwork quilts found in every poor man's home.

Another appealing aspect of simple village life is that villagers do many things out of doors rather than being cramped up inside all day. Bathing, washing clothes, answering nature's call, sitting and talking to people, or quietly reading — all functions executed indoors in most places — are often done outdoors in Bengali villages. Even eating is often done on the veranda or in the courtyard of a house. Those accustomed to this sweet simplicity can appreciate why the Supreme Personality of Godhead in His ultimate feature prefers village life to royal opulence.

Morning Bathing

The day begins early in villages. Most people rise with or before the sun. Before dawn we would hear the lilting, formal summons in Arabic from a local mosque, calling the faithful to prayer. Sometimes this would be followed by a less formal exhortation in Bengali: "Come on, get up! Praying is more important than sleep!" For someone to sleep till mid-morning would certainly be considered strange, although in cities, television is changing people's lives.

Upon rising the first duty for villagers is tending to nature's call. They are regulated to evacuate at that time either in the field or a latrine, generally just a hole in the ground without drainage, the stench of heat-fermented stool and urine attracting millions of maggots and flies. Even water-flushed toilets, which are the norm in towns, are at floor level for squatting on, which posture is natural and therefore more effective for defecating than are Western commodes.

After evacuating, bathing is compulsory. Villagers go either to a tube well or open well, draw a bucket of water, and throw it over themselves with a *lota;* or bathe in a river or pond. By

Kṛṣṇa's arrangement, in the early mornings of winter days, water taken from a tube well or open well is as warm as if heated. Yet on torrid summer days, water from the same wells is cool, this effect being more pronounced in deeper wells. When after an arduous journey we would arrive at a village during the midday heat, someone would vigorously pump a tube well and fill bucket after bucket with cool water, which we would throw over our heads. On a hot summer's day there's nothing as invigorating and refreshing.

Man-made ponds *(pukurs)* are important amenities in Bengal; almost all villages have at least one, and some have several. Many relatively affluent families have their own. *Pukurs* are generally square or oblong. They are used for bathing and for washing clothes and cooking utensils. Some are reserved exclusively for drinking water. At the edge of *pukurs* are bathing ghats with steps of mud, or preferably stone or brick. The best *pukurs* are large and deep and therefore do not dry up during summer. They also remain relatively clean even if many people bathe in them. Our devotees would often enjoy swimming and cavorting with village boys in the water of a deep cool *pukur*.

Men and women bathe at separate *pukurs,* or at least at different times or at different ghats at the same *pukur*. While bathing, men wear lungis or long *gāmchas* and women wear *sārīs*.

By mid-morning women cluster at a ghat beside a *pukur* or river. "Thwack! Thwack!" reverberates as they wash clothes by hitting them against large stones at the waterside. Women often also scrub their household pots in a *pukur* or river and simultaneously collect water for the day's cooking.

Down at the *pukur* just after sunrise men cheerfully chat with each other, chewing on neem twigs and rubbing mustard oil on their bodies before their daily bath.[20] They also slip some oil up their noses to help clear out mucus. Mustard oil applied on the body helps keep it warm in winter and protects the skin from drying, and also contains vitamins and minerals which enter through the pores.

Sunset Duties

Sunset in Hindu homes is heralded by ladies' sudden banging of gongs, blowing of conches, and making *ulu-ulu* sounds. These auspicious vibrations counteract the ominous effects of the hours of darkness, when ghosts and malevolent spirits become active. The malignant influence of that hour is further offset by offering *ārati* to family deities, thus making everything propitious. Sundown is also time to light *dhuna,* a frankincense mixture burned with coconut husks in a clay or brass chalice. It produces purifying smoke that wards off subtle malefic influences, and its fragrance keeps at bay the teems of mosquitoes that become active at dusk.

Another duty at twilight is to light lamps, either crude contraptions made from used tin cans, or slightly sophisticated hurricane lamps. Even in homes where there is electricity, lamps are usually lit because the current often cuts out. After everyone retires for the night, one or two lamps are kept burning on low wick, to be found easily when rising in early pre-dawn.

20. Neem twigs are a natural antiseptic toothbrush.

Social Structure and Dealings

Typical Bengal scenery is flat fields interspersed with clumps of trees, especially coconut, betel, and palm, on higher land. Yet there are people everywhere. Under every clump of trees are several huts, each giving shelter to a household of many members. Sometimes we would stop our van in what appeared to be a remote spot in the middle of empty fields, but within a few minutes we would be surrounded by crowds of villagers curious to see the "sahibs" who had suddenly appeared in their midst.

There is little privacy in Bangladesh; anyone's business is everybody else's. Simple village folk have no qualms about standing together in a group and staring, on and on, totally fascinated by everything a foreign visitor does. Many foreign devotees, including myself, would be quite unnerved by this. Sometimes I felt like an animal in a zoo. But eventually I grew accustomed to it.

Even after bathing we would have to dress in crowded rooms, with women also present. For most families there is no question of having private quarters; there's simply not enough space. So people learn how to dress in the presence of the opposite sex, keeping their bodies always covered with cloth in the process.

Loneliness is unheard of in Bengal, not because people get lost in the crowd, but because they know how to live as persons. Bengalis like nothing better than to get together and go on talking and talking, though often their discussions are of little practical value. Boredom also is unknown. Bengalis like to be and do things together. Everyone gets involved and has his part to play. It's a different kind of pleasure than that derived from an endless variety of external stimuli, the norm of modern society.

Development-minded Westerners often become frustrated at the apparent foolishness of the Bangladeshi, who appears to lack common sense regarding his own best interests. Bangladeshi culture does not promote individual dynamism, competitiveness, or the type of efficiency required for technological advancement. Rather, although not uninterested in economic development, a Bangladeshi is more concerned to preserve the indigenous group culture which fosters the sharing and cooperativeness necessary for a traditional labor-intensive agrarian society.

I was once in a village that had recently been devastated by a cyclone. The residents were cheerfully helping each other rebuild houses from mud. That's how village life works. People are obliged to cooperate throughout the year, and they happily help each other harvesting, irrigating, organizing festivals, or building a wall against a rising river.

Necessity also dictates maintaining good relationships with neighbors. Most people aren't well situated economically, so those who have more are expected to help those with less. It's a culture of sharing and responsibility toward others. Despite ill-feeling sown by politicians between Hindus and Muslims, even today in many villages the two communities live together cordially — although it's cordiality mixed with wariness.

Bengalis feel close to each other, especially to members of their own group. They're quick to make new acquaintances and ask each other questions. Due to my Western sensibilities, initially I felt my privacy being invaded by their constant probing — "What is your age?" "How many brothers and sisters do you have?" "Are you married?" "How do you get money?" — not knowing that in Indian culture to take such personal interest in a person is complimentary, indicating that he is considered important.

Western culture romanticizes the rugged individual who struggles alone in a harsh world. Bangladeshis emphasize dependence on others and a sense of group identity. They usually say "our house" and "our country" rather than "my house" or "my country." Bangladeshis do not like to be judged as individuals, but as members of the group to which they belong.

The first and foremost group with which a Bangladeshi identifies is his family; then caste and village. To offend an individual Bengali is to arouse the ire of his group, because he stands for the group and thus also is upheld by it. Group solidarity assures protection of a member if he is attacked in any way. Even an entire village may seek revenge for the sake of an individual member.

The group lends support when a member is in difficulty, whether moral, social, or economic. Reciprocally, members have obligations to the group, one of which is conformity. In fact, the pressure to maintain fellowship with the group is extremely strong. In this way the group regulates the behavior of its members, keeping them within the bounds of acceptable conduct. What one person does reflects upon his group. A wrong action brings shame upon the entire group, and similarly success brings honor to all. If someone is behaving improperly, the elders of the family or village will tell him, "You will give your family (or village) a bad name." That will be a compelling reason for him to rectify his conduct.

Bengalis are anxious to maintain honor and respectability. They uphold their status in society by keeping relationships with others, especially superiors. They also keep their clothes clean and dress as neatly as possible, even if they have only few, or not very nice, clothes.

Especially Bangladeshis ascribe much importance to etiquette. For a Bangladeshi to say that a person's behavior is good indicates high appreciation. On the other hand, to state that a person doesn't know how to behave expresses strong disapproval. For example, a person becomes much scorned behind his back if due to wealth or status he behaves neglectfully or disdainfully toward others.

In every culture certain activities are considered repugnant or reprehensible. It is sometimes difficult for a foreigner to live amidst cultural standards different from those of his native land. One example is that Bengali men sometimes walk together holding hands as a simple expression of friendship. Whereas in the West this would indicate a homosexual relationship, at least previously widely deemed as disgusting, there is no such connotation in Bengal. Or if a Bengali feels shocked or shamed, as when rebuked by a senior, he may express remorse by holding his tongue tightly between his teeth. But in British and American culture, such showing of the tongue is considered rude. And I got in trouble a few times for making the "thumbs up" sign. For although in the West this is considered a friendly, positive affirmation, it's a vulgar gesture in Indian society.

A newcomer to Bengali culture must learn many fine points and taboos. For instance, it's considered rude to sit with one's foot pointing toward someone else. So when sitting on a chair, the feet should be tucked in underneath so that one's toes do not point out. And the Western practice of signaling someone to come by waggling the index finger up and down is considered rude by Bengalis. Their method is to hold the hand out with the palm down and make a gentle indicatory motion. Also, in Bengali and Indian culture shaking the head from side to side is equivalent to saying yes, whereas in the West it indicates no.

Even drinking from a glass held in the left hand is incorrect, because the left hand is used only for inauspicious and unclean activities, such as washing the backside, whereas the right hand should be used for everything clean and auspicious. It is an insult to give or receive anything with the left hand. Once when selling Śrīla Prabhupāda's books I was routinely giving change to a man, but with my left hand. In front of a crowd of people, he took the money and placed it into my right hand and then waited for me to give it to him with that hand. It was embarrassing but instructive.

Coming from the land of *mlecchas,* I did not easily adjust to Bangladeshi standards of behavior. Being unfamiliar with the culture, I often made mistakes, and many people, usually older than I, would tell me so. Because of egotism it wasn't easy for me to learn the finer points of that culture which others all around me had imbibed from childhood.

It was difficult for me to accept instruction from persons who presumably weren't following the more important regulations of spiritual life.

Personal dealings among Bengalis tend to be subtle. Although known as emotional, they don't always "wear their hearts on their sleeves." Thus a Western newcomer must learn the subtle nuances implied in Bengalis' gestures, glances, inflexions, and indirect speech. Straightforwardness and frankness, considered axiomatically desirable by Anglo-Saxons, are seen by Bengalis as brashness and indicative of ill breeding.

Bengali culture is especially delicate regarding misunderstandings and chastisement. Although they may be forthright with family and close friends, Bengalis are roundabout when dealing with others, except when angry or quarreling. Potentially schismatic issues are handled indirectly, with every effort to avoid causing shame, anger, discord, or an unnecessary rift in the relationship. This is practical in a village community, in which people must continue living together and cooperating.

If one Bangladeshi must correct another, he does so in private, in a euphemistic and reassuring manner, for it's considered important to keep others satisfied even when there is cause for disagreement. Generally correction is done only by seniors. Even then, rebukes are cushioned with tact, showing great concern over the rebuked party's family welfare. *Kichhu mane korben na* ("Please don't mind") is an important phrase to precede a topic that will not be palatable to the hearer.

He who is correcting will first ask questions about personal matters, to ease the harshness of the rebuff and to indicate that the misbehaved one is still accepted and being treated on the same basis as before but being warned to improve his behavior. The admonisher will speak in a sweet tone of voice with words designed to make the erring party feel good, even though what is being said may not be palatable to him.

Bengalis are typically Oriental in that they sit and chat about lighter subjects before they begin to talk about more serious matters on their minds. Even then, they may talk around the point instead of directly addressing it. If in a group there is some feeling of dissatisfaction between two men, it will most likely be expressed by subtle hints. And if he who is the cause of dissatisfaction to another doesn't respond to the indirect messages, then the dissatisfied man may request a mutually respected senior to approach the other to relay his discontent.

If offered an apology for improper words or behavior, the correct etiquette is to respond, "No, no. You didn't do anything wrong. I didn't think badly of you," even though both know that there was indeed wrongdoing.

Although Bengali culture is based on respect and behaving in such a way that others aren't offended, saints are few, and Bengalis sometimes devise ways to inflict hostile feelings upon others. Indeed, social boundaries are all too often transgressed, leading to the loud arguments common in Bengal. Arguments between individuals inevitably attract a crowd and become group affairs.

Seniority

In Bengali culture "senior" means father, mother, paternal grandfather and grandmother, and other elderly persons. The older brother is respected almost equally to the father. Teachers are also much respected. Juniors are not allowed to argue with seniors. Even if a junior has a point of contention, generally he will not submit it. If someone needs to submit a complaint to a senior, he must do so most respectfully, and if the senior adamantly disagrees with him, the junior must simply accept. If an elder calls a junior, he will reply, *ājñe:* "I am at your order."

Whenever I would enter a room where juniors, such as disciples of my Godbrothers, were sitting or reposing, they would immediately stand up, as a gesture of respect. They would not remain sitting while a senior was standing. And whenever I visited the residence of the head of the Sanskrit department of Dhaka University, I would see his students touch his feet upon entering and him touch their head in return.

Affection and Family Life

Affectionate feelings are as much part of Bengali life as respect. Men have no qualms about saying they love another man or that another man loves them: *amake bhalobashe.* When friends and relatives meet they feelingly embrace each other three times. Each person's head goes first over the other's left shoulder, then again they embrace with their heads over the right shoulder, and then again back to the left shoulder. Of course that is between two men or two women. Men and women never embrace each other in public, even if husband and wife, or mother and son — unless the son is very young, in which case he will be held in his mother's arms much of the time.

The typical Bengali family is a joint interrelationship. Perhaps five brothers will live together with their wives and children. Each man treats the children of his brothers with all affection, practically as if his own. The elders have many children with whom to be affectionate; thus children grow up receiving love and care from many.

In Bengal a male is not considered a man until he is at least thirty. Until then he is referred to and treated as a boy. Even if married with children, he still has limited independence.

Men and women have distinctly dissimilar roles in Bangladeshi society. Their dress, disposition, social position, and duties are clearly delineated and clearly different. Women are socially subordinate to men, yet honored and fully cared for and protected. Women throughout India and Bangladesh have not been infected by the Western madness of trying to be manlike. Despite working hard and having little financial resources, they nonetheless maintain natural femininity by dressing themselves attractively with colorful sārīs, bangles, jewelry, *sindura, bindi,* and *alta.*[21]

The role of women in Bengal, or in any traditional culture, is as wives and mothers — not sex symbols trying to attract every man who comes within their vision. Bengali women's

21. *Sindura* — natural red pigment applied to the hair part of married women; *bindi* — the same tincture applied as a dot in the center of the forehead; *alta* — red dye applied to the soles of the feet.

pleasure is in serving their family and guests. They're especially enthusiastic for social and religious occasions. They delight in making preparations for festivals, including dressing themselves up and meeting their village friends.

First thing in the morning Bengali village women sweep all the floors of the house and courtyard. Next they wash them with a mixture of cow dung and water. Then they have many other chores: milking the cows, cooking, feeding the family, threshing grains, washing pots, and so on. Along with these different duties they take complete care of the children twenty-four hours a day. Since the work load is shared among the many household women, it doesn't seem burdensome or a strain.

Nor could Bengali women ever imagine children to be a burden. Rather, it is their prime happiness to care for and raise children. Bengali women are profusely affectionate toward children in general, but especially to their sons. Most Bengali mothers have several sons, but should they have only one then all their attachment focuses on him, and he becomes completely bound by it. Among several sons the youngest is usually the object of special motherly tenderness. Even as adults men feel deeply for their mothers. Every village man who has gone off to work in the city has a photo of his mother in his wallet.

In villages women would come in groups, never alone, to see me. Invariably they would ask about my family and home, for these are the most important concerns for Bengalis, especially the women. When I would tell them that I was an only son, they could not understand how I could have left my mother and not even seen her for many years. And they would grieve for the separation which they were sure my mother must be feeling. They could not realize that in modern Western society, feelings of affection are so reduced that mothers often drive their sons out of the home: "You have been here long enough. Get out." So I would truthfully tell them that although I had left one mother behind, I had found so many more in Bangladesh. On hearing that, their hearts would melt and they would affectionately accept me as a son.

In Dhaka I once saw a family group waiting on the roadside. They were mostly women with several children, and one or two men. It was obvious that they had just come from the village, for they were visibly confused and frightened by the traffic and bustle of the city. The children were milling around and one of them strayed into the road. Seeing this, one of the older women ran out, grabbed the small child, and brought him back to the group, clutching him tightly to her breast. Then she feelingly chastised a younger woman who had been closest to the child but hadn't seen him drift off: "How could you let him wander out into the street like that?"

These motherly and domestic instincts are developed almost from the cradle. From the age of four or five, girls begin to help in bringing water, cooking, serving meals, and looking after younger children. Unlike their counterparts in the West who play with toy dolls, girls in Bangladeshi villages carry around and care for real babies — their own younger siblings or the children of an aunt or neighbor. Five-year-old girls commonly carry babies almost as big as themselves. Thus from the beginning of life children grow up having many mothers, not just one. Even after an older sister is married and her younger relations have grown to adulthood, she still retains maternal feelings toward them. It's no wonder that Bengalis revere their older sisters.

Children are corrected by verbal chastisement and social pressure. I have never seen or even heard of Bengali parents slapping or beating their children. Bengali children do not cry very much, and grow up self-confident and unabashed, if not rather undisciplined.

Children are taught what is unacceptable behavior by the expression *chi-chi:* "For shame!" Training in the many rules of Bengali culture starts from an early age. A tiny child is warned, "Don't put your feet on anyone or on a holy object," "Don't give things to people with the left hand," "Don't call an older person by his given name or use the familiar form of speech with him," "Don't step over the rope that tethers a cow." As a child grows older he learns that there are severe sanctions against taboos like answering back to an elder or staring at a person while talking to him.

I remember seeing women bringing tiny babies to our *āśrama*. The mothers would bow the babies' heads to the floor in front of the Deity and put *caranāmṛta* in their mouths.[22] Even though the children could not have known what was going on, their mothers were concerned that they get the benefit of performing pious activities. The mothers would also bow their babies' heads at our feet and tell their younger children, *pranāma koro* ("Bow down"), upon which the children would immediately prostrate before us. The

22. *Caranāmṛta* — water that has washed the lotus feet of the Lord's Deity form and which is later drunk by devotees.

already trained older children would automatically offer obeisances without having to be told.

Bengali women's love for their children is paralleled by that for their husbands. Young girls imbibe the qualities considered most important for women: chastity, submission, and faithfulness to the husband. I was once in a Bengali home when an elderly woman started speaking about her sick and aged husband, who was sitting a little elevated from us. "Of course we all love Kṛṣṇa," she said, "but my husband is my god. He has protected and cared for me throughout my life. He is a great devotee of Kṛṣṇa, and I am eternally grateful to him." Her voice cracked as she continued, "Now he will be going to Kṛṣṇa. I also want to go to Kṛṣṇa, but only with him."

Obviously the Bengalis' idea of marriage is far removed from the Western concept. We knew one modernized young man who dressed in fashionable Western clothes and spoke English well. Yet the Vaiṣṇava spirit with which he had been raised was still strong within him. He was an expert *mṛdaṅga* player and regularly participated in evening *kīrtanas* at our Dhaka *āśrama*. Eventually he got the opportunity to go to America to study. He was excited before he left, but when he returned a year later he expressed dismay with American ways. "They make a big show of love," he said disgustedly. "When a man drops his wife off to work, they do this big kiss.[23] But then they fight and divorce as easily as they kiss. In our country we never even talk about love and certainly don't make a big show of it. There's no need; it's

23. Public kissing, even as an affectionate gesture between husband and wife, is unthinkable in Bangladesh.

automatically there. There's no question of a wife not loving her husband. Naturally she loves her husband, because he's her husband! Many Americans asked me about arranged marriages: 'How can you marry someone you never met? How can you love that person?' I tell them, 'Your system is to fall in love before marriage, but we fall in love after marriage. The difference is that afterward you fall out of love as easily as you fell into it. And you think nothing of falling out of marriage also. That we don't do.'"

Forms of Address

In the Bengali village two males of the same age are called brothers. In the beginning I was confused when someone would introduce every male of the same age in the village as his brother, but then I learned that in Bengal that is what a brother is. Brother may mean someone from the same district, a friend, an old school colleague, or so on. Thus young men are not allowed to marry girls from their same village, having grown up together as brothers and sisters.

Seniors are never called directly by name. They may be called *dādā* (older brother), or *dīdī* (older sister). *Mejo bhāi* means a middle brother, who is older but not the eldest. Any person who is a little older will be called with the appellation *dā,* meaning "elder brother." For instance, a boy called Nripendranath becomes Nripen-dā, Kamal Bhushan becomes Kamal-dā, and so on.

Proper etiquette is for men to refer to all women other than their wives as *mā* (mother). But this practice has been compromised and so men now often refer to women as *dīdī,* as women address each other.

Women are addressed as the mother of their eldest son. If her eldest son's name is Gokula Chandra, a woman will be called Gokuler Mā. The given name of a woman, such as Bhāvanā or Prīti or Rādhikā, is hardly used, except in religious functions or official matters. Others living in her village may not even know her actual name.

Bengalis use different names to define their connection with people outside their family. They establish friendly relationships with elderly people by designating them as *māmā* (maternal uncle), *māmi* (maternal aunt), *kākā* (father's younger brother), *kāki* (paternal aunt), and so on. Senior Muslims will be referred to as *chāchā* (paternal uncle) and *chāchi* (paternal aunt). Little boys are called *khoka,* little girls *khuki.*

Language

Language and culture are intrinsically linked. Without speaking the local language a foreigner remains like an extraterrestrial, neither able to directly communicate with people nor enter into an understanding of their lifestyle. Therefore most of our Western devotees who spend much time in Bangladesh learn Bengali to better relate with and live among the people.

Knowing Bengali also gives one access to the treasure house of Gauḍīya Vaiṣṇava literature. Nowadays only a few Bengalis are familiar with this tremendous cultural asset. But the great Vaiṣṇava *ācārya* Śrīla Bhaktisiddhānta Sarasvatī Ṭhākura predicted that a time would come when people throughout the world would learn Bengali just to read *Śrī Caitanya-caritāmṛta.* Now *Śrī Caitanya-*

caritāmṛta and many Gauḍīya Vaiṣṇava songs and poems have been translated into English. Yet even rudimentary understanding of Bengali reveals many subtle nuances in these transcendental compositions, enhancing appreciation of their sweetness.

Most Indian languages are based on Sanskrit, and Bengali especially so. Therefore as is Sanskrit, Bengali is quite appropriate for expressing the subtle philosophy of the *Vedas*. Bengali is particularly suitable for *rasa vicāra* (analysis of liberated souls' personal exchanges with God). The topmost relationships in spiritual existence are between Kṛṣṇa and the residents of Vṛndāvana, and between Caitanya Mahāprabhu and His intimate associates. At that level, philosophy is superseded by overwhelming affection. Bengali is most suitable for expressing such loving exchanges. It can precisely convey the mood of selfless spotless love in a way that is not possible in English or other Western languages, none of which are separate from the culture of lust.

As Śrīla Bhaktisiddhānta Sarasvatī Ṭhākura wrote:

> The Gauḍīyas are not only residents of Gauḍa (West Bengal) but by the help of the Gauḍīya language (Bengali) they become expert in the language of the eternally liberated inhabitants of Goloka and thus understand themselves as associates of the Lord.[24]

Bengali *kīrtana* style has evolved in intimate link to the language. The words used and the way they are sung combine with the music to perfectly awaken, express, and

24. Commentary on *Caitanya-bhāgavata*, Introductory Notes.

enhance spiritual emotions. There are literally thousands of *padāvalī kīrtanas* composed in Bengali which describe the form, pastimes, qualities, feelings, and so on of Kṛṣṇa, Lord Caitanya, and Their associates.[25] Even though some of these songs are now translated into English and other languages, their original expression of *rasa* (spiritual sentiment) can be conveyed in no languages other than Oriya and Maithili, which are close to Bengali. Even Hindi and other Indian languages do not have the same charm.

Bengali is known as a sweet language. The style spoken in Bangladesh is particularly pure, having been little influenced by outside dialects. Even those who don't understand it can appreciate its beautiful, almost musical cadence, especially when spoken by cultured persons. The sound of the words, intonation of the voice conveying respect and affection, and the very structure of the language combine so that even ordinary day-to-day talk is pleasing to the heart and mind. It is reminiscent of the spiritual world, where talking is singing.

Of course when rough people squabble, which they often do, they sound coarse and nasty. Low-class women are particularly expert in quarrel, being well-practiced at launching barrages of expletives to outdo their opponents in volume, audacity, vitriol, and misplaced wit. I could hardly stop laughing when I heard a woman cackle about another, "She thinks the sun is shining through her anus." Even the vulgarity is unique.

---

25. *Padāvalī kīrtanas* — devotional verses composed especially for singing in a distinctive style.

Bengali script is also very attractive. Many Bengalis take care to write so that the dots and curves of the letters combine to look like (as Caitanya Mahāprabhu compared Rūpa Gosvāmī's handwriting to) a row of pearls.

Hindu Religious Life

With over 100 million Muslims, Bangladesh is the third most populous Muslim country, after Indonesia and Pakistan, and also has the second largest Hindu population, around twenty million.[26] There are also a few Christians and Buddhists. In Bangladesh religion is more than a formality; it is a fundamental force in everyone's life, in the social structure, and in the national psyche. Almost every Bangladeshi practices religion in some form or another. Throughout the entire country hardly an atheist can be found. Even if there were one, due to strong social censure he would not profess openly. Especially in the villages everyone has strong faith in God, as natural for them as breathing.

I used to visit a village in which there was an elderly Bengali gentleman who reminded me of the description Śrīla Prabhupāda gave of his own father. The man worshiped his tiny Rādhā-Kṛṣṇa Deities for several hours a day. He was old and bent over, had thick white hair, and couldn't walk without the help of a stick, yet he was very strict. No one in the home was allowed to eat anything until it had been

26. Official census figures put the Hindu population at around 10 million, but most educated Hindus of the country believe this to be a deliberate underestimate. My experience tends to corroborate this, as I have traveled extensively throughout the country and come across large numbers of Hindus in most areas.

offered to the Deities. He had a brass shop in the village where he would go for a few hours every day, but mostly he seemed to be happy just doing *pūjā*.

One evening it so happened that everyone of the household had gone out except him and me. So he handed me a copy of *Śrī Caitanya-caritāmṛta* to read aloud by the light of a kerosene lamp. The book was quite worn out from a lifetime of constant use, but now my host could no longer read it, for his eyes were also worn out and obscured by the lids and white hairy brows which drooped over them. I asked from which portion I should read, and he said, "Anywhere." As I recited, he chanted the verses along with me; it appeared that he knew it all by heart.

In another household where I was staying the youngest son's name was Viṣṇu. All day his mother would call out, "Viṣṇu, Viṣṇu, Viṣṇu." It seemed that she couldn't be happy unless he was at her side. I was reminded of the story of Ajāmila in *Śrīmad-Bhāgavatam*.[27] Even though the woman was not thinking of the Supreme Personality of Godhead, she, her son, and everybody else in the neighborhood were benefited by always hearing the name Viṣṇu.

Many towns and villages in Bengal are named after the local presiding Deity of Kṛṣṇa. Examples in Bangladesh are Gopalganj, Gopaldi, Narasimhdi, and Madhavdi. In West Bengal there is Krishnanagar, which is named after a king whose name was Kṛṣṇa.

---

27. Although greatly sinful, Ajāmila was saved from hell because he chanted the holy name of Nārāyaṇa, being attached to and always calling his son of the same name.

The religious element in Bengali society is not restricted to the simple and uneducated. I discovered this the first time I met Paresh Chandra Mandal, the head of the Sanskrit department of Dhaka University, at his residence. When I arrived he was sitting with several students. After sitting me down he started to advance different atheistic arguments, asking why we should believe in God and why we should accept Kṛṣṇa as God. After politely answering his questions for ten or fifteen minutes, I became a little frustrated, and declared, "I am surprised. Although you are a learned person and well-respected in Hindu society, you are not accepting the statements of *śāstra* and instead are advocating these strange theories." Professor Mandal and his students then burst into laughter, upon which I realized that they had been testing my knowledge, conviction, and patience, albeit in a light and humorous way. And judging from their good-natured laughter it appears that I passed the test.

Every sizable Hindu village has a Hari-*sabhā*.[28] At least once a week the residents come together to chant the holy names and perhaps read together from *Śrīmad-Bhāgavatam* or *Śrī Caitanya-caritāmṛta*. Śrīla Prabhupāda explains, "In Bengal there are still many places called *hari-sabhā*, which indicates a place where local people gather to chant the Hare Kṛṣṇa *mahā-mantra* and discuss the pastimes of Lord Kṛṣṇa."[29]

Dharma-sabhās are popular throughout the eight-month dry season. Especially during summer, people are prepared to sit for hours throughout the night listening to various speakers discoursing on religious topics. In Bangladesh

28. Hari — name of Kṛṣṇa; *sabhā* — meeting.

29. *Caitanya-caritāmṛta, Madhya-lila* 1.227, purport.

still today religious topics are of more interest and more certain to draw a crowd than politics, current affairs, sports, or other such ephemeral subjects.

Every formal Vaiṣṇava function must begin with offering sandalwood paste. By moistening a coarse stone and vigorously rubbing a stick of dried sandalwood against it, one gradually produces a pale pink, fragrant pulp that is highly cooling. This is transferred to a small copper dish. A male devotee will then dip a flower into the paste and apply it first to pictures of worshipable Deities, next to sacred books, then to the *mṛdaṅgas* and *karatālas* used for making spiritual music, to the most senior Vaiṣṇavas present, and finally to all other male members of the assembly. After the men have received this sandalwood *prasāda* it is passed to the ladies, who similarly apply it among themselves.

At a larger function, a senior and prominent member of the community will take up the service of applying sandalwood pulp. Often those he applies it to will embrace him, take the dish from him, and then smear it also on him. Sandalwood pulp is generally applied on the forehead but sometimes also to the arms and chest, especially of more prominent devotees.

Unfortunately, despite their inherent belief in God few Bangladeshis are actually serious about self-realization, one reason being that Bengali culture makes people feel peaceful and secure. They feel that life is passing on nicely and there's no harm in continuing in this manner indefinitely. Without preachers stressing that life is meant for seriously trying to understand God, even such an advanced platform as Bengali culture does not help one to understand the essence of religion, as described in *Śrīmad-Bhāgavatam* (1.2.10): "Life's desires should never be directed toward sense gratification. One should desire only a healthy life, or self-preservation, since a human being is meant for inquiry about the Absolute Truth. Nothing else should be the goal of one's works."

Muslims

On launch journeys I would see Muslims silently chanting the names of Allah on beads. At prayer times, such as at midday or in the evening, many of them would go to the back of the boat, spread mats out, pump up water from the river, wash their hands and legs, and then perform *namaz* right on the boat.[30] Unlike most Westerners, they had no compunction about showing their faith in God. One evening while driving in a rural area we saw a young boy alone in a field dramatically falling down on the ground to offer his prayers.

The Muslims of East Bengal follow Vedic culture in many ways, even more so than most Hindus in India. For example, in our neighborhood in Dhaka we once saw a Muslim family going to the street to receive and touch the feet of elderly members of their clan who were arriving from the village.

Many Bangladeshi Muslims are so cultured that they also respect Hindu sādhus, even though they don't know what to make of the "Western Hindus." Sometimes when I was walking on village paths in Bangladesh, Muslims who were cycling in the opposite direction would get down from

30. *Namāz* — prayers recited by Muslims five times a day while bowing down toward Mecca.

their bikes as a gesture of respect. At that time I was in my early twenties and some of them were old enough to be my grandfather. But their culture was so deeply ingrained that they would dismount to offer the one-handed Muslim salute of respect.

During the 1971 war of liberation, genocidal Punjabi Muslim soldiers from West Pakistan especially targeted Hindus but they also killed hundreds of thousands of Bangladeshi Muslims. Their "justification" was: "These people are not Muslims at all. Their language is written with a Hindu script and is predominantly derived from Sanskrit. Their customs and culture are Hindu." Indeed many Muslims in Bangladesh hardly use their given name — for example, "Manzurul Khan" — but are better known by a Hindu nickname, like Kamal or Dilip.

Another Hindu cultural practice widely adopted by Bangladeshi Muslims is astrology, despite its being forbidden in Islam. Many Bangladeshi Muslim politicians and businessmen seek astrological advice before making important decisions. And the more affluent consult astrologers before arranging marriages, as do Hindus.

But some Bangladeshi Muslims want to move closer to Arabian ways, not liking that their compatriots have retained so much of their forefathers' Hindu culture (after all, Muslims in Bengal were originally converted from Hinduism). In particular, fundamentalist Muslims deplore the prevalence of gurus among Bangladeshi Muslims. Certain Muslim religious leaders, known as *pīrs,* dispense blessings and advice, and are treated reverentially, just like Hindu gurus.

I even heard Muslims performing *kīrtana* in praise of Allah, although music and singing, even in praise of God, are supposed to be forbidden in Islam. But these are so integral to Bengali life that the ban on music in Islam is somchow not implemented in Bangladesh. Drama is similarly proscribed in Islam but is central to Bengali life even for Muslims.

Yet there are significant differences between the habits and outlook of Muslims and Hindus, the most prominent being that Muslims kill cows, which Hindus consider a great sacrilege. And they do other things oppositely. An example is the use of banana leaves, which being large, flat, and approximately oblong make perfect natural disposable plates. Yet Hindus eat from banana leaves while keeping the darker side upward whereas Muslims turn it downward. And when bathing with a bucket and jug, Hindus start from the head, Muslims from the feet.

Once when newly in Bangladesh we arranged to meet a highly placed government official, mistakenly thinking that he might be pleased to learn of our preaching activities. When we told him that our movement was spreading Bengali culture all over the world he replied, "Yes, but not Bangladeshi culture." He was making a distinction, although at that time even the very concept of a country known as Bangladesh had existed for less than ten years.

Music and Kīrtana

Practically the whole population of Bengal loves music. For Bengalis, especially simple folk without pretensions to maintain, any time or place is good for singing. Boatmen especially are known for singing loudly as they ply their craft. Once while riding on a rickshaw in Dhaka, I started to softly sing a *bhajana* and the driver turned around with a big smile, happy that I was singing.

Bangladeshis have both strong religious belief and ingrained love for music, so it is natural for them to communicate with God through music and song. Although Caitanya Mahāprabhu's *saṅkīrtana* movement is meant for everyone in the universe, it seems especially appropriate for Bengalis, who are full of verve and spirit and both laugh and cry with spontaneity and vigor.

Indeed *Caitanya-bhāgavata* states that because of the good fortune of Lord Caitanya having visited and been well received in East Bengal, the inhabitants still perform *śrī-kṛṣṇa-saṅkīrtana*. That benediction is visibly present even today, at least among Hindus. Although a plethora of imaginary mantras have been introduced by unscrupulous cheating "gurus," still by far the most popular *kīrtana* in Bengal is the *mahā-mantra:* Hare Kṛṣṇa, Hare Kṛṣṇa, Kṛṣṇa Kṛṣṇa, Hare Hare/ Hare Rāma, Hare Rāma, Rāma Rāma, Hare Hare.

Although other Vaiṣṇava traditions give more stress to temple worship, Gauḍīya practices center on *kīrtana*. Bengal has an enthralling *kīrtana* culture that is difficult to describe in words. For example, in the middle of one song another may be sung as explanation of a line in the original. After finishing that entire song, the singers go back to the original composition and in this way weave together several lyrics in an elaborate, mind-enchanting mixture of *rasa* (emotions), *tattva* (philosophical truths), *bhāva* (expression of feelings), *sura* (melody), and *tāla* (rhythm). Accomplished musicians in Bengal can converse for hours on the intricacies of Indian music, in technical Sanskrit terms incomprehensible to the layman.

Sometimes we would arrive in villages in the evening and find residents engaged in *kīrtana* even though they weren't expecting us. I was once staying for some days at an *āśrama* in Sylhet town during Kārtika, when Vaiṣṇavas follow special observances and there are many *kīrtana* functions. I would visit various homes in the evenings, and while returning either on foot or by rickshaw to the *āśrama*, I would hear *kīrtana* coming from any of the many Vaiṣṇava temples in the town as well as from homes where devotees had gathered to sing the names of the Lord. As one *kīrtana* would fade out of earshot another would fade in. This would continue until I reached the *āśrama* at about 11 p.m.

Unfortunately many traditional Bengali *kīrtana* styles have been lost. Yet whatever remains is still wonderful and mind attracting. Śrīla Prabhupāda liked it when the Māyāpur *gurukula* boys would sing the Hare Kṛṣṇa mantra in typical Bengali fashion.[31] But he didn't like another common Bengali technique, the artificial drawn-out manner of singing by which the Hare Kṛṣṇa *mahā-mantra* is almost lost in long notes. Prabhupāda called it "howling."

In practically every village there are experts in the Bengali style of singing in high pitch. In the morning it is common

31. *Māyāpur* — birthplace of Caitanya Mahāprabhu and site of ISKCON world headquarters.

to hear the sound of singing and harmonium practice within homes.

Flute playing is also popular. Cheap bamboo flutes are hawked on town streets and at country fairs. Even in big cities it's not unusual to see a person playing a flute while walking along. Other instruments common in Bengali music are the violin and *ektara,* a simple indigenous stringed instrument.

Many Hindu villages have at least two or three superb *mṛdaṅga* players. A real master can produce more than a hundred varieties of sound from the two heads of the drum. One drummer we knew could make his *mṛdaṅga* "talk" and say Hare Kṛṣṇa. Even many five- or six-year-old children are quite deft on *mṛdaṅga,* although they can hardly stretch their hands to reach the heads. When I was new to Bangladesh, I once attended a temple *kīrtana* and was surprised to see a small boy nonchalantly playing *karatālas* in a brilliant manner that I had never before heard or imagined.

Our *āśrama* in Dhaka became a place of *kīrtana.* Some devotees whom we had recruited were expert musicians and at any time could sit down with harmonium, *mṛdaṅga,* and *karatālas* and sing and play wonderfully. Evening was prime time for *kīrtana,* when people from outside would come and our tiny temple room would be packed. The tempo would start softly and slowly, then gradually build. Or sometimes it would suddenly go fast and the rhythm change.

Oh, the dancing — and the jumping! It was tremendous. We could sing for hours together. Our whole bodies and even our clothes would become drenched in sweat yet we would hardly notice. Sometimes after such *kīrtanas* I would have to wring out my dhotī. Afterward we'd go up to the flat roof of the building to catch the night breezes. Finally we would take rest late at night, with the intricate *mṛdaṅga* rhythms and beautiful melodies still echoing in our minds.

Western Christian missionaries are sometimes alarmed at their Bengali brethren exuberantly singing and banging drums, for fear that they are reverting to their "old heathen ways." The standard Christian approach to God is with solemnity, but for the Bengali, worship of God is something to be enthusiastic about. Bengali Christians cannot give up worshiping God with *mṛdaṅgas* and *karatālas*.[32]

In Sylhet district resides a community of Manipuri Vaiṣṇavas who migrated there a few hundred years ago. They practice Gauḍīya Vaiṣṇavism in their own regional manner. At appropriate times of the year, they have performances in which children dress up as Kṛṣṇa, Rādhā, and different *gopīs* and dance pleasingly to the accompaniment of devotional songs. Manipuris have somewhat Chinese-looking features; their Gaura-Nitāi Deities also have slanted eyes, and mind-captivating beauty.

Manipuri *kīrtana* tends to be more subtle and less intense than its Bengali counterpart. The former is soft and

32. In our early days in Bangladesh, a Hindu leader told us that wherever in Bangladesh Western devotees go, the tendency for Hindus there to convert to Christianity completely ceases. When the Hindu villagers come to know that Kṛṣṇa consciousness is spreading all over the world and being accepted by Western Christians, they take renewed pride in their own culture and cannot give it up even at the offer of so many material inducements (a standard feature of Christian conversion in poor countries).

charming, with highly intricate rhythms and elaborate long beats. Bengali *kīrtanas* mostly employ simple two-beat and three-beat patterns, but Manipuri *kīrtana* is often so complex that it is difficult to trace the beat. Sometimes the emphasis comes only on the fourteenth beat. They use a drum that looks like the Bengali *mṛdaṅga* but made of wood instead of clay and giving a less resonant sound. Manipuri *kīrtana* is sung in their own language, significantly different from Bengali.

Nāma-yajñas (sacrifices of chanting the holy names) are important events in Bengali Vaiṣṇava culture. Every Bangladeshi Hindu knows Caitanya Mahāprabhu's teaching that in Kali-yuga the only authorized *yajña* (sacrifice) is the chanting of the holy names. Festivals of nonstop *kīrtana* by rotating groups last at least a full day — or three days — or even seven days. Unfortunately these *yajñas* have become commercialized. Groups of businessmen in towns vie with each other to see who can make the most ostentatious show, attract the biggest crowds, and feed the most people. Professional bands make an entertainment business out of the holy names of the Supreme Lord.

Previously *nāma-yajñas* were organized on a small scale, with purely religious motives. The singers would be local residents who relished chanting and hearing the holy names. The organizers would happily feed everyone without making a spectacle of it. Such *nāma-yajñas* are still held in some villages wherein people either do not want to or cannot afford to pay for professional groups, and who instead themselves chant the holy names.

Bengalis are also intensely fond of drama. In villages especially during summer, performances continue all night. The dialogue is highly expressive, with much gesturing, and the tone tends to be heavy on pathos. The actors wear incredibly gaudy outfits and make-up. To me the cntire theatrical style seemed comically overblown, but Bengalis take it most seriously. If any, the props are simple, and the stage is often just an open area. A few musicians in the background lend accompaniment, sometimes with a little singing.

Food

Annual floods wash down from the rivers alluvial deposits that make Bengal's earth black with vitality. The rich soil combines with plentiful rainfall and a tropical climate to make the whole country like a lush garden. This verdant land produces an apparently inexhaustible variety of leaves, shoots, roots, stems, creepers, and flowers, some cultivated and some wild. For instance *śāk* (green leafy vegetables akin to spinach) is a nutritious Bengali favorite of which there are at least thirty varieties. Some are cultivated, and others grow wild, to be collected from riverbanks and jungles.

Even after years of traveling in Bangladesh I would occasionally come across some kind of vegetable that I had not yet seen or heard of, or a familiar vegetable prepared in a unfamiliar manner. Bangladeshis are expert in combining diverse types of vegetables in apparently limitless culinary varieties. And though their cooking techniques were simple, the results were naturally tasty because the food was grown in excellent soil, without fertilizers and insecticides (when I was there).

Despite their limited financial resources, Bengalis love many kinds of food. Previously the regular daily meal was rice, *dāl,* and three vegetable preparations — one dry, another wet (i.e. very juicy), one semi-wet. Extras such as *pāpar,* chutney, or pickle might also be given. About fifteen minutes after the meal some fruit with milk or *khīra* (boiled down, thick, sweetened milk) would be served. This was the standard even in less affluent families.

The saying "Eating only rice and *dāl*" used to indicate a family's being extremely impoverished. Although most people are not so poor, and at least in recent years nobody starves, nonetheless malnutrition is widespread. Children with bloated bellies and matchstick limbs — symptoms of Celiac disease, a chronic nutritional imbalance — are a common sight.

In a land where few can afford to eat luxuriously, being fat is considered prestigious and healthy. In Bangladesh to say that someone looks "healthy" means that he would be considered overweight by Western standards.

Rice is the staple food of Bengalis, and inseparable from their lives and culture; it is eaten morning, noon, and evening. Nowadays many city folk eat chapatis at night instead of rice, but the standard Bengali meal is heaps of rice with a little something else on the side. Vegetables and *dāl* are usually hotly spiced, so generally a small portion of each is taken with much rice. Normally, cooked rice is served at midday and evening. While chewing one mouthful, Bengalis like to prepare the next by rolling the rice with their fingers and mixing it with *dāl* and vegetables. They say it makes the food more tasty. In the morning villagers often eat *pantabhat*

— rice left over from the previous evening kept overnight in a pot with plenty of water. By morning it becomes slightly sour. *Pantabhat* is taken with salt and chilies and maybe also a little curry or something else. It has a cooling effect on the metabolism, so is not eaten during winter or the monsoon.

Dietary habits also largely depend upon occupation. Office staff may not eat much in the morning, whereas field workers can eat piles of rice up to four times a day. Despite being usually quite short and of slight build, villagers work hard in the fields and carry heavy loads. Their appetite is commensurate with their labor.

Many dry rice preparations, such as *muri* (puffed rice), *chira* (flat rice), and *khoi* (fused rice) are kept in airtight tins and are convenient to eat any time. Puffed rice is made by boiling rice in the husk, drying it again in the sun, and then heating it within sand in a *korai* (shallow metal cooking pot). The sand becomes completely black, and as the rice gets hot it goes "Pop! Pop!" After the rice is puffed the sand is removed through a sieve. It's like Rice Krispies of the West, but naturally white. If eaten just after being made, its delicious flavor rivals that of many complex and costly dishes. *Khoi* is made by a similar process but is soft, not crispy like *muri*.

Another permutation of rice is *chira*. The rice is first boiled and husked, then flattened with a wooden mortar — "thump, thump, thump" — and finally dried and stored. If soaked in water for a few minutes *chira* can be eaten uncooked.

Muri, khoi, and *chira* are often taken with *gura,* a favorite village confection. If to any of these combinations are added hot milk, or sweet yogurt, plus some freshly grated coconut pulp and maybe a few slivers of ginger root, it becomes a royal breakfast even though made from everyday ingredients. *Gura* mixed with ground coconut and made into balls or bars is another village favorite.

One more among dozens of such simple yet superb treats is *dāl boris,* made by grinding soaked *dāl* with certain spices, rolling it into balls, and drying them in the sun. Fried *boris* are added to vegetable and liquid *dāl* preparations.

Being a land of rivers and ponds, Bengal is full of fish, which Bengalis are well known to be fond of. Although poverty forces much of the population to follow a predominantly vegetarian diet, most of those who can afford it eat meat or fish along with their rice, *dāl,* and vegetables. When our devotees first went to Bangladesh, fish eating was considered normal and acceptable even for Vaiṣṇavas and gurus. Now that has changed. Many Bangladeshi Hindus have reformed their lifelong habits and people have come to know that true Vaiṣṇavas don't eat fish or other flesh foods.

If a guest arrives unexpectedly and his host wants to give him a special food, he is asked to wait while puris are quickly prepared. Fried potatoes or eggplant — both of which are tasty and can be cooked quickly — also go well with puris.

Generally, frying is done with a minimum of oil, which is better for health and also economical. Traditionally mustard oil was used for frying, but nowadays many people cannot afford it. Cheaper, imported soybean oil and palm oil are now widely used, but are less flavorsome.

By and large Bengalis are content with the same simple fare every day, yet for festivals or special guests the women take great pleasure in preparing many items. In such elaborate meals, which we were often given wherever we went, the Bengali style is to serve a heap of rice with many small preparations around it. A typical feast might consist of two or three fried dishes, a bitter vegetable, perhaps two or three types of *śāk,* and two or three other vegetables. Or there may be many vegetable preparations given in tiny portions.

Bengali milk sweets are renowned throughout India. There are many varieties, with names like *rasagullā, rasa malai, chamcham, rabri, sharbhaji,* and unlimited variations of *sandeśa.*

Some sweet shops are named *Jala Khabar* ("to take water"). In Bengal's tropical climate it's common for travelers to request water from a local villager. The tradition was to give not only water but also a sweet along with it. Even today in many homes of the affluent, guests are given both water and a sweet. Others will often give at least some grains of sugar, to uphold the tradition.

A delectable sweet is *mishti doi* (sweet yogurt), which is made by adding yogurt culture to sweetened condensed milk. And a winter favorite is milk boiled down slowly until there are thick pieces of cream floating in it, served hot with sugar or date *gura.* Yet milk is no longer as plentiful as in former days. One elderly gentleman told me that when he was a child milk was never sold in villages, because everyone had sufficient supply. And if anyone needed more he would just ask a neighbor.

Coconut and date palms grow profusely in the south of Bengal. In winter the sap from date trees is extracted by boring a hole in the trunk and inserting a short wooden pipe. This sweet juice can be taken as a beverage, but soon starts to ferment and turn sour. Thus the system is to boil down most of the sap into *gura*. The most common source of *gura* is the juice of sugar cane, which is widely cultivated, but the sweetest *gura* comes from palmyra sap, and the most delicious from date sap. Simply by combining date *gura* with grated and fried coconut, two profusely available ingredients, an incredibly tasty sweet is produced.

On a hot day *dābs* (unripe or slightly ripe coconuts) are the best thirst quenchers. A *kachi dāb* is fully unripened and has no pulp, just slightly salty water inside. *Kachi dābs* are the most cooling, and contain valuable electrolytes that are lost in perspiration. Slightly riper *dābs* have a creamy, jelly-like, white pulp around the inside shell, and the water is sweet. A few dexterous swathes of a machete at the top of a *dāb* make a hole from which the water is drunk. Then the *dāb* is chopped in half and a piece of the shell sliced off to make a spoon for eating the pulp.

I remember once arriving at a village after a long hot journey. Upon entering the courtyard of the house where I was to stay, my host seated me on a wooden chair in the shade. His approximately eight-year-old son came and offered obeisances to me immediately without being told. The father then told him to bring a *dāb*, so taking a machete he deftly climbed about fifty feet up the nearest coconut tree. After three or four rapid hacks, there was a brief silence — while we watched the green missiles plummet down, land with a thud, roll around a bit, and come to a halt. Two were enough to relieve the arduousness of travel.

Another popular drink is lemonade (called *sharbat*). Many village homes have a lemon tree in their courtyard, from which lemons may be plucked at any time. The juice is mixed with cool water and sugar, and sometimes a little salt, to make a great refresher that is especially invigorating on hot days.

Cooking

A typical Bengali village kitchen is a tiny mud-walled room with a stove consisting of a hole in the ground with earth raised up around it. Generally cooking is done over a wood fire or by burning dried cow dung patties. This method educes a special flavor that cannot be derived from coal, gas, or electric stoves. Cow dung fire gives the best flavor of all. The pots are usually aluminum, although brass used to be the norm. Prior to cooking, a layer of mud is rubbed on the outside of the pot so that soot from the fire may easily be removed afterward just by washing off the mud — thus saving much scrubbing.

All kitchen work is done on the floor; there are no sinks or sophisticated machines. Vegetables are cut with a foot knife, which is held stationary under one foot while the vegetables are pushed onto it. Cooks use merely a few simple tools, pots, and utensils, most of which would be unfamiliar in Western kitchens. Differently shaped pots are suited for cooking different preparations, and a *korai* is used for frying and cooking vegetables. With these simple arrangements, Bengali women can produce practically unlimited varieties of dishes that in quality and flavor far surpass that of internationally famous gourmet kitchens. One woman told me that she knew thirty-two ways to cook the vegetable *kochu,* using the leaves, stem, and root.

The women of a household generally prepare meals together and serve them to the members of the joint family. Because they routinely cook in quantity, and always a little extra, they're always happy to receive even unexpected guests. But if there happens to be any shortage, the women, who eat last, will often serve out their portion and simply eat more at the next meal. Or they may dilute the *dāl* and cook more rice, or rustle up a quickly prepared item such as fried eggplant or fried potatoes.

Guests

Bengali villagers derive great pleasure in receiving guests. Not having many diversions like so-called civilized modern folk, they enjoy simply being together with other people. In the course of our party's travels, people went to much trouble to accommodate, feed, and serve us. *Athiti Nārāyaṇa* ("The guest is as good as God") is an important principle in Bengali and Hindu culture. Sometimes we would tell our hosts, "Oh, you are taking so much trouble to look after us," and they would happily reply, "Not at all. It is our pleasure to have you. Please excuse us for not better caring for you. Whenever an unexpected guest arrives, we consider that God has personally come to visit us.." And when guests are about to leave, the host will ask them to stay longer, or at least to come back again.

Bengalis are prepared to sacrifice to whatever extent necessary to serve guests properly and in the best possible manner. For them it is a matter of prestige. One who does not receive others well cannot be a very important person. The extent to which a person or family receives others is a vital factor in determining social status. Indeed it is common for people to host others well beyond their means and think nothing of the debt incurred.

We experienced how hosts are eager to serve guests, especially Vaiṣṇavas. Automatically people would come and fan us by hand. One time I arrived in a village on a very hot day. After being served a midday meal I laid down to rest. A boy was appointed to fan me because it was so hot that without being fanned, falling asleep would not have been possible. I told him to fan only until I fell asleep, but when I woke up over an hour later he was still there patiently fanning away.

Bengalis love to feed their guests to full satiation and beyond. The idea is that if the guest eats plentifully, he must be enjoying the food. Bengalis are expert in inducing guests to eat more and more, serving different preparations little by little, saying, "This is very tasty; you'll surely like it. And it's excellent for health." If one objects, "But now I am full," they may playfully retort, "Oh, this is something to help digest your food."

And when the guest says no, his actual intention is understood from the tone of his voice. If there's any indication that he is willing to eat a little extra, the host will understand that and serve more. So when one *really* doesn't want any more, he must fold up his leaf plate and maybe also get up. When we visited homes in Bangladesh our hosts liked to serve us more than we could eat, because they rarely got the chance to receive sādhus. They would give more and more, to make sure that there would be enough remnants to share with others, at least those of the family — if not the entire village![33] Persons would even request our remnants before we had finished eating. Although that is actually not proper, it was an overbubbling of good-natured enthusiasm.

Health Care and Occult Miscellany

Villagers generally get plenty of fresh air, fresh food, and physical work, and are consequently usually strong and healthy. Even though Bengalis are not very stout, they can toil all day in the hot sun. Many men and women continue to work even in old age, for instance by milking the cows, tending the fields, or sweeping the courtyard. Although not obliged, they still feel energetic enough to want to.

Once an elderly man with a black, ferocious countenance was trying to touch my feet. In order to avoid getting dumped upon myself what appeared to be a lifetime's worth of rather heavy karma, I ran. But he followed determinedly. I thought that being so old he would quickly give up — but he didn't. Other than leaving the village altogether, I had no alternative than to submit to him. He caught my ankles in a painfully strong grip. Although bent and wrinkled, his body was still full of strength and stamina.

---

33. In Hindu tradition, to eat the leftover food of saintly persons is considered a highly pious activity that bestows great blessings. This practice is particularly observed by Gauḍīya Vaiṣṇavas, especially in Bangladesh.

In the towns and larger villages of Bengal there are qualified physicians, but very few throughout the balance of the country. Health care in rural areas is based primarily on knowing how to live according to nature's laws. How to keep healthy by eating properly is common knowledge — which foods heat or cool the body, what should be eaten at different times of day, which foods bind or loosen the belly, and so on.

An everyday topic of discussion among Bangladeshis is the condition of their stomachs and intestines; particularly, what kind of stool they've been passing — whether liquid or solid, what color it was, how quickly it came out, and so on.

Basic medical needs are administered at home, for every grandmother knows how to treat minor ailments and wounds and even more serious conditions such as rheumatism and fever. For instance, they know that for stomach upset, drink the extract of such-and-such plant. In one village when a member of our party had severe diarrhea, an elderly lady went out to the field and soon brought back different kinds of grasses and leaves. She extracted the juice on a flat stone mortar, as found in every Bengali kitchen, and told him to drink it. Within ten minutes he was back to normal.

Kajjal, a substance made by mixing an oil lamp's soot with a little oil, is applied to children's and women's eyes for its cooling medicinal effect and also as a decorative mascara. Mothers commonly also put a spot of *kajjal* on their children's faces to ward off the evil eye.

Foo (blowing) is a traditional cureall. Once when I had stiff and painful joints from the cold weather, a local woman brought some mustard oil, chanted mantras over it, had me rub it on the affected parts, and then blew on the joints: *Foo! Foo! Foo!* All the stiffness and pain immediately went away. Equally fantastic, but also well accepted, are tantric methods for discovering thieves. Once some money disappeared from our *āśrama* in Dhaka. We deduced that the culprit must have been one of two residents — but which one? So some local devotees called in a tantric. To the suspects and several others he gave a little uncooked rice over which he had chanted some mantras. He told them to chew it for two or three minutes and then spit it onto some newspaper he had put down. Naturally the chewed rice was broken up and mixed with saliva. But that which came from the mouth of one of the two prime suspects was hardly broken and completely dry. Thus everyone concurred that he was the culprit.

Animals and Insects

Up until the early twentieth century much of Bengal was covered by dense jungle, in which tigers, wild boars, elephants, and other dangerous animals roamed. Now most forests have been cleared and eighty percent of the land is under cultivation. In the far south, where the Gaṅgā finally splits into multiple substreams before reaching the sea, there are dense mangrove forests on the innumerable uninhabited islands therein. And in the hilly narrow panhandle bordering Burma are many thick woods. Except for snakes, outside of these forests dangerous wild animals are nowadays rare.

Domesticated village creatures include goats, cats, chickens, and geese — and scrawny cows, often no bigger than large dogs of the West.

The dogs of Bangladesh are of the mongrel genus common to the subcontinent — neither truly domesticated, nor exactly wild. They live close to humans in villages and towns. But there are relatively few of them compared to the huge population of miserable street dogs in India, probably because dogs are officially abhorred in Islam. In villages they're thrown some scraps of food, allowed to sleep on verandas and in outhouses, and are generally tolerated. But they aren't petted or given names, what to speak of being hailed "man's best friend" as in the West.

Legions of fat grisly-looking cockroaches emerge at night and swarm through kitchens and latrines. Similarly hideous are the little green lizards that run about walls and ceilings, chasing after insects to eat and after each other for sex. Sometimes they fall — plop! — on the floor. They are called *tik-tikkis* because of the loud ticking sound they sporadically make. Bengalis believe that a *tik-tikki's* ticking just after a person has said something is confirmation of his statement. One of the less memorable sights of Bangladesh is that of a *tik-tikki* stalking a cockroach, each running a few paces and then stopping. If the lizard manages to catch the roach, he'll swallow the struggling vermin bit by bit, stretching his jaws to fit the little monster inside. After ingesting it whole, the outline of the roach shapes the victorious lizard's bloated belly.

Rainy season means ant season. Their cities quickly devastated by flooding, ants seek shelter within the homes of humans. Their constant marching to and fro is a constant source of annoyance, for they invade sheets, beds, clothing, and food, and also use human bodies as their highways.

Just after rainy season comes bug season. For a few days millions of *gadhipokas,* large flies prevalent at this time of year, teem into existence. They come out at night and swarm in clouds around lamps. Since their bodies are larger than their wings, and not very aerodynamic, these bugs often fall to the floor and then gyrate around, trying to get back into flight. But they don't, and every morning small heaps of these dead bugs have to be swept away.

There are many snakes in Bengal and death from snakebite is not uncommon. People working or walking in fields may accidentally tread on a snake and get bitten. During the rainy season, when their holes get flooded, snakes move into granaries and houses. Muslim fakirs know how to cure snakebites by mantra.

When Bengali villagers see dangerous snakes they cry out, "Garuḍa, Garuḍa, Garuḍa ..." invoking the protection of Lord Viṣṇu's eagle carrier, the great enemy of snakes, until the danger has passed. Catching snakes by their tails and swinging them around is a pastime of Bengali village children. I don't know how they do it; they're quite fearless. They also know how to slowly and repeatedly hit a snake on the head with a stick to kill it. Then the dead snake is chopped into pieces and burned. Otherwise, it is said, it may come back to life. Or its mate may come, see the reflection of the killer in the dead snake's eyes, and take revenge.

A devotee once told me this story which he personally witnessed: A snake was killed but for some reason not burned. The next day at noon, at the same residence, there was a knock at the front door. Everyone in the household thought it strange that someone would be calling at this hour, when the extreme heat normally kept everyone indoors. The man of the house looked out an adjoining window to see who was there yet saw no one. But at the base of the door he espied a cobra, presumably the dead snake's mate, knocking with its head.

Scorpions are rare. I came across only two during my years in Bengal and each time instantly killed them with my shoe.

Village Set-up

The vast majority of arable land in Bangladesh is divided into innumerable little family farms. Ownership keeps people on the land and out of the cities. Even if a family plot is small, it accommodates a home to live in, a measure of respectability, a sense of identity, and the hope of stable sustenance.

Rice, two or three yields of which can be grown each year, is the leading food crop in all regions. Pulses, the main source of vegetable protein, are the next most important produce. Bright yellow mustard flowers are a common and pretty sight. Mustard is cultivated for the seed, which is used as a spice and for production of mustard oil, the favorite cooking medium of Bengalis. Jute is a major cash crop, as more than fifty percent of the world's jute is produced in Bangladesh.

Many prosperous village families own a group of small houses clustered together. There will be a house for each of the married brothers and his family, perhaps a separate one-room house for cooking, and a similar small construction for a temple. The typical Bengali village home is a mud hut with thatched roof, which although hardly luxurious is quite pleasing to live in. The thick walls render such homes somewhat cool during summer and warm in winter.

The houses surround a courtyard — a place for children to play and for all to relax in the evenings. It's also used for drying clothes, *dāl,* and rice. And a sacred *tulasī* plant will be there upon a small plinth.

Women clean their residences with a mixture of cow dung and water. Every morning they smear it with a rag over the floors and walls. I once heard a Bengali Christian criticizing this practice as dirty, ignorant, and primitive, but actually cow dung has antiseptic, cleansing, and purifying properties, as verified by modern science. And its smell is pleasing, not offensive. Wherever cow dung is smeared, no flies will come. It's also an excellent fertilizer and cooking fuel. Throughout India, village women collect cow dung and shape it by hand into patties, which they slap onto tree trunks and walls for drying in the sun.

People generally sit on the floor, either directly or on mats of straw or cotton. Other than maybe a few shoddy benches and chairs, most homes have little furniture. Except during winter and monsoon, people generally sleep outside — but whether inside or out, they sleep either on grass mats spread on the ground or on simple wooden beds. Sleeping on beds gives some protection from snakes. Residences being perennially congested, beds are also useful for storing items beneath.

Apart from their hereditary fields, most families have a little garden plot near the houses, every inch of which is utilized to produce vegetables, flowers for offering in worship, and spices and herbs, especially chili and coriander leaves. They may also have fruit trees, most commonly banana, mango, jackfruit, coconut, lemon, and papaya. Creepers straddle outer walls of dwellings, yielding vegetables like pumpkins and squashes. It's remarkable how much the villagers produce from their small patches of earth.

Except for the most destitute, all families possess some valuables, usually locked away in steel trunks or in cupboards. For security against financial difficulties, families stash jewelry and ornaments, which they rarely display or talk about, but which may be sold or pawned in an emergency or otherwise passed from generation to generation. It is also common to bury such treasure under the earthen floor of homes even without other family members knowing about it. Considering paper money and bank balances unreliable, villagers have always preferred to keep their savings in precious metals and jewels, although attitudes are now changing.

Nowadays jewelry and ornaments are mostly worn only by women, although in previous times men also would wear ornaments. Although married women must wear jewelry — at least some silver anklets, gold earrings, and maybe a nose ring — they don their more elaborate ornaments only on special occasions, such as marriages.

While most people struggle just to survive, not everyone in Bangladesh is poor. Some landholders own extensive properties, and many merchants also are prosperous. Affluent Hindu men are usually somewhat portly and dress in fine cotton dhotīs, compared to the rough cloth of the common man, and many chew pan incessantly. They are addressed as *babu,* maintain several servants, and are influential and highly regarded.

Handicrafts are made throughout Bangladesh, each region with its specialties. Tangail is renowned for *sārīs,* Nator for certain milk sweets, cane furniture mostly comes from Sylhet district, and so on. A certain type of grass that grows primarily in Sylhet is made into thin mats that are cooling to sit or lie on, a definite relief in the long hot season. And Dhaka was long famous for extraordinarily fine cloth, until the British cut off the weavers' thumbs to eliminate competition with English mills.

Village shops are usually little ramshackle structures and dispense all kinds of items, mostly at prices less than one US dollar. There are no fast-food joints, but rural shops sell biscuits and other prepared edibles such as *channa chur,* crispy noodles made from chickpea flour and ground spices.

The once-weekly market brings chaos to the already disordered country towns. Sitting behind mats or cloths spread higgledy-piggledy on the ground, traveling peddlers displaying their wares — medicines and herbs from other regions, expensive spices like cinnamon and cloves, forest honey, trinkets, curios, and crude homemade toys. Vendors raucously hawk their goods, yelling in croaky voices long since worn out from overuse. And common are hucksters with amazing cure-all medicines, promising miracles and attracting gullible crowds. Villagers jostle and push through the throng, everyone eager to get as much as he can for as little as possible, and prepared to haggle over a few paisa.

In Bengal, shopping means bargaining. Generally this is difficult for a Westerner to adapt to, for he naturally assumes that the retailer is trying to cheat him by quoting an excessive price. But that is the system. Initially the merchant will quote a figure too high for his goods — be it apples, vegetables, a cooking pot, a shopping bag, whatever — expecting the prospective customer to offer a lesser amount. The seller then reduces the rate somewhat, but the buyer again rejects. In this way it goes on until they agree on an amount and clinch the deal. Or if the shopper isn't satisfied with the vendor's final offer he may try his luck elsewhere. It's a contest to see how much the purchaser can lower the sum. It adds some fun to life, although in a poor country where every paisa counts, it's not exactly a game.

Approach to Life

Lord Caitanya most mercifully appeared in Bengal, but unfortunately most Bengalis do not take His benediction seriously enough. Instead they eat flesh and worship bogus incarnations. Thus they must suffer severe karmic reactions in the form of poverty, floods, droughts, cyclones, tidal waves, epidemics, and so on.

Most Bangladeshis spend their entire lifetime struggling to scrape together bare necessities for existence and are constantly on the edge of ruin. Climatic vicissitudes, political instability, and a "might makes right" rule of law add to the uncertainty. Protracted hardships and the insecurity of below-subsistence living have fostered cheating, lying, and exploitation, all of which have become an integral part of modern life in Bangladesh despite its otherwise great culture. Land disputes and forcible occupation are common. No one knows what will happen tomorrow, but tend to expect calamities. Hindus suffer even more, being treated as second-class citizens and an easily exploitable minority.

During the terrible era of the Bangladesh Liberation War no one was safe. An estimated million people, mostly defenseless, were slaughtered between March and December of 1971. At any moment the Pakistani Army could arrive in a town or village and wreak devastation. Soldiers especially targeted Hindu villages, dragging people from their homes, slitting their throats, raping and strangling women, and performing other such loathsome crimes. A standard question to ask a Bangladeshi is his father's occupation, but often the reply is, "He died during the *gandagol shomoy* (disturbed period)."[34] Occasionally people would tell me some horrific stories, but mostly they didn't want to talk about it.

Early death is not remarkable in Bangladesh. When asking a Bangladeshi how many siblings he has, it's not unusual to be told, "We are three brothers, but the eldest died of diarrhea when he was two years old." Upon an untimely death the relatives grieve piteously for some time but then adjust and get on with life. Yet a woman who has lost her husband or a child will remain sorrowful for the rest of

34. Even after the war was over, chaos continued for several years after the establishment of Bangladesh as an autonomous nation. Land-grabbing and political opportunism contributed to the disorder. In 1974 massive flooding destroyed crops and led to an enormous famine, establishing in the minds of television viewers worldwide the name Bangladesh as synonymous with poverty and wretchedness.

her life. Not that the men are heartless, but they tend to accept difficulties stoically. If a woman loses her husband, generally her father or a brother will look after her and the children.[35] Yet many single women strive against great adversities to put their children through school and get them established in life.

Bangladeshis have a composed manner of accepting hardship, which helps them adjust to all kinds of trials. Their sense of resignation toward unavoidable calamities is combined with a feeling of satisfaction and appreciation for God's gifts. They're not rife with anxiety like Westerners, despite living in circumstances that few Westerners could tolerate. Their hard and bitter struggle for sustenance does not make them hard and bitter. Instead they persevere, remaining confident that whatever may happen, somehow or other they will go on. Inner resilience carries them through even the greatest adversities without their becoming overwhelmed. Thus Bangladeshi villagers are far happier and psychologically sounder than their affluent brothers of technologically developed nations. Even the crazy people in Bangladesh are generally happily crazy, not dangerous, and thus rarely locked away.

Life is slow in the villages of Bangladesh. People have time for each other. Time is only relatively important. Exact to-the-minute accuracy is not required. Time is approximately ascertained by the sun's position. If a villager is asked,

35. In Bangladeshi culture "single mother" means a widow, not a divorcee. In Hindu culture a woman who has prematurely lost her husband returns to her father's household. But if her relatives have been washed away in a flood or have migrated to India, a single mother will have to manage alone.

"When will you come?" he'll not give an exact time, but will reply, "In the afternoon," or whatever. The day is divided into early morning, late morning, midday, afternoon, and evening, and few Bangladeshis feel a need to be more specific than that. Even in town life, with its schools, factories, and offices, there is but vague punctuality. If a town dweller is asked, "When will you come?" he may reply, "Around four o'clock." But that is understood to mean "some time after four," because timeliness is not intrinsic to the Bengali lifestyle. It's not unusual for Bangladeshis to arrive fully one or two hours later than they said, which in the West would be considered irresponsible and insulting, but which is quite acceptable in Bangladesh. Indeed an important person often deliberately arrives late at an event just to show his importance — that other people have to wait for him, not that he has to wait for them.

This languid approach to life is often frustrating to Westerners, who take it as mere laziness. But their urgent and busy lifestyles strike the Oriental as frenzied. It's difficult for Bangladeshis to understand the Western proclivity for being constantly active. A visitor to a Bengali's home is expected to remain for some time — to sit and chat and partake of some food or drink — not just rush off, which would seem rude to Bangladeshi hosts, as if the visitor had no regard for them or was anti-social.

Westerners like to lead a life packed with variety and excitement, whereas Bangladeshis prefer to live by tradition, doing things in basically the same way that their fellow men do, and indeed as their forefathers have done since time immemorial. Often when missionaries or so-called social workers try to teach Bangladeshis something new, such as a modern farming technique, they will be challenged, "Why do you want to do in this way? Do you think you're some great person to teach differently than our ancestors of thousands of years?" And that will be the end of the matter.

Generally Bangladeshis, especially villagers, don't appreciate when their own people adopt a different or modern lifestyle. Although nowadays in the towns of Bangladesh many men wear Western-style shirts and pants and consider it prestigious to speak English, they still don't want to become fully Westernized. And it's still considered improper for women to dress in modern, overly attractive styles. But contemporary ways are affecting even Bengalis; thus Western fashions for women are gradually becoming accepted in the cities of Bangladesh.

More modernized Bangladeshis are now adopting Western concepts of progress and success based on individual performance, accomplishment, and competitiveness. Yet even today most Bangladeshis have few ambitions. They're not motivated to prove or improve themselves. They might aspire for higher education or a government job, but generally not more than that. They're concerned about maintaining status in society and procuring enough food for their family, and perhaps also a few luxury items like a tape recorder or television. Most Bangladeshis don't expect much materially and are more or less content with what they already have.

Growing Up in the Land of Jagannātha

Braja Hari Dāsa recalls memories of his childhood in Orissa, a state of eastern India. He describes the intimate family relationships and interdependence of different levels of Oriya society. Braja Hari gives insights into the spiritual culture of Orissa and discusses how modern ways have quickly eroded it.

B.V. Swami: Braja Hari Prabhu, you're from a *brāhmaṇa* family in a village in Orissa?

Braja Hari: Yes. I was born in 1953 in a *brāhmaṇa* family. In our house we worship Lord Kṛṣṇa and recite *Śrīmad-Bhāgavatam* every day. From the time of my grandfather we have been reciting the Oriya version of *Śrīmad-Bhāgavatam* by Jagannātha Dāsa.[36] When I was a child my father's elder brother used to read from palm leaves, because books were written on palm leaves in the old days. No printed books in Oriya were available. We still have

36. Jagannātha Dāsa's edition of *Śrīmad-Bhāgavatam* is widely known and revered in Orissa. However, it is not accepted as bona fide by strict followers of Caitanya Mahāprabhu. Jagannātha Dāsa composed his version with thirteen cantos (the original has only twelve). He is therefore known as *ati-bari* ("one who makes too big") Jagannātha. *Ati-bari* is one of thirteen *apa-sampradāyas* (deviant groups) listed by Bhaktivinoda Ṭhākura. Despite its shortcomings, Jagannātha Dāsa's rendition nonetheless inculcates a tendency toward Kṛṣṇa consciousness.

that old palm-leaf manuscript in our home and worship it daily. We also worship *śālagrāma-śilā* and pictures of Lord Kṛṣṇa in our home.

B. V. Swami: What is the name of your village?

Braja Hari: Gulugunde. It's in a remote part of Dhenkanal district, in a hilly area at the edge of the Jharikhanda jungle. The nearest proper road is the Cuttack-Sambalpur National Highway 42, about twenty-two kilometers away.

B. V. Swami: Still many Indian villages are quite a long walk from any road. Many people even live far away from any but the most basic shops.

Braja Hari: Yes. Our family has a medicine shop, but we have to go four kilometers from our home to get to it. My younger brother runs it. The name is Medico Hare Kṛṣṇa.

B. V. Swami: So he has to carry all the goods four kilometers.

Braja Hari: He has a motorcycle.

B. V. Swami: So nowadays it's easier.

Braja Hari: Before, everybody used to walk. Previously there were people who would daily carry big baskets of vegetables maybe fifteen kilometers to sell in the town. Then they would walk back in the evening with empty baskets.

B. V. Swami: They were so strong. Who were your family members living at home?

Braja Hari: We were three brothers and four sisters. Three sisters are older than me and are now all married. Ours was a joint family. In my father's family there were also three brothers. So my father and his brothers were staying together in separate houses in the same compound.

B.V. Swami: Did you have a courtyard?

Braja Hari: Yes. The courtyard in every home would have a *tulasī-mañca.*[37] Everyone would water *tulasī* at least once daily, bow down to her and circumambulate her — even those who were not Vaiṣṇavas, like the *śāktas.*

B.V. Swami: Yes, the courtyard system is there in Bengal also. The members of the joint family live in cottages around a courtyard, with other cottages serving as the common kitchen and so on. You were telling me earlier that the teachers were very affectionate to you.

Braja Hari: Yes. When we were children the teachers treated us like our own father would. They gave us work to do, and sometimes if we couldn't do it they would punish us. But they also loved us and were very affectionate. They sometimes visited our house to tell our father and mother what we were doing, and whether there was any difficulty.

Parents were very concerned that their children be brought up properly. They preferred teachers who were strict, and gave full license to them to punish and beat their children if they misbehaved. No one complained about such strictness. Rather, they wanted it — "Spare the rod and spoil the child."

B.V. Swami: So you must have been afraid of your teachers.

---

37. *Tulasī-mañca* — plinth for the sacred *tulasī* plant.

Braja Hari: Afraid, yes, but we also loved and respected them like our own parents, because they cared for us as if we were their own children. Even after we were grown up and married, they would be concerned with our welfare and always ready to guide us. Even more than teaching us the ABCs, they wanted to see us become good people, to have the proper values in life. The teachers would even want news of those children who later moved to the towns, to hear how they were doing. Teaching was not just a job for them, like a job in a factory. They were selfless. They wanted to give us whatever they knew. They didn't just forget us after we left school. And we can't forget them either. You can hardly find such teachers nowadays, and even if you do, the children are brought up so badly that they don't appreciate them.

So the parents and teachers were concerned that the children be brought up properly, that they be honest and not steal, tell lies, misbehave, or insult their elders. They brought them up in such a way that they became honest. It depended upon the family — it is not that everybody taught the best morals — but if the father and the mother were good, they would teach it.

I can give an example: One farmer we know has no time to look after his children. He goes out in the morning to work in the field and comes back late. It is the mother's duty to give the children breakfast in the morning and get them ready for school. Naturally children don't like to go to school, but it is the duty of the mother to send them. And the mother also keeps in touch with the teacher, and asks how the child is doing, whether he is fighting or stealing. If he is misbehaving then he gets punished.

When I was in the sixth or seventh standard I once stole ten rupees from my father's pocket. My father had just received his salary and had it all with him. We belonged to the lower-middle class, and my father was the only person earning an income, with seven children. Although we had property and everything, it was still a struggle. My father was a very honest person. He made sure he never had to borrow from anybody. But my grandfather borrowed many things. He was forced to borrow again and again with accruing interest, and my father struggled hard to repay his debt.

The Indian system is that the debts of the father are passed on to the son at death; and my grandfather died in debt. So at that time our landlord came and took whatever paddy we collected from the fields. After my father got his job we were leading a very austere life, but he wanted to maintain honesty. That's why he finished all his debts first. He would give us the bare necessities, but he never allowed us to lead a luxurious or extravagant life. After that struggle, my father took a vow not to borrow a single paisa in his life, so as not to pass a burden on to his children, such as he had been given.

So why did I steal the ten rupees? In our school the students would go to the market and buy *boris* and so on, and my father used to give me twenty-five paisa every Monday. In those days twenty-five paisa was a large amount. But I had a habit of buying something to eat and then sharing it with my friends. So one day we thought we would make a feast, but when I asked my father he didn't give me money. So I just stole ten rupees from him and we made a feast.

B.V. Swami: In those days ten rupees was a lot of money.

Braja Hari: A lot. And when my father discovered it missing he asked me why I took it. Then I told a lie, that I didn't take it. But he found out that we had had a feast and everything, and he asked me to tell the truth. I said, "No, I have not taken it." Then he beat me with a stick. He said, "Unless you tell the truth ..."

B.V. Swami: On your hand?

Braja Hari: Yes. So I put my hand up to protect myself and he beat me — ten, fifteen times he hit me. And my mother and my father's eldest brother's wife, who is very affectionate to me, came and held me to protect me. After that I promised I would never do such a thing again, and I really meant it. So they gave strict instruction and punishment. When I went just a little wrong they would scold me like anything.

B.V. Swami: Now you are grateful for that.

Braja Hari: Yes. The last time I went home we were discussing my childhood, and I told my father that I am grateful to him. He was very happy.[38]

---

38. Braja Hari Prabhu has been a leading manager at ISKCON's Śrī Śrī Rādhā-Rāsabihārī Temple in Mumbai since 1995, and is known for his honesty and selflessness. Thus I was surprised to learn that he had ever stolen anything. His story demonstrates how Oriya children were strictly trained in moral principles. And the effectiveness of such training is evident today in Braja Hari's character. Another feature of his honesty is his openness regarding his childhood waywardness. Braja Hari still likes to arrange feasts for his friends, but nowadays does so by licit means.

All the children in those days felt grateful to their parents, uncles, aunts, older brothers and sisters, and teachers — who all loved them from the heart.

B.V. Swami: We were discussing about the teachers. They took a personal interest, almost like a guru-disciple relationship.

Braja Hari: Almost like a guru. And we would also treat them like that. In the morning when we came to school we would first touch the feet of the teacher, and in the school we used to sing a prayer to Kṛṣṇa from a book called *Varṇabodha*, by Madhusūdana Rāya. Everything was in that one prayer. The meaning is very nice. And from the very childhood they would teach us from this *Varṇabodha* about how Kṛṣṇa is taking care of all living entities.

Another observation from this story is the differing responses by Braja Hari's father and the womenfolk. Both acted out of affection for him. But out of sentiment the women demanded leniency, whereas out of anger his father was determined to punish him. His anger was not spiteful but motivated by concern for his son's welfare, that his character not be spoiled. His father let it be known that he was deeply displeased and would not tolerate such misbehavior.

Such Indian villagers never studied psychological books on child-raising. Yet the training was so nice that generation after generation was well-adjusted and morally upright, with a natural, inbred proclivity toward devotion. The training was simple, uniform, and consistent: that certain things are right and others wrong. Elders set good examples and punished digressions by juniors. Everything was conducted in an atmosphere of selflessness. There was no need for complex psychological advice, nor could the villagers have understood or related to it.

B.V. Swami: Did they teach *kṛṣṇa-līlā* as part of the syllabus in school?

Braja Hari: No, they were not allowed to do that, due to secularism. When we were promoted from third to fourth class, however, one of our teachers took about a month to tell detailed stories from the *Mahābhārata* and *Rāmāyaṇa* — *Mahābhārata* fifteen days and *Rāmāyaṇa* fifteen days. He would teach us every day for two hours. It was interesting, and he described the stories very nicely. He taught with real feeling. It made such an impression on us that we could never forget it.

We were so lucky. We got such nice teaching in our childhood that the impression of Kṛṣṇa will remain with us throughout life. We cannot forget Kṛṣṇa. Not that we are perfect or highly elevated or cannot get into *māyā,* but that impression of Kṛṣṇa will always be there, at least in the back of our minds. We cannot give it up. Now we are also hearing *Śrīmad-Bhāgavatam* class every day, but it doesn't affect us as much — the impression that we got in childhood carries up to the end of life.

I can never forget one teacher in particular, Jaya Krishna Mishra, a professor at Ravenshaw College in Cuttack. He was an M.A. in Oriya literature and a great poet also, a highly respected figure. He was proficient in Oriya as well as Sanskrit and English — a renowned personality who would get invitations from all over India to give lectures. He used to teach us Bhakta-caraṇa Dāsa's *Mathurā-maṅgala* and many other literatures.[39] *Mathurā-maṅgala*

39. Bhakta-caraṇa Dāsa was an Oriya Vaiṣṇava poet. His Mathurā-maṅgala, written in thirty different prosodic styles, contains a brief account of Uddhava's role as a messenger after Akrūra brought Kṛṣṇa to Mathurā.

is the story of Kṛṣṇa in Mathurā, told in the elevated language of Sanskritized Oriya. Nowadays nobody uses such words, but when Jaya Krishna Mishra explained it to us it had deep meaning, so it was very interesting to hear. He taught us in such a way that everything was related to God, or Kṛṣṇa. He was a great devotee. When he was explaining some parts of *Mathurā-maṅgala* he used to cry.

B. V. Swami: He would cry!

Braja Hari: Not for show or anything like that, but out of strong feeling. And the students would cry also. In our childhood almost all the people were very religious, spiritual — not like now. Nowadays teaching has become a formality, just another job. The teacher cares nothing for the pupils and vice versa. In those days we had so much respect for the teachers, because they taught in such a way that it had a long-lasting effect. When we returned to the hostel at night we would go on thinking deeply about what our teacher said, because it touched our hearts. And sometimes the students would discuss all these things in the hostel.

Like in our ISKCON society, devotees sometimes come to consult the *sannyāsīs* or gurus and ask questions, we also used to go to our professor's house to ask more about *kṛṣṇa-līlā*. He was such a nice man. He would call everyone, give each a place to sit in his room, and explain the subject — and ask his wife to give us some *prasāda,* whatever they were cooking. A very sweet exchange.

B. V. Swami: Even in your college life would you touch the feet of your teacher?

Braja Hari: Not all of them, because some teachers were not good examples. But Jaya Krishna Mishra was a senior man, from the older generation. When we were young he was in his late fifties. But younger teachers didn't have such status. It also depended on their behavior.

B.V. Swami: One thing about Orissa is how everyone is attached to Jagannātha. As soon as you enter Orissa, Jagannātha is everywhere — His Deities and pictures in homes, shops, and even buses, with His huge transcendental smile. In the morning when the pan shops open, they play beautiful *bhajana* cassettes glorifying Jagannātha — before they start the continuous cinema music.

Braja Hari: Lord Jagannātha is the worshipable Lord of Orissa. I don't know how it happens exactly; when I was a child nobody told me to worship Him, but spontaneously we liked Lord Jagannātha. It is in our heart. Even now we also pray to Rādhā-Rāsabihārī, Rādhā-Śyāmasundara, and Kṛṣṇa-Balarāma, but when I see Lord Jagannātha or hear about Him, immediately I feel something ecstatic.[40]

B.V. Swami: Did you go to Puri in your childhood?

Braja Hari: My father is a devotee of Jagannātha, so he took me — not every year, because it was too expensive. I went with him two or three times.

B.V. Swami: At *Ratha-yātrā,* or some other time?

Braja Hari: Other times. Also nowadays the *upanayanam* ceremony has become very expensive, so some people go

40. Rādhā-Rāsabihārī, Rādhā-Śyāmasundara, and Kṛṣṇa-Balarāma are Deity forms of Kṛṣṇa at major ISKCON temples in India.

to Jagannātha Puri and celebrate it there, where they can do everything with a minimum of expense.

B. V. Swami: You were telling me a story about how you were saying, "Rāma, Rāma, Rāma..."

Braja Hari: That was when I was studying in fourth class.

B. V. Swami: That means you were nine years old?

Braja Hari: Yes. In our village there is a school, but my father sent me to a school in another village because he thought if I studied in the same school, with the same family or children, then I would be spoiled. So a man from our village was a teacher in that other village, about four kilometers from our home. Half a kilometer from our village the forest starts. Nowadays the forest is not very thick, because everybody is cutting the trees, but in those days it was very thick. There were tigers, elephants, lots of wild boars, and everything.

B. V. Swami: Still?

Braja Hari: Yes, but they didn't come to the villages. They kept away from human habitation. If by chance a tiger or ferocious animal came, then people became very scared. Once the villagers told us a tiger had just come. Everybody was scared. And in the night a young teacher left and didn't come back, because he was afraid. But our teacher stayed.

I told my mother, "I'm not going to school, because everybody is saying that a tiger is there and it will kill me. I don't want to go." But my mother said, "No, you should go. Why are you afraid of the tiger? The tiger will never touch you if you just chant Rāma's name." So the two of us went to school, chanting, "Rāma, Rāma, Rāma, Rāma, Rāma, Rāma ..." all the way along the forest trail from our house to the school. But we were still afraid.

I used to stay in a hostel in that village and come home once a week. My father was a government servant and went to work in the town. He would come home on the weekends, so I would also.

B.V. Swami: You were saying how you were taught to respect your family priest. Even though you are *brāhmaṇas,* still another *brāhmaṇa* would come and do your *karma-kāṇḍīya* activities.

Braja Hari: Yes, like *śrāddha* and other such observances.[41] We still celebrate the death ceremonies of my grandfather and grandmother. On *śrāddha* day we call the priest to do the *piṇḍa* and various other rituals, and invite other *brāhmaṇas* and feed them. When I was a child a family priest would come. He was a very old man, but still he would come. My father and mother first washed his feet and dried them, then they asked all the family members to go and touch his feet, and he would put some *akṣata* on our heads. And then he would give his blessing, reciting some Sanskrit verses.

The *brāhmaṇas* were respected. They maintained their principles properly. Now that old man's grandson, a young man, is coming. Although my father is now seventy years old, he also touches his feet. That is the tradition, to

41. *Śrāddha* — ceremony observed on death anniversaries of departed relatives. The ceremony has several aspects, the most important of which is offering *viṣṇu-prasāda* to departed forefathers and distributing *prasāda* to guests, especially to pure *brāhmaṇas.*

give respect to superiors. The boys from *smārta-brāhmaṇa* families would study *karma-kāṇḍīya* rituals, apart from attending the village school. They would learn how to perform *śrāddha, anna-prāśana,* and other ceremonies, astrology, the Oriya editions of the *Rāmāyaṇa* and *Mahābhārata,* and all the other branches of knowledge they needed to become village priests.

B. V. Swami: Tell us more about the ceremonies.

Braja Hari: When the children are about ten months old *anna-prāśana,* the first grains ceremony, is held. Before that they are given only milk — mother's milk and cow's milk, and nowadays buffalo milk. Especially mother's milk is very important to help the child grow up stout and healthy. Women would generally breastfeed their children up to the age of five years. In many communities *nāma-karaṇa,* the name giving ceremony, is held at the same time as *anna-prāśana.* According to the astrological chart, the *brāhmaṇas* would recommend certain names.

Part of the name-giving ceremony is a vocational inclination test. The priests would put different items on a platter. They would put a copy of *Bhagavad-gītā,* some pieces of gold, a knife, and a box with *kumkum.* Whatever item the child selected was supposed to indicate his future propensity. If he picked up the *Gītā,* he was expected to be pious and scholarly, like a *brāhmaṇa.* If he grabbed the knife, he was supposed to become noble and bold, a leader, like a *kṣatriya.* If he went for the gold, he was expected to become business-minded and wealthy, like a *vaiśya.* And if he took the *kumkum,* that would indicate that there would be no major difficulties or calamities in his life.

Cūḍā-karaṇa, the first hair cutting, was another auspicious ceremony. Parents let their boys' hair grow until they could bring him to a holy place, especially to Puri, to have it all shaved off.

B. V. Swami: Puri is 150 kilometers away from your village. How would people go there?

Braja Hari: By walking. They would pack up some raw rice. Anywhere they could get wood, and vegetables for cooking. Those days vegetables were never sold. There was no big trucking business bringing vegetables to the big city to sell. So people grew them locally, and if any travelers on the way took a few vegetables to eat, they were welcome.

B. V. Swami: What about birth ceremonies?

Braja Hari: The first thing is, in those days everyone was born at home. There was no question of being born in the hospital. Living in the village, we had not even seen a hospital. A lady who was expecting was ceremoniously sent to her father's placc for delivery. There'd be some function, a ceremony overseen by the family priest. They would hold the usual kind of ceremony with *akṣata,* mantras, some *prasāda,* like that. Then the ladies would put *mahendi* on their hands and there would be plenty of flower garlands.[42]

B. V. Swami: After how many months of pregnancy was this?

---

42. *Mahendi* — henna; red coloring extracted from a certain plant, widely used throughout the Indian subcontinent for making decorative designs on women's hands and feet, especially on festive occasions. It is not the same as *alta,* mentioned in the essay on Bangladesh.

Braja Hari: It depended upon the caste. In my family it was in the seventh month. The mother was ceremoniously sent to her father's place. So my mother was sent to her father's place, my maternal grandfather's place, where the delivery would take place. The elderly ladies knew how to look after pregnant women and all the problems they are likely to have. They had already had so many children themselves.

Women used to keep busy with all family duties right up to the point of delivery. That way, by keeping active, the delivery would be very easy. Sometimes we would hear stories like this: A pregnant woman went to the forest to collect wood, delivered right there in the forest, and came back carrying a bundle of wood and a baby.

All the elderly ladies would look after the mother-to-be nicely, and if there was any pain or anything, they knew the right herbs to give her. They would call the pregnant lady and have her sit while they read *Bhāgavatam, Rāmāyaṇa, Mahābhārata,* like that — especially these three books. Sometimes the elderly ladies would read, or sometimes the older men. And that's one of the reasons, I think, why even the young children in India used to have spontaneous attraction to hearing about Rāma and Kṛṣṇa, because they already started hearing about them in the womb, even before birth.

B.V. Swami: Can you tell us something about the *upanayanam* ceremony?

Braja Hari: The sacred thread ceremony is very important in a *brāhmaṇa* family, like a marriage. The usual age is about ten or twelve. If there are two half-brothers or cousins of similar age in the family, they may be given *upanayanam* together in the same ceremony.

Before the thread ceremony we would go from village to village to beg alms for seven days. The people would give rice, fruit, vegetables, money. We would collect everything, and after some days the collected items, along with other things from the house, would be given back to the people. When they came to the festival they were fed nicely, and they gave money to the priest.

For the *upanayanam* ceremony the boy's head would be shaved to make him look like a nice *brahmacārī*. *Upanayanam* is supposed to mark the boy's going to *gurukula* for beginning Vedic studies. But nowadays, it's simply a formality and a social occasion. The family priest does a fire sacrifice and everybody wears a dhotī and *chaddar*. The family spends a lot of money for the *upanayanam* ceremony, and after the fire sacrifice they give a huge feast to all the villagers and their relatives. If there is a feast in the village, they have to invite everybody.

After the ceremony the priest and villagers take the boy to the end of the village where there are no more houses, and they chant a mantra and put three lines on the sand. Then they ask the boy, "Do you want to remain a *brahmacārī* or do you want to take the renounced order?" Actually it is just a formality. The elderly people teach the boy not to say that he wants to accept the renounced order.

If the boy chooses the renounced order, then he has to cross those three lines, and he will never come back home. Hardly anyone ever does that, but we know of some very rare cases, who left to become sādhus. Near our village a boy just left. He never came back.

B. V. Swami: All the village people must have been very sorry. Had he planned that?

Braja Hari: He was fourteen years old at that time. He always went when there was a *kīrtana* festival in a nearby village. He was very fond of chanting Hare Kṛṣṇa. He just took off from the *upanayanam* ceremony. He took the thread, the mantra, everything. When you cross the lines, your father and mother cannot bring you back. They cannot call you to come back over those three lines. To do that — take *sannyāsa* and then return to home life — is extremely sinful.

After the initiation ceremony we would sleep outside for seven days. And after taking initiation (*upanayanam*) everyone had to take bath, at least once, if not twice or thrice in a day. Even on the cold winter mornings it was a strict practice, especially in *brāhmaṇa* families, to take an early morning bath.

B. V. Swami: What about other festivals throughout the year?

Braja Hari: One of the big festivals is Makara-saṅkrānti.

B. V. Swami: How do they celebrate that?

Braja Hari: For Makara-saṅkrānti they make a feast in everybody's house and people exchange the different preparations.

B. V. Swami: Life in the village is very simple. Is there electricity in the home?

Braja Hari: Now we have it.

B.V. Swami: But when you were growing up there was no electricity.

Braja Hari: I remember at that time everybody had cows. A milkman from another village used to come about six-thirty a.m. All the people would free their cows, because they kept them in the house, milk them, and then let the cows and calves go to the forest for grazing. It was a very nice scene, especially in the rainy season. I clearly remember in the morning the milkman would come with his flute, and when he played the flute all the cows would come. That man took all the village's cows out all day. Because everybody worked on their land, they didn't have time. So we would just pay the milkman every month.

B.V. Swami: And he milked the cow also, or would you do it yourself?

Braja Hari: No, we would do it. But he took care of all the cows and took them to the forest, because the forest grows nice grass. They used to take care of the cows so carefully, better than the proprietors themselves. They would take them to the river and wash them very clean. Their twelve- or thirteen-year-old children would tend the cows, taking them to the field and coming back in the evening. The cows were healthy and we had respect for them. We were following what is done in ISKCON today very nicely, and we did worship also — Govardhana Pūjā, everything.

At that time money wasn't always used. The main activity in the village is, of course, farming, so we would often pay people, at least partly, in grains. Especially farm laborers would get paid like that. That cuts out the need for the middleman and makes it more economical for everyone. Or at harvest time we would give the barber a certain amount of paddy, then every so often he would come to our house and do haircuts and shaving for whomever needed it.

We used to have about a hundred mango trees on our land. Nowadays many people just steal things, and we ourselves don't have the manpower to take care of everything. But when we were children everybody had trees. Nobody ever bought or sold mangoes because everybody had enough. We would go to the mango garden, about two kilometers from our house. In Orissa almost every day in the summer there would be a huge storm with heavy wind. About five p.m. it would suddenly become very still and hot, and then a strong wind would blow for five or ten minutes and blow so many things down. All the ripe mangoes would fall, and we would collect them and bring them to the house in a bullock cart. Every day we would bring back more than thirty kilograms. How much could we eat? Hardly a fraction of it. So my mother and all the ladies used to make pickles and keep huge quantities throughout the year. They still make them.

And in our garden we grew our own vegetables, which tasted very nice because they were fresh from the ground. We used only cow dung — no fertilizer, no insecticides. We had a huge garden, so generally we didn't buy anything from outside.

In Orissa they make all kinds of fried foods from pumpkin seeds, all kinds of seeds. What is considered waste and thrown away elsewhere they know how to prepare as tasty, nutritious items.

B.V. Swami: There is wonderful, unique cooking in the villages in Orissa. How did you get water? Was there a village pond or well?

Braja Hari: Every village had at least one pond. In our village we have a very big pond, and people from three or four of the surrounding villages come and take bath there. It is a first-class pond. It's very cool, and in the summer you go deep down inside. In winter it seems too cold to take a bath, but when you dip in it is quite warm and pleasant, because it is a big body of water, fresh and calm. And in summer it is very cool. That is Kṛṣṇa's arrangement. Everybody has at least one well for the garden and for drinking water. Having separate, extra wells is better. In our house we have three wells: two for the garden and one for drinking water.

The original village system worked in an eco-cycle. There were no plastic bags or tin cans to create pollution. They used traditional machines: just one or two types of plow; a hand-operated apparatus for flattening rice; gardening, farming, cooking, and fishing utensils; like that. All very simple. People ate from freshly-cut banana leaves that were used once then thrown away. Or they used stone or metal plates. A plow, cooking pot, or anything else fully or partly made from metal was repaired if necessary, not thrown away. If something went beyond the point of repair, the metal was sold for scrap. There were even people who came around and collected garbage, like old bottles, and they would give you a few paisa for them.

Among the poor people, old clothes were sewn and patched again and again. When they got too old to function as clothing they were used as rags or for making a *kantha,* a patchwork quilt made from pieces of old cloth and stuffed with rags. Rich people didn't patch their clothes; they gave them to their servants. Nothing was wasted.

We would grow our own food, make our own cloth, or get it from the village weaver. There was a village potter, a blacksmith, a barber. The village shop sold odds and ends, nothing very fancy — candles, matches, some fancy spices, like that. We got oil for lamps and cooking from mustard seeds, which were grown at home and pressed in the village oil mill — simple.

B.V. Swami: In your childhood, please don't mind me asking, did you wear shoes or not?

Braja Hari: We used wooden shoes. In every village there was a carpenter. They made very nice shoes, good quality shoes with elephant teeth around the edge.

B.V. Swami: Ivory. And the strap would be made of cloth? Or what?

Braja Hari: No, no strap.

B.V. Swami: Wooden peg. Everyone was using that?

Braja Hari: Yes.

B.V. Swami: That's very nice. I ask this because I saw myself that even twenty years ago in India many people did not wear shoes. Even today some respectable *brāhmaṇas,* especially in South India, prefer not to wear shoes. Twenty years ago also, most men in the more traditional cities of

South India wore dhotīs in the typical South Indian style, double folded and straight down the back without a *kacha* (length tucked in at the back). Towns like Vijayawada and Madurai would be a sea of dark faces and white dhotīs. Nowadays it's all pants and shirts; you hardly see a dhotī. Did you used to wear a dhotī in your childhood?

Braja Hari: No, short pants. But my father never wore Western clothes in his life. Only dhotī, *chaddar,* like that.

B.V. Swami: In the generation before, would the children have worn dhotīs and the girls have worn *sārīs*?

Braja Hari: Yes.

B.V. Swami: In your generation would the girls wear *sārīs*?

Braja Hari: Up to sixth standard they wore pant-shirt (*salwar khameez*), and after that, when they were a little grown-up, they wore *sārīs.*[43]

B.V. Swami: Another thing: the separation between the sexes was very strict back then. You were telling me that even your younger brother's wife couldn't speak to you.

Braja Hari: Oh yes, that was there also, in Orissa especially. I think separation was there in all caste communities, even in the lower classes.

B.V. Swami: The younger brother's wife could not speak to the older brother.

Braja Hari: All older brothers. If it were important that the eldest brother talk to the wife of the younger brother or she to him, they couldn't talk face to face. The wife of

43. *Salwar khameez* — originating in Muslim countries, a loosely fitting trouser-suit worn particularly by unmarried girls.

the younger brother would be on the other side of a door or screen, and they would talk in such a way that they couldn't see each other. She could cook *prasāda* for him, but she could not serve it. So now in our house we have a problem because my mother is very old. Whenever I go, nobody is there to serve but my mother, who is unable to walk. But she still brings *prasāda* and gives it to me, instead of my brother's wife.

B.V. Swami: What is the reason for that?

Braja Hari: It is a sign of respect to the eldest brother, who is treated like a father. If the father in a family dies, then the eldest brother becomes the head of the family. As long as the father is there, he is the head. Even now, if my father dies I will be the head of the family, and all the brothers will have to pay respect to me.

B.V. Swami: They have to follow what you say.

Braja Hari: Even they may be married, they may be elderly and have grandchildren, but still they follow the eldest brother.

B.V. Swami: I was told that in some families even brothers and sisters are not supposed to mix together too much. When they become eight or nine years old, the brothers are not allowed to play with the sisters.

Braja Hari: When the sisters become a little grown up, then the boys and girls don't sleep together. When they are young, up to five or seven years, we sleep and play together, everything; but after six, seven, eight, nine years, they sleep separately.

B.V. Swami: They may not even talk so much together.

Braja Hari: No, no, they talk. It is an affectionate relationship, but still nothing like that between two brothers. The older sisters also behave almost like a mother to the younger children. That's nice, because even after they are married, they treat the younger brother or sister nicely. They exchange a lot of affection and respect — more affection than respect.

And family ties are very strong; they are maintained. For example, if the eldest sister's daughter or son marries, or if there is a thread ceremony, she will invite everybody in the family. The relatives may be married and living in another village but they all come for the ceremony. The visitors will bring a gift, and in return the hosts will prepare some *prasāda*. After the function is over, when they are going back to their village, the hosts give them some *prasāda* to take — not a small amount. And when the visitors are back in their village, they will distribute the *prasāda* so that everybody can share in the program, even if they didn't personally go. That is still practiced also. In addition, the elder who invites the guests will give them gifts, like dhotis, *sārīs,* or children's pants and shirts.

Nowadays some people think it has become very burdensome because everything is more expensive, but the tradition of exchanging gifts is still there. Everything is costly and sometimes it's difficult to meet all the expenses. But I have seen that many people will make a loan or sell their land so that they can give gifts and observe these functions nicely. It is a prestige issue.

The village people knew each other intimately. It wasn't like modern cities, where next-door neighbors don't know each other's names or even talk to each other. People would invite each other for festivals and family ceremonies. When there was a need, neighbors would help each other in the fields, in house rebuilding, or whatever. Sometimes there was a lot of hard work, especially during the sowing and harvesting seasons. All the family members joined in and worked together happily for days on end. It was like a big family. If there was no food in a certain home, the people wouldn't have to say anything; someone would quietly send some rice for cooking. Of course they couldn't go on helping them forever — no one was rich — but there was a sense of concern. How could you eat and live comfortably if your brother over the way was starving?

We were brought up with a sense of concern, generosity, and service: "Don't just think about yourself. Think of others too. We've all been put here together by the will of God, and if we all live peacefully and cooperatively together, that will please God." Problems were there; it was not Vaikuṇṭha. But even the worst disagreements would be settled quickly. There were no courts, legal fees, bribes. That kind of thing was all far away in the town. If there was any serious dispute in our village, the elders would listen to whatever the protagonists said, and everyone had to accept their judgment, whether they liked it or not. Nothing was private. If there was a quarrel or disagreement the whole village knew about it. But the prevailing mood was one of friendly and natural cooperation. Life was simple and austere, yet people were content. Now that is all spoiled by modern life, by the rascal politicians.

B.V. Swami: Was there any feeling of caste-ism or anything like that?

Braja Hari: Yes, caste-ism is always there. Now also it is there.

B.V. Swami: Some bad feeling.

Braja Hari: Not bad feeling.

B.V. Swami: But the caste system was rigid, wasn't it? Formerly, for a Hindu, caste determined his occupation and social status and affected in one way or other every aspect of living. Nothing could change it. A man born a *śūdra* had to live and die as one. No riches or power that he might acquire could raise him to a higher status, and his children and grandchildren, and their children after him to the end of time, would always be *śūdras.* The misunderstanding was that only a life of great piety and good works might, after his death, make it possible for him to be reborn as a member of a higher caste. Apart from that, there was no way to escape his destiny.

Braja Hari: That's true. But even the perversion of the caste system wasn't always bad. A boy born in a traditional family of potters, weavers, barbers, or whatever, would have his life's profession chalked out. There was no anxiety about his livelihood and no struggle against others in a competitive work market. His father would train him at a young age, and he would later on train his own sons in the same craft.

B.V. Swami: But there was separation between the castes.

Braja Hari: Some separation, yes, but generally there was cooperation. Like, if a lower-caste person had a marriage, we would go to his house but wouldn't eat anything.

B.V. Swami: You'd go there anyway.

Braja Hari: We would go and bless them, but not eat there. They could give us fused rice only.

B.V. Swami: In Bengal it is called *khoi*. It is always considered auspicious, pure.

Braja Hari: *Khoi* mixed with *gura*. That we would accept. But we heard that in some places certain *brāhmaṇas* were so strict and rigid in their rules that they would not allow anyone else to come near them. They didn't mix with anyone and looked down on and despised others. I don't think you'll find such *brāhmaṇas* nowadays. Social conditions have changed. People won't tolerate such behavior any more.

B.V. Swami: How have things changed in your village since your childhood?

Braja Hari: It is changing rapidly. Previously people didn't have much money and depended mostly on agriculture. Nowadays village boys want to get a modern education, live in the towns, get a job in an office or factory, and in this way become modern, civilized, and advanced. They think it backward to live in a village without modern amenities, doing farming and following the customs and culture. Even those who remain in the village no longer care to rigidly uphold the traditional practices. Now agriculture is neglected there because all the young men from the villages are getting jobs in the towns and factories. Even the farmers are becoming lazy. Festivals used to be nice family affairs; now you get half-dressed young girls dancing on stage to lusty film songs. Still, the interior villages are better. But those close to towns, to which the villagers go to work in factories, have almost completely lost their culture.

Drunkenness is everywhere in the villages. People work in the factories, get money, and drink, mostly illegally made "country brandy." *Daru* means brandy, you know? Everywhere. Young boys go to work and by age twelve, at the latest, they're smoking; by fifteen, it's *daru*. Then sex and abortion. There are signs all over the villages advertising cheap abortion.

Previously we were more innocent. We would hear the *Śrīmad-Bhāgavatam* for entertainment or do *kīrtana* ourselves, and from time to time drama troupes would come around. The cinema, transistor radio, and now TV, have changed the way people act and think and dress, everything. It started with the cinema. It was a big treat for the village people to go to town with the family to see a movie.

B.V. Swami: Religious themes?

Braja Hari: Of course. The first films were meant for families. Sex, even kissing, was taboo. The films upheld our traditional values of devotion, self-sacrifice, and so on. Then they gradually introduced different ideas, and now the cinema is totally, totally materialistic and degraded. Even though people live in conditions actually not meant for humans, they would rather live in a hovel in a town than in a village because they want to imitate the high life they see in the movies, dressing in jeans and all these things. They look down on village life and the farming their forefathers did for countless generations. They no longer want to respect any authority. There are so many machines now in the villages, like mechanized water pumps, tractors, and the like. They're getting the mentality that hard work is a curse. Most of the people have motorcycles, because they are making money, whereas previously they didn't even have bicycles. They simply work in a factory, earn money, drink and smoke, and go to the cinema. They will have a cassette recorder and listen to cinema songs all day and night. So this industrial revolution has gradually destroyed the innocent life of the village.

Factory-produced goods such as plastic plates and mass-produced clothing have destroyed the traditional livelihood of the potter, weaver, tailor, and others, driving them to the towns in search of work. Now their children become drivers, factory workers, or mechanics.

Much has been made of the sufferings of the poor and backward caste people in India, and much of it is true. Ignorance and apathy led in many cases to their gross exploitation. They used to accept it all as their karma and not grumble much. Modern education and politics has changed all that, but overall, in terms of real human happiness, there's no real improvement. Exploitation still goes on. But now it's the government officials and politicians who do it more than the landed gentry.

Even the least educated people nowadays are more aware about what is going on. They get the whole world, especially the worst of it, right in their homes on the TV. But in those days people hardly used to go outside their village. To go somewhere would be a big event, bringing all the family. Mostly they would go only for a marriage or a pilgrimage. For us Oriya people, pilgrimage means to go to Puri for *darśana* of Lord Jagannātha. Otherwise, people hardly went to towns. They didn't need to. Everything was there in the village.

It was Mahatma Gandhi who said, "If the village perishes, India will perish too. India will be no more India." Well, the villages are still there. The cocks still crow at dawn and the breezes still gently blow. But the old spirit is all but gone. The village is now hell. The kind of cruelty that goes on, both to animals and humans, you wouldn't believe. The real India is dead, or at least in a very deep sleep. We used to have genuine good will for everybody, but now we cannot afford to. It is difficult to trust anyone, even within the same family. Politics, which we never knew before, is everywhere. Village life is now full of greed and envy. Before, our doors were open to strangers. Now they're bolted against our neighbors. Life goes on, but it's chaotic and frustrating. We've lost our soul. We have votes and so-called rights, but we don't have good feeling, trust, or respect for others. We have TVs, motorcycles, tractors, and all the things we dreamed would bring a better future. But actually the past was in some ways better. All these machines were supposed to make life better and more comfortable, but even if we get enough money to buy them, we don't have peace to enjoy them. There are so many quarrels these days. People drink and fight. There are wine shops in every village, which we could not have imagined in our childhood. They don't respect elders like they used to. In our generation we even respected our enemy. Suppose in our village some other *brāhmaṇas* were there and my father did not have a good relationship with them. We considered them an enemy; our father's enemy meant our enemy. But still, as a matter of respect, whenever we would see them we said *namaskāra*. Even if they didn't talk to us, we still said *namaskāra*.

B. V. Swami: It's interesting that despite so much culture there was still consideration of friends and enemies.

Braja Hari: [laughs] That's natural. It's still the material world.

B. V. Swami: But the culture is so nice that even enmity is tempered with dignity.

Braja Hari: Yes, that's the value of our culture.

Lokanātha Swami's Childhood Home

The following are excerpts from morning walks with Lokanātha Mahārāja at his birthplace, Aravade, Maharashtra, in December 1996.

Outside the house

There is no air pollution here; the air is fresh. There are no vehicles. We hear only the bells that hang from the buffaloes' necks. In the past, every farmer had an ox cart with bells. The bullock carts used to have bells attached to them, so whenever they were returning from the farms, that's the only sound you would hear. There was a system to get water out of the well with the help of the bulls. There was no electricity, no electric motors, no oil engines, and no vehicles. Now these vehicles make such horrible sounds.

The farmers used to sing. Some bulls would not do their job unless the farmer sang some songs. They would sing for hours. I remember that when I was a little boy I used to hear so many farmers singing, including my father, and I was also learning some of those songs.

Visiting the kitchen

In every house the mother used to do the grinding with her hands. There was no grinding machine. The mother would grind only the amount of flour that was required for the day, for making *bhakari* (chapatis made from millet flour). My body is made of *bhakari*. During the first twenty years of my life, till I went to Mumbai, I was eating *bhakari* thrice a day. We would eat wheat products, like chapatis, only on festival days, once in a few months. Rice was also a festival item. Farmers do not grow wheat and rice in this area, so they have to purchase them.

Grinding is a very good, natural exercise. That kept the women's bodies healthy. To do the grinding they had to wake in early morning, because unless they did the grinding there would be no breakfast for the family. The mother would do the grinding and cooking and then send the breakfast out to the father, who would be working on the farm land. I used to bring the breakfast for my family. Some farms were quite a distance away from the house, up to five kilometers. Those were the good old days — very healthy, cultured, civilized ways.

Walking toward the village

This road we are walking on is new. It is not really an improvement. I was eleven years old when I first went to Tasgaon, the nearest town, in Sangli district. It would take two and a half hours to walk one way and another three hours to come back. Now children just jump in some vehicle and go to the town to see and hear some nonsense.

My father used to walk to Pandharpur, a hundred kilometers to go and a hundred to come back. So many people from the village would go several times in a year. It is the tradition that those who go for *darśana* also touch the feet of Lord

Viṭṭhala.[44] The Pandharpur *darśana* is not just seeing the Lord. It is complete when one touches the body of Viṭṭhala.

Those who did not go would wait at the entrance of the village, expecting the return of the villagers who had been to Pandharpur. So as soon as the pilgrims would arrive back, the villagers who had stayed back would touch their feet. To them, touching the devotees' feet was the same as touching Lord Viṭṭhala's feet. You will never succeed in stopping anyone from touching the feet of one who has had the *darśana* of Lord Viṭṭhala.

Passing by the village hospital

Here is the village hospital. The mothers stopped grinding the grains, so they're getting more sick, and now they need a hospital for the village. Thirty years ago, while I was in the village, we had one doctor coming once a week. He would come in the afternoon, and all those who needed medicines would get their treatment then. There was very little sickness, because people ate fresh grains and led a healthy life with less complications. But now things are getting difficult, with more air and noise pollution.

At Mahārāja's birthplace

This property is divided into two parts; to the left was my father's house and to the right was my uncle's. We are sitting in the middle. I was living here during my first fourteen years. I was born here. This is where I crawled and cried as a baby. Lots of things were different in those days; there was no electricity. I was ten years old when the village was

44. Viṭṭhala — name of the Deity of Lord Kṛṣṇa at Pandharpur.

first connected with a big powerhouse and got electricity. Before that we just used kerosene lamps and lanterns. Candles were not so popular.

Tasgaon is ten kilometers away. My mother and father never allowed me to go there. There is a big Gaṇeśa temple in Tasgaon, and on Gaṇeśa's appearance day they have a big *Ratha-yātrā* for Gaṇeśa. So once, on the occasion of the Gaṇeśa festival, I was allowed to go. That was the first time I went to a town. I was eleven years old, and the longest distance I had traveled was ten kilometers.

Walking through the village

You see the hill over there? Atop the hill is a big rock. The hill is known as Chilamkara. *Chilam* means "pipe." The elders used to tell us that there was a big demon who had a pipe. Once he emptied his *chilam* there and the ashes formed that hill. On the top of the hill the large rock is his *chilam,* that he stuck into the ash. You can imagine the size of the demon. From generation to generation they keep repeating this story.

At the school

I went to school here in the village for seven years. Then I went to high school in the nearby town and stayed there for four years. On the weekends and vacations I used to come back here and help the family with farming and herding buffaloes. At that time we had more buffaloes. When my family became Kṛṣṇa conscious they got more cows. You see those tall mountains? There are fields everywhere there.

We would take our buffaloes around the mountains and graze them in the fields.

Later on I went to Sangli town for my college education. My family wanted me to be an engineer, so that one day I would come on a motorcycle to the village. In those days only engineers and doctors had motorcycles; everyone else walked.

Arrows, Monkeys, and Mangoes

A picture of life in Andhra Pradesh, a state in southeast India. Narmadā Swami's memories range over many topics, including Rāmāyaṇa dramas, relations between the sexes, cowherd boys, childhood pranks, and more.

B.V. Swami: Narmadā Mahārāja, you were born in Nellore, in Andhra Pradesh. Today it is a large, busy city, but formerly it was a small market town.

Narmadā Swami: Yes. Then it was a small town, peaceful.

B.V. Swami: So you were living on the edge of the town, near the temple. The town is situated on the bank of a river, is it not?

Narmadā Swami: Yes, on the bank of the river Pennar.

B.V. Swami: There is a beautiful temple of Raṅganātha Swami in Nellore.

Narmadā Swami: Yes. A big Deity of Śrī Raṅganātha is there, sleeping.

B.V. Swami: Similar to the Deity at Śrī Raṅgam.

Narmadā Swami: Yes, the same as Śrī Raṅgam, but a little smaller.

B.V. Swami: Are you from a *brāhmaṇa* or non-*brāhmaṇa* family?

Narmadā Swami: A non-*brāhmaṇa* family. Choudhary, Naidu — officially *śūdra,* but a wealthy and powerful community in Andhra Pradesh. On my mother's side they were Śrī Vaiṣṇavas. So even though they were officially from a lower caste, because they were accepted as devotees they were allowed to chant various mantras and observe different rituals, much like the *brāhmaṇas* did. We were traditionally landholders, but my father got into the trucking business. We still had land, but my father also had a big fleet of passenger and goods transport trucks, which was nationalized in 1970.

B. V. Swami: As a prominent businessman in the city, he must have been well known.

Narmadā Swami: Yes, a well-known person. He was one of the few people in the transport business. Previously towns were few and not very big. Every region would have a market town where villagers could bring their excess produce and procure items that were not available in the village, such as ornaments and fine cloth for special occasions. On market day, villagers would throng to the town to buy, sell, and socialize. But when I was born the whole pattern of trade was changing. Those who were first to change with the times, like my father, were able to earn plenty of money.

B. V. Swami: I suppose Nellore was a big agricultural market.

Narmadā Swami: Of course.

B. V. Swami: Rice, tobacco?

Narmadā Swami: In our district mainly rice. Tobacco developed later, but mainly rice paddy. Nellore rice is famous in South India. They like it everywhere.

B.V. Swami: It must be long grain.

Narmadā Swami: Yes, very good rice. And *dāl*. After harvesting the *dāl* they would dry it in the sun for a few days and then husk it and roast it in big open pots. That was to make it last, so it wouldn't go bad. It had such a nice flavor after being roasted that you could just eat it like that, without cooking. I liked to keep some in my pocket and chew it all the time.

B.V. Swami: Maybe that's why you're so big and strong.

Narmadā Swami: There was a Telugu *paṇḍita* who was my tutor. He would ask me, "What is in your pocket? Give me some." In this way he would finish off my whole pocketful of *dāl*. [Laughs] He enjoyed it too.[45]

All the food was tasty in those days. I'm disgusted with the food you get now. It all tastes the same. Rather, none of it has any flavor. Even the so-called fresh vegetables have no life in them. Vegetables that are cooked a few hours after picking them have lost most of the flavor and nutrients, what to speak of the old frozen or half-rotten vegetables sold in the city. The real way to take vegetables is to prepare and eat them immediately after picking. Vegetables sold in city markets are lifeless and tasteless, grown with artificial fertilizers, and coated with dangerous pesticides.

People don't know what food is anymore. Neither the food has any flavor, nor do people know how to cook it. They used to prepare so many types of food for festivals. Who

---

45. Throughout this interview Narmadā Mahārāja often laughed in simple appreciation of his childhood days.

knows how to prepare such varieties now? The mothers are working; they don't have time. They want fast-food. Previously the ladies would keep themselves looking nice by putting turmeric mixture on their face at night. Now they spend two thousand rupees to go to a beauty parlor to do the same thing. They have a beauty expert tell them how to spend all their money. But before, every grandmother was a beauty expert and an everything-expert. They knew how to cook, how to clean, how to look after the children, how to handle the husband, everything. They were doctors and managers without ever going to medical school or management school. The home was the school.

About two generations before us, children were trained in traditional Indian style, that is, only in what they needed to know. A farmer's son would learn about different types of soils, seeds, and farming tools; when and what to sow according to season; when and how to harvest, thresh, and store grains; all about the weather; training animals for plowing; the ins and outs of caring for cows; and so on. A farmer's son would learn everything by working with his father. There was no need for wasting time going to school, learning so many things that would be of no use to him.

Likewise, the carpenters, goldsmiths, blacksmiths, artists, musicians, and others would receive on-the-job training from an early age. Only those who were to be *brāhmaṇas* received extensive schooling. The *brāhmaṇas* received extensive philosophical training according to the *sampradāya* they were in, and also learned the stories in the *Mahābhārata, Rāmāyaṇa, Śrīmad-Bhāgavatam,* and other *Purāṇas.* The *brāhmaṇas* would impart knowledge to other castes mainly by telling illustrative stories. It wasn't unusual for a *brāhmaṇa* to know some thousands of stories. Such tales were repeated at home, especially by the grandmothers to children, so that everyone grew up knowing of the exploits of Kṛṣṇa, Rāma, Hanumān, and the Pāṇḍavas.

Sons of merchants would learn as much arithmetic as they needed to know for trading. They would learn on the job how to distinguish between top quality and faulty goods, and how to deal with customers, suppliers, and tax collectors. Everyone received religious instruction.

B. V. Swami: So traditional village life in India had a strong spiritual and intellectual base.

Narmadā Swami: Oh yes, a lot of intellectual activity in the villages, because that's where most *brāhmaṇas* lived. And although there were some renegades, most of them were committed to maintaining the traditions. All the great *ācāryas* — Rāmānujācārya, Madhvācārya, even Śaṅkarācārya, what to speak of Caitanya Mahāprabhu — how did they spread their teachings? By walking village to village. They would meet the *brāhmaṇas,* debate, and convince them. And the *brāhmaṇas* would guide everyone else.

B. V. Swami: You've told us about the training for the different castes. What about for women?

Narmadā Swami: Women's training was first and foremost to be chaste and faithful to the husband, and to cook, clean, spin, look after guests, care for children, and whatever else was required of a dedicated housewife.

Extensive education for women was generally frowned upon, although higher-caste women might learn to read and write.

B.V. Swami: Cooking was very important for women. Girls learned from a young age how to cook nicely.

Narmadā Swami: That way their husbands would be obliged. If they always cooked nicely and served sweetly, what wouldn't a man want to do for his wife? The women would cook and feed everyone. *Woman* meant mother, and everyone was happy with that, not least the women.

The men had little or nothing to do with bringing up children, especially young children. It would be considered unmanly for them to carry around and fondle their offspring. It was entirely the women's job. Only when the children got older did the father come into the picture, as a disciplinarian and guide. Generally the fathers would be affectionate more to their daughters and strict with their sons. And the mothers would be the other way — strict with their daughters, affectionate to their sons.

B.V. Swami: So either way the children got a mixture of affection and discipline.

Narmadā Swami: And the women were not playgirls; they were mothers.

B.V. Swami: Instead of being sex oriented they were motherly, care oriented. The word *sex* was taboo.

Narmadā Swami: Taboo? We had never heard it.

B.V. Swami: Today it is considered advanced to talk about sex openly.

Narmadā Swami: [making a sound of disgust] All this talk of love and beauty and Miss World. They don't know what beauty is. In the past they were really beautiful people — all-round beauty, not just this skin beauty. Even physically they were more beautiful than today's young women. These poor girls, they spend so much time trying to be beautiful, but they simply look grotesque with their hair all splayed out like a *piśāci* (witch). They can never be truly beautiful because they're always full of anxiety. Maybe they look lusty, but not actually beautiful.

Even if they are beautiful, what business have they got showing that off to the world? That's not proper. Cāṇakya Paṇḍita says a woman's beauty is her chastity, not her hairstyle. Even now in the villages women always wear *sārīs* and ornaments, even to do manual labor. They would never want to be seen in something as unattractive as men's trousers. They would think that unwomanly and inauspicious.

B.V. Swami: Did most women cover their hair back then?

Narmadā Swami: Most of the women, say before 1960. Some of the more traditional women never came in front of any man, even though we were younger. They were supposed to be completely covered up, so that they could just see with their eyes.

B.V. Swami: To see their son also?

Narmadā Swami: Even to see their son. They were so strict. They kept just enough open so they could see.

B.V. Swami: At what age did girls start covering their heads?

Narmadā Swami: At an early age. By the time they reached twelve, at the latest, they always had to keep their heads covered in public. We saw all the old traditions. It was so strict that women could not eat until after their husbands. Even if he came in very late at night, they would wait up patiently, serve him, and only then take. Women were respected for following these things. Old men would address young girls as "mother."

B.V. Swami: The woman's place was in the home. They were required to be submissive and work hard. From early morning until late at night they would be busy. These days there's a lot of protest against this. Women are asking for liberation and equal rights in business, and opportunities in jobs, and that they shouldn't be dictated to. Modern women think they'll be happier if they have equal facilities — and on the surface these may appear to be fair demands — but we see that society is becoming chaotic due to the breakdown of the family. It seems that in the past, despite their clearly delineated inferior status, women were happier, and family life more stable.

Narmadā Swami: By all means it was more happy and more stable. There was no divorce. Very rarely. In my childhood I had never even heard of it. And families were joint families, the father and three or four sons' families all living under the same roof. If the unity in the joint family was appreciated, they didn't make any differentiation or discrimination between the children of one brother and the children of another brother. There was no restriction on having children. Back then there was no family planning. It was thought good to have more children, not less. Pregnancy was considered auspicious, not something to be avoided. So three to four sons, their wives, and their children all lived together, shared everything together, dined together, and pursued their destiny together. And it wasn't that women were despised, nothing like that. A woman biding by the traditions of her family was respected in society. It was required. A woman who didn't follow that was a disgrace.

B. V. Swami: One thing which is common these days is the mixing of men and women, which was very restricted before.

Narmadā Swami: Completely. They used to give so much importance to chastity. Until girls were teenagers they could come out and go to school, but when they came to puberty there was no question of them coming out. Their education was finished; everything was stopped.

B. V. Swami: And then they got married.

Narmadā Swami: Yes, always.

B. V. Swami: By what age?

Narmadā Swami: Between twelve and sixteen. Some higher caste girls would get married at nine or ten years old, although they continued to live with their parents for three or four years. They used to give girls education also, but when they came to puberty, and before sixteen, normally twelve, fourteen, then the marriage.

B. V. Swami: So girls were married early. Did the boys also marry at an early age?

Narmadā Swami: Normally at eighteen years.

B.V. Swami: So young. They lived with their wives immediately?

Narmadā Swami: No. But when a girl was married after puberty, she was sent to her husband's house within a few months.

B.V. Swami: So girls were instructed and sent away very young.

Narmadā Swami: Very young.

B.V. Swami: And they had many children.

Narmadā Swami: Yes.

B.V. Swami: How many brothers and sisters were in your family?

Narmadā Swami: Just myself.

B.V. Swami: Oh, that is unusual.

Narmadā Swami: Yes, that runs in our family, to have only one son. Otherwise at least five or six, plus of course some daughters, was the norm.

B.V. Swami: There is propaganda that this causes so many problems, overpopulation.

Narmadā Swami: But it is nowadays that we see so many marital problems, and in those days no problems. No marital problems and no breakdown of marriages. I don't think they ever had a divorce. Nobody. Even in some of the worst cases, in rare cases of misbehavior, the women tolerated everything. Even if the wife was suffering, she could never go back to her father's place. That was strict.

Once she was married she had to spend her life with her husband.[46]

B.V. Swami: Did the husbands sometimes mistreat the women?

Narmadā Swami: Sometimes. But even if they were having so many problems, the women would never talk about them. I have seen so many of them tolerating so much. They would never speak a word about what was happening. Even when the parents came and inquired whether the girl was happy or not, they always said, "I am happy. No problem." When they were suffering they never said so. That was the system.

B.V. Swami: So nowadays there is a dowry system.

Narmadā Swami: Slowly the dowry system has become a business. At that time they were not that much after the dowry. There was a system according to social position, but no compulsion. They used to feel ashamed to ask for any dowry. If the other family was ready to give according to their position, then they would accept. That was the system. But slowly, slowly it has become a business.

B.V. Swami: In Hindu tradition a man can have more than one wife. Did you ever see anyone like that?

Narmadā Swami: That was there. Normally we could have only one wife, but if they did not get children they might marry another wife.

B.V. Swami: Oh, only then.

---

46. In Bengal, a woman having too many problems in her husband's home may go back to her father's home — not permanently, but temporarily.

Narmadā Swami: Otherwise, I know of some cases in rich families somebody married the elder sister and the younger, because that family was not so rich and one more daughter was there. There are cases like that. But normally only one wife.

B. V. Swami: And those two sisters lived peacefully?

Narmadā Swami: Yes, because the society was such that women could not be independent. They could not even speak out boldly. That way everything was arranged so nicely; they were peaceful. And there would be exchanges. Somebody would marry a girl, and in the same house a boy would marry a girl from the first house. It was like that in my father's case. My father was an only son, so they exchanged. My father's sister married my mother's brother.

B. V. Swami: The women were disciplined.

Narmadā Swami: They were not allowed to speak roughly. Low-class women would talk loudly, but in higher society they were very soft-spoken. They would not even come out before a man.

B. V. Swami: They would not speak with an unknown man?

Narmadā Swami: No. There was no question of women speaking with unknown men. When I was married I did not see my mother-in-law's face for six months.

B. V. Swami: She was always covered up?

Narmadā Swami: I was so young. I married very young. She was like my mother, but even then it was the custom.

I saw her face only six months after my marriage. They used to follow all these things. That's why they were peaceful. They were satisfied. Whatever the system was, they would follow and accept it, that's all.

B.V. Swami: What about poor people. Were they also satisfied?

Narmadā Swami: Yes. The poor people used to work hard. In the villages they worked mostly in the fields and rich people's homes. When I went to my mother's place I would see two to four people working there, very happily. They worked hard. They were supplied clothing and everything and were looked after just like family members. When the crop came they got a quota of grain, so they were happy. There was no complaint. Everything was based on love and affection.

Every family followed the traditions handed down from generation to generation, and hence, the customs being equal in all the families, the society functioned according to more or less identical customs and traditions. Everyone was trained what to do from the beginning, and everything worked in harmony.

People also worked hard. They were stout and healthy and ate good food, not necessarily luxurious food, but whatever they ate nourished them and they digested it easily. They didn't have to go to fitness clubs [laughs]. The women would grind the rice and *dāl* by hand for making *idlis.* Have you seen that big stone and mortar? And churning milk, cleaning the house, so many things. It kept them healthy.

Now they do everything by machine, and they have an exercise machine also [laughs heartily]. A bicycle with no wheels [laughs more]. When they want to go to buy some useless stale vegetables with no flavor they go by car, and when they come back they take a lift up to their apartment and pedal a bicycle with no wheels [laughs uproariously]. And this is progress! Advancement!

Back then, we didn't have many machines; we had animals. Every family would have at least one or two pairs of oxen and one or two cows or buffaloes. The animals were also just like family members. They had to be fed and cared for and sometimes chastised if they misbehaved. They would paint the horns of the oxen and cows in bright colors and keep bells on their necks that jingled as they worked in the fields. Often the farmers would sing as they guided the oxen. The fields would be full of song, with one farmer singing in this field, another in the next, and so on. This combined with the sounds of the bells and larks' singing to make it seem as if the whole world was full of happiness. I used to see so many cows and bulls going out every day at about eight a.m.

B.V. Swami: Everyone's cows together?

Narmadā Swami: Everyone's cows all together. They would go out and come back in the evening, and these boys would take their lunch out in the pastures.

B.V. Swami: Like Kṛṣṇa and the cowherd boys.

Narmadā Swami: Yes, I have seen all these things. All the cows had names. The boys used to give names to all the cows and call them by name.

B.V. Swami: What names did they give to the cows?

Narmadā Swami: Sometimes the names of flowers. I have forgotten now. Some cows would have names like Lakṣmī and Sarasvatī, and the bulls Bhīma and Arjuna. Nowadays people don't keep cows, so you might think cows are all the same, but when you live with them you get to know them like people. They are all different. They all have their own personalities. Some are gentle, some proud, some tricky. But if brought up with affection, they all respond to it, and expect it and feel a need for it just like people, because they are people, but in different kinds of bodies.

In my house we had three very special cows. One white cow they called Mallemogga [laughs]. Jasmine flower is called Mallemogga in Telugu. There was another cow called Kanchana [laughs].

B.V. Swami: "Gold."

Narmadā Swami: Her color was like that [laughs].

B.V. Swami: So they all loved cows.

Narmadā Swami: Yes. Then the young bulls would fight in the fields and they would all come and watch. They used to take the cows to the river and clean them and take bath there. Sometimes we would go with them down to the river and give the cows a bath. And we would bathe too, and swim and laugh and splash. In the evening the boys and the cows would all come back. The calves would come jumping with their tails up [laughs]. When I was young I loved to join in these rural activities. I was attracted to playing games like that with the schoolboys. We were all friends. In the evening we came home, took bath, and again ran out to play.

B.V. Swami: What did you play? Sports?

Narmadā Swami: Yes, I used to play tennis sometimes. We spent most of the time in the playground in the evening, but in between we would regularly go to the temple. And early in the morning also, after going to the river to take bath. But by my tenth year I went to high school and became disconnected from religious life. During the next four years I was at home only during vacations. From that time I visited the temple only rarely, for special occasions.

B.V. Swami: You were saying that your mother was a Śrī Vaiṣṇava.

Narmadā Swami: Yes, she was a Śrī Vaiṣṇava. We were not *brāhmaṇas,* but we were vegetarian. We followed all the rules and regulations, especially for cooking.

B.V. Swami: Like cooking only after taking bath.

Narmadā Swami: Yes. I used to see my grandmother cooking wearing wet cloth [laughs]. She would cook and then at the time of serving, come to the other room and take *prasādam.* In this way she was very strict.

B.V. Swami: Among *brāhmaṇas* ...

Narmadā Swami: Most of them were initiated.

B.V. Swami: The women had to be initiated. Young boys had to take initiation also. Otherwise they could not cook, or even serve *prasādam.* I have heard that the women could serve. Could they do *pūjā* also?

Narmadā Swami: My grandfather on my mother's side worshiped many Deities. My father also. He used to worship "all the gods."

B. V. Swami: Gaṇeśa, Śiva...

Narmadā Swami: Yes. Viṣṇu, Gaṇeśa, Śiva, Lord Rāma.

B. V. Swami: He did *pūjā* himself?

Narmadā Swami: Yes, and every morning and evening he used to practice breathing exercises, yoga, and so on.

B. V. Swami: But your mother worshiped Viṣṇu exclusively.

Narmadā Swami: Yes. Our relatives in my mother's place were *brāhmaṇas*. The three brothers from that family used to take care of the whole village.

B. V. Swami: All priestly functions, giving advice.

Narmadā Swami: Yes. Giving advice, arranging *pūjās*, doing *nārāyaṇa-vrata* in every house, and all the offerings to the ancestors.[47] At that time they ran the schools also, every morning from ten a.m. to three p.m. There was one common hall where they used to come to guide the people.

When we were children we used to go to my mother's family's place during summer vacation. Everybody had to take bath in the afternoon before taking *prasādam;* then we would apply *tilaka* [laughs]. We used to do all of this. One of my uncles used to always do some chanting after taking bath.

B. V. Swami: What did he chant?

Narmadā Swami: He was chanting a Rāma mantra.

B. V. Swami: Before taking *prasādam*.

Narmadā Swami: Yes.

---

47. Nārāyaṇa-vrata — a Vaiṣṇava observance of worship.

B. V. Swami: That's very nice. Why were people inclined to chant like that? Did they do it for *mokṣa,* or *bhakti,* or what?

Narmadā Swami: Well, *śāstra* states that the name of Viṣṇu is all-auspicious and should always be chanted. That was well known. Even the *smārtas* followed that, what to speak of the Vaiṣṇavas. "All-auspicious" means auspicious for everything: protection from calamities, protection from evil spirits, protection from all kinds of misfortune, bringing in good fortune in this life and the next. I think that was the main consideration for most people. And Viṣṇu's name frees you from sinful reactions. Just like Ajāmila. Everyone knew the story of Ajāmila.

This chanting of *harināma* was deep-rooted in the culture. My one old uncle used to keep me awake with chanting. In the summer we slept outside, usually on the flat roof of the house. The cool breezes felt so nice after the heat of the day. Sometimes, if there were no wind, it was too hot to sleep, so we would lie half-awake swishing ourselves with hand fans, talking about this and that until early morning. When we visited our mother's house I couldn't sleep at night, because there was an old uncle who would simply lie down and chant, "Hari! Rāma! Govinda!" and so many names of God, off and on throughout the night. I would just be falling asleep when he would call out, "Nārāyaṇa! Hari!"

So people had faith and made it a habit to chant. They were brought up with it. If your father always says, "Hari! Govinda! Nārāyaṇa!" and your grandfather says it, and your uncles and aunts and your mother say it, then you also will start calling out, "Hari! Govinda! Nārāyaṇa!" When we children made a disturbance, an old man in our village always used to say, "Any moment passed without remembering the name of Lord Hari is the greatest loss, the greatest tragedy."

Anyway, exactly why they chanted *harināma* I can't say. It might have been different for each person. With a lot of our customs people didn't think why. They just did it because everyone had always done it that way, and they supposed it was the right thing to do. And they felt good doing it.

Everyone believed in God. As the day-to-day life was natural and simple and pleasant, so was the acceptance of God's hand in everything. The thought of God was never far away from anyone, so mention of Him followed naturally in the course of normal activities. It wasn't reserved for formal occasions or for special people.

Even in ordinary conversations, the common people would frequently mention Kṛṣṇa or Rāma, because their minds were full of *Mahābhārata* and *Rāmāyaṇa*. They used to hear from the *paṇḍitas* or from elder people at home. A father might chastise his son by giving an example from *rāma-līlā:* "Just see, Sītā said like this," or "Bhīṣma did like that." Or in a conversation someone would make a point by citing *kṛṣṇa-līlā* and someone else would come back with another quote, like that. Or if something extraordinary or unexpected happened they would praise God, how wonderful He is. Even if anything bad happened they would say it is all God's wish. When people met each other or left each other's company they would say, "Jaya Śrī Rāma," or something like that. They could not avoid saying the names of God.

Our life was like what we read in *Śrīmad-Bhāgavatam* about Kṛṣṇa's village life. I was just reading about how Kṛṣṇa and Balarāma received Akrūra, and it reminded me of how relatives used to visit our home, or how we would visit our relatives. When meeting after a long time, we could go on all night asking about the welfare of this relative and that one and another one. And we would not only talk about relatives. The older people, especially, would break into a spontaneous discussion of Kṛṣṇa's pastimes, or some philosophy from *śāstra,* or something like that, talking for hours and hours. We youngsters would wonder when they would finish, because none of us could eat until the elders had been fed.

Almost all used to follow some vows, either personal or traditional, perhaps to please Lord Śiva or some other god, or simply to enhance their piety by restricting sense enjoyment. Women especially used to follow vows to protect and benefit their husbands and children. On Ekādaśi the pious people used to fast, at least from grains. Quite a few fasted from all kinds of food, and some even from water. Similarly, almost everyone used to accept some kind of austerity during Caturmāsya. People followed vows like eating only once a day, not eating after sunset, not eating sweets or ghee, and so on.[48]

There wasn't a person, at least among the higher castes, who didn't do their *pūjā* or recite Sanskrit prayers in the

48. Strictures like refraining from eating meat, fish, eggs, garlic, onions, and taking intoxication are not mentioned as vows, because they were regularly practiced.

morning. Walking around the village in the early morning you'd hear bells ringing — *ting-ting-ting* — and see clouds of incense coming from the windows. The sound of Sanskrit mantras would come from every home.

They would chant *Śrī-sūkta* and *Puruṣa-sūkta,* or some people had *pāṭhas* for the different demigods.[49] In the bigger cities some of the modern educated people may have given it up, but otherwise most people would spend one or two hours in the morning for all these things. They would be up before dawn, take bath (never mind if it's cold), put on fresh dhotī, and then do chanting or meditation. Meditation wasn't so popular, but chanting was. At the very least someone would chant one chapter of the *Gītā* every day. But mostly they liked to do more.

In South India *Viṣṇu-sahasra-nāma* was the most common one. Just by chanting these names — Jyeṣṭha Śreṣṭha Prajāpati [sings a few lines from *Viṣṇu-sahasra-nāma*] — you automatically remember the qualities of Viṣṇu. *Ananta-kalyāṇa-guṇa-viśiṣṭa* — He is possessed of unlimited auspicious qualities. So by meditating on those qualities and hearing the holy names, naturally your spiritual feelings, or Kṛṣṇa consciousness, become aroused. People got real spiritual pleasure from it.

B.V. Swami: Why?

Narmadā Swami: Well, they believed it conferred peace and prosperity, that sins would be overcome and difficulties would go away. It was a kind of insurance for the next life also. The ultimate aim was to get *mokṣa,* and the grace of

49. *Śrī-sūkta* and *Puruṣa-sūkta* — certain Sanskrit prayers in praise of Lakṣmī and Nārāyaṇa respectively; *pāṭha* — scriptural recitation.

God. So it was not totally self-motivated. *Bhakti* was there too. It wasn't considered a drudgery or dry ritual, as some rascals brainwashed us later. Their belief wasn't forced or adopted out of fear. Still, not to believe in God would have been socially reprehensible. People felt the need to spend time with God, to forget everything else and just be immersed in Him. They were God conscious, and that's how they wanted to be. Mostly they weren't pure devotees — they were praying for prosperity and family happiness — but they didn't want those things without God. And if they did get money they spent a good part of it for God. Their family happiness was God-oriented too. People wanted their children to be well educated and materially successful, but they wanted to see them of good character and believing in God too.

Naturally people were brought up with a sense of personal pride. They prided themselves on their character, on their principles — that even if they could take advantage of someone by telling a lie, they would never do it. Nowadays people are proud if they have a tin-can motor car. But that's a different kind of pride — demoniac, foolish.

And the *brāhmaṇas* were much respected, not just as a formality, but because they were actually learned, cultured, and renounced. Even a well-to-do, educated *kṣatriya* or *vaiśya* would be respectful to a young boy of *brāhmaṇa* caste. In those days there were still typical village *brāhmaṇas* who would call all the children under a tree and teach them. They never demanded anything from anyone, but the villagers gave them whatever they needed, without any fuss or contracts or unions, or anything of the sort.

I remember an old *brāhmaṇa* used to visit our home. He would drink milk or buttermilk out of a silver cup we kept specially for *brāhmaṇas.* Very affectionately he would ask about all our family members. We would give him some uncooked rice or *dāl* when he left. In this way everyone would give the *brāhmaṇas* a little of this or that, so without strain on anyone they would live very simply, just the basic requirements. Not only the *brāhmaṇas,* almost everyone lived just with what they needed, and little more.

We were trained to be polite and respectful toward *brāhmaṇas,* and they would bless us. People believed in their blessings. And actually they had some power, probably due to the pure and renounced life they led. We also heard of *brāhmaṇas'* curses. I never personally knew of any such curse, because people were careful not to upset *brāhmaṇas,* while the *brāhmaṇas* themselves were tolerant and overlooked minor offenses. But we heard that just about the worst thing that could happen to anyone was to be cursed by a *brāhmaṇa.*

Although they have been much maligned, and although some of them misused their positions and had human defects, on the whole the *brāhmaṇas* were special people. It's not just that we were trained to respect them; we automatically felt like respecting them. They were called *bhū-devas,* gods on earth.

Sādhus were given tremendous respect. Saffron cloth was taken very seriously. Later on so many rogues took advantage and posed as sādhus to cheat people. Naturally people lost faith and became disgusted, and that was one of the causes of the downfall of religion. But you see even now the tendency is to respect sādhus.

B.V. Swami: So it was a completely God-conscious atmosphere.

Narmadā Swami: Always thinking of the spiritual side, completely.

B.V. Swami: Was Māyāvāda also strong at that time?

Narmadā Swami: Not so much. Generally Māyāvāda was seen only among the educated *brāhmaṇas*. The common village people were mostly God-conscious and pious, irrespective of caste.

B.V. Swami: The educated *brāhmaṇas* had modern education?

Narmadā Swami: Yes. They would go to town and get a modern education, then they went to work in government offices. Somehow or other they followed Māyāvāda. The higher education influenced them to adopt it. A select few would leave the villages, saying that the lifestyle was not correct. They used to discourage the common people, who were traditionally *bhaktas*.

B.V. Swami: They were *bhaktas*.

Narmadā Swami: Yes. They did not believe in Māyāvāda. If anyone spoke like that, others would consider him fallen and would not mix with him.

B.V. Swami: Weren't there any skeptics or atheists?

Narmadā Swami: Very few. I never met anyone like that.

B.V. Swami: Yes, but when the British-influenced people started attacking all these rituals as meaningless, the *paṇḍitas* had nothing to say, and the whole culture collapsed.

Narmadā Swami: That's a very simplistic analysis, but there's truth in it. Today if you tell people to do anything, they want to know why. In some ways that's good, but on the whole, modern education has done tremendous damage to our culture. Intellectual hooliganism. They are worse than dacoits. Ordinary dacoits may take all your money and even your life, but they can't touch your soul.

B.V. Swami: That's a very big subject, how we got from what you are describing to where we are today — in just two generations.

Narmadā Swami: A very big subject. You should write a book about it [laughs].

B.V. Swami: Now everything has changed in India.

Narmadā Swami: Yes. Most of the people from the villages have shifted to towns. Because the new generation wants to go to town for higher education, the whole family gets shifted. People also go to the city looking for jobs.

Previously town life was also cultured and civilized. There were not so many towns, and they were mostly not very big — market towns. Not like the industrial hellholes of today. They had administrative, commercial, and educational functions for largely agrarian societies. Towns upheld the life of the village, and the same dignified way of life prevailed in both.

We didn't realize what a good way of life we were giving up until we had totally destroyed it. Still we don't realize. We didn't appreciate it, but those were wonderful times, at least compared with life today. What nice things we have given up. And for what? What is the benefit of this modern way of life? All this running around, building factories, drilling into the earth, making pipelines under the sea — for what? You have to work so hard, with so many difficulties, so much anxiety. But for all that, your basic needs are the same: something to eat and somewhere to sleep. For this they are working so hard. "Fools and rascals," Śrīla Prabhupāda used to say. "Simply fools and rascals."

B. V. Swami: Well, if it was so good, why did people give it up? How was this great culture eroded?

Narmadā Swami: That's a very big question with no simple answer. You yourself have analyzed it in detail in your *A Message to the Youth of India*. You see, it was a gradual process, almost insidious. With the advent of modernization, India didn't lose her culture immediately. It was not possible to give up everything just like that. There was a period when the old fairly happily blended with the new.

Some Britishers noted in their memoirs about the Raj how the village stationmasters and postmasters were just like gurus. Intelligent, educated, and responsible men were needed for such positions. Especially in those days, born *brāhmaṇas* were the natural candidates. In the course of reading letters or taking dictation for replies on behalf of the mostly illiterate villagers, the postmasters would give advice on family affairs and would sometimes intercede between quarreling parties. Stationmasters often used to keep *śālagrāma-śilās* in their offices and perform regular worship throughout the day. It was only gradually that values declined. And as the saying goes, "When character is lost everything is lost." It was a simple life, but quite strict also.

B.V. Swami: Many people today would think the kind of life you are talking about to be pretty dull. No fast cars, bars, parties, TV, and telephones means no fun.

Narmadā Swami: It's true that there was no rush to always do something or go somewhere. Life was slow and easy, so I suppose your overly hyped-up types would find that tedious. But we weren't bored. We took pleasure in simple things. Meeting with relatives, seeing a new calf born, eating good food — these were our day to day pleasures. And I told you about those dramas and the festivals — not very sophisticated maybe, but not dull. Yes, simple, but a more wholesome kind of enjoyment. What is this "fun" you are talking about? Simply titillation. No substance.

B.V. Swami: But what about all the restrictions you mentioned? People today wouldn't go for that. Especially children were restricted and couldn't go here and there as they liked.

Narmadā Swami: That's good. That's how it ought to be. Children need guidance, training. They need to be restricted from activities that will spoil their character and degrade them. Not only children, everybody.

B.V. Swami: It seems that women had a life of drudgery, like slave labor.

Narmadā Swami: You don't believe that and I know it. No. Women worked hard, and that kept them out of trouble. Their pleasure was in serving their husband and looking after the children. They took pleasure in cooking and feeding everyone and seeing everyone happy — a selfless kind of life. But selflessness brings happiness; selfishness doesn't.

And the women had the security of knowing that they were cared for and protected. On festivals and social occasions they enjoyed dressing up in their best clothes, with ornaments, and meeting their friends and relatives.

B. V. Swami: What you were saying about working hard to keep out of trouble wouldn't be very well received today.

Narmadā Swami: But these "liberated women" are working hard too. They go to a job and still have to cook and clean and everything else. They don't have proper time for their children. And without mother's love, the kids grow up as brats.

B. V. Swami: Now that's simplistic.

Narmadā Swami: But it's true.

B. V. Swami: Did the people have any bad habits? What about meat eating?

Narmadā Swami: Some people ate meat. Non-*brāhmaṇas* ate meat, although only once in ten days, once in a month. They would offer it to the goddess.

B. V. Swami: Goddess Kālī?

Narmadā Swami: Yes. And then they shared. Nobody would eat it by himself. In one area they offered a goat or sheep, something like that, and then they shared.

B. V. Swami: *Kṣatriyas?*

Narmadā Swami: Yes, *kṣatriyas* and low-caste people.

B. V. Swami: Low-class people.

Narmadā Swami: They were all non-*brāhmaṇas*. But Śrī Vaiṣṇavas would not eat meat, not even eggs. They didn't even eat at another's place.

B. V. Swami: Right, right.

Narmadā Swami: Even non-*brāhmaṇas* who ate meat were very few. Once or twice a month, that is all.

B. V. Swami: So the number of people eating meat was a small percentage.

Narmadā Swami: Yes, very small.

B. V. Swami: What about *śūdras* and those even lower than *śūdras?*

Narmadā Swami: The lowest *śūdras* and Muslims stayed outside the village. They were separated from the main society.

B. V. Swami: Like those who ate meat?

Narmadā Swami: They would eat meat once in ten days and offer it. Also, the people who offered were special. Not everybody could offer, only certain people.

B. V. Swami: *Brāhmaṇas* also offered?

Narmadā Swami: Some kind of officials did brahminical work, but they were not *brāhmaṇas*. They did this offering and then they distributed it to that area. Very rigid rules.

B. V. Swami: What about smoking?

Narmadā Swami: In those days people used to smoke cigars.

B. V. Swami: Tobacco?

Narmadā Swami: Yes, tobacco, but only elderly people. I never saw young people smoking. That practice was not at all there. They would have been chastised. Any young boy smoking would have to go somewhere very secluded. He could not smoke outside.

B. V. Swami: Not before thirty.

Narmadā Swami: Not even thirty. Only people above fifty. A few of them used to smoke cigars.

B. V. Swami: But Śrī Vaiṣṇavas never smoked.

Narmadā Swami: Never.

B. V. Swami: At that time they didn't even take coffee.

Narmadā Swami: Nor even eat anything outside. They were very God conscious, God fearing. There was no question of eating outside, and normally in the houses they did not prepare coffee and tea and all those things. I never saw anybody making tea or coffee. But those who were not very strict used to take coffee or tea outside. Nobody was addicted to them. Now they make coffee in every house.

B. V. Swami: Did you used to live close enough to the temple in your childhood to go daily?

Narmadā Swami: When I was young, in Nellore, we were very close to the temple. We used to play in the temple itself [laughs].

B. V. Swami: How did you play?

Narmadā Swami: [laughs] We used to play *Rāmāyaṇa* stories and *Mahābhārata*, because we used to hear all those stories. Somebody took the part of Bhīma, somebody took the part of Arjuna, or somebody would be Rāvaṇa.

B. V. Swami: How did you hear those narrations?

Narmadā Swami: They would be read regularly in the evenings, and we would also see dramas performed by traveling troupes at festival times. The readings were not just ritualistic. In the *Rāmāyaṇa* itself it is told how Lava and Kuśa used to sing the *Rāmāyaṇa* so beautifully and with feeling that the listeners would become enchanted with indescribable bliss that pervaded their minds, senses, and every limb of their bodies, and made them forget everything else.

Wonderful, isn't it? That description is exactly correct, even now, if the speaker is good. The speaker has to really feel for Rāma. In those days all the speakers did. We couldn't even think of leaving. There is a system for reading *Rāmāyaṇa:* twenty chapters a day, no more. I think that was made because once you started, you could never stop. Everyone would just forget everything and continue all day and night. We never wanted it to stop, but even when the speaker did, we couldn't stop thinking of Rāma, Sītā and Hanumān. We were saturated, intoxicated. We went to sleep thinking of *rāma-līlā* and woke up thinking of *rāma-līlā*.

All would forget that they were in their village. We were not in our village; we were in Laṅkā with Hanumān! When we heard about the fighting we felt like jumping in and joining the monkeys. Whenever Hanumān did anything we would all cheer like anything. The Telugu people are very fond of Hanumān. They call him Añjaneyālu, "the son of Añjanā." Añjanā is his mother's name.

B.V. Swami: What about other epics? The *Mahābhārata*?

Narmadā Swami: We heard those also. Of course we liked them all. But the *Rāmāyaṇa* is easy to follow. It's one clear story, unlike the *Mahābhārata* and *Bhāgavata,* which have many stories. And it's easy to tell who is good and who is bad. The *Mahābhārata* is very complex [laughs]. Just like Karṇa. Karṇa is supposed to be bad, but you can't help sympathizing with him. He had many good qualities also. Then Ghaṭotkaca, who was basically a *rākṣasa* and a troublemaker, fought on the right side.

They say that with *Mahābhārata* you have to be careful. They'll tell it only in the temple, not at home. If you tell it in the home, quarrel will come.

B. V. Swami: Why?

Narmadā Swami: That's what they say. Not just now but from long ago, no one would discuss *Mahābhārata* in the home. It's all about a family fighting among itself, so I suppose that's why. But maybe that's some atheistic propaganda. Actually, by studying all these scriptures, you will get all your problems permanently solved.

Rāmāyaṇa and *Mahābhārata* were so popular that everybody knew them. Everybody was familiar with them from seeing the plays, especially *kṛṣṇa-līlā*. The performances would go on all night because people had time. They didn't have to rush to the office in the morning. Also, the actors were so expert and made-up with such nice costumes. The actor playing Duryodhana wasn't acting as Duryodhana — he was Duryodhana.

[At this point, Narmadā Mahārāja became absorbed and started excitedly recounting stories from *Mahābhārata*.]

Kṛṣṇa-līlā and *Mahābhārata* were so popular that although the people had seen them many times, they wanted to see them again. When the players performed, the villagers would give them some charity and feed them. In a big village they would stay for a few days or even a week.

There were *haridāsas,* who were like *sannyāsīs,* only not officially. They were mostly from the Śrī *sampradāya* and were fully dedicated to God. That's why they were called *haridāsas.* They would be decorated with *tilaka* and everything. Every day throughout January they would come in the early morning for alms. They would sing instructive songs in sweet tunes. Depending on their position, somebody would give them rice, someone *dāl,* and so on.

B. V. Swami: They were local people, or travelers?

Narmadā Swami: Some local, some travelers.

B. V. Swami: They came in January, and the rest of the year they did not?

Narmadā Swami: No, they did not. The rest of the year they just did their regular activities.

B. V. Swami: Which were?

Narmadā Swami: Mostly to sing about Kṛṣṇa. There were many songs they sang that were famous, that everybody knew. [Sings a Telugu song]. That was one of my favorites. It means, "My dear brother, everyone has to suffer the reactions of his own karma. No one can escape. You must suffer all the distresses of carrying the burden of your own body. Others will not suffer for you."

The *haridāsas* were very austere. They collected during that month only and then not again for another year. I have actually seen how *haridāsas* live very strict lives. Continually, year after year, we used to see all these things going on, without any change.

There was also a well-known Telugu *paṇḍita*, Deepala Pichaiah Shastri. He was so brilliant. He used to hold meetings in school courtyards or in the town hall. One hundred people would ask him questions, one after another, and he would answer them all. They would ask him complex questions, from Telugu literature or on fine points of grammar. He would not miss any question. He would answer them all.

B. V. Swami: How could he remember them all?

Narmadā Swami: That was some special ability given by God. Just like some people have mathematical genius by the grace of God. Give them any mathematical question, and right away they will give the answer, faster than a computer. Not only him, there were quite a few *aṣṭavadhanis* in those days. That means they could talk to eight people at a time. But Deepala Pichaiah Shastri was the only *śatavadhani*. One hundred people would each ask him a question, and when they had finished he would answer them all one by one. People were amazed. How could he catch all the questions? How could he know all the answers without fail? The meetings would go on and on, at least for four hours, and often five or six. But no one would want to go away. That *paṇḍita* was very well respected. Wherever he went people would bow down to him.

In those days the tradition of scholarship was still strong in India. There were Sanskrit *paṇḍitas* in every village. They were good scholars, too. It's hard to find anyone like that today. Even an ordinary scholar, if he was serious, had vast knowledge of philosophy and *śāstra*. Most of the few people who are supposed to be big scholars of Vedic philosophy today couldn't stand up to an ordinary *paṇḍita* of the past. And the really learned people were simply amazing. They knew so much. They could quote inside out, upside down. Those were the days when two *paṇḍitas* could accidentally meet and get into an informal debate over something like the meaning of *tat tvam asi*.[50] And they'd just go on and on for hours and hours quoting this, quoting that, putting each other's points down — all excited, as if the world depended on it.

B. V. Swami: Was there a lot of this intellectual rivalry?

Narmadā Swami: It wasn't just intellectual rivalry; they were philosophical enemies. They were committed to what they argued about. We are talking about devotees and impersonalists. You know about it very well.

B. V. Swami: Yes. The enmity is still going on and probably always will.

Narmadā Swami: Undoubtedly. But at least in those days they were cultured enemies. You know the saying "Better to have a learned enemy than a foolish friend."

B. V. Swami: Those debates sound exciting.

---

50. *Tat tvam asi* — "thou art that;" the interpretation of this quote from the *Upaniṣads* has been controversial for centuries.

Narmadā Swami: But it wasn't simply quick wits and bravado. It required vast learning in the *śāstras* and their commentaries, and in the science of interpretation. No one would dare enter a debate unless he could back up each minute point of his position with numerous quotes from *śāstra,* was well versed in logic, and was prepared to reply to the similarly erudite thesis of his opponent.

B. V. Swami: Did you get to learn any of these things?

Narmadā Swami: No. We were brought up with the Telugu *Bhāgavatam,* called Potana *Bhāgavatam.* It is still well known among the Telugu people.

B. V. Swami: Potana?

Narmadā Swami: Potana was a poet a few hundred years ago. He rendered the *Bhāgavata* into Telugu. It is not a direct translation, with the same order or the same details, but all the main stories are there. It's a mixture of Telugu and simple Sanskrit. He wrote in the beginning [quotes Telugu verse], "I'm writing this so the scholars will be pleased and the farmers will also be pleased." [Quotes more Telugu] "Since the narrations of Hari deliver us from birth and death, why should I describe any other subject?" Beautiful, very devotional. In those days there were certain verses from Potana that everybody knew. So many of the early films came out of Potana.

B. V. Swami: You were taught Potana in school?

Narmadā Swami: Of course. There was no secularism like today. They had to teach it in school.

B. V. Swami: And did they teach Sanskrit?

Narmadā Swami: Yes, from the primary level up. I wanted to go on and do higher studies in Sanskrit and enjoy that nectar more and more, but I was pushed into science. Such horrible things we had to do: cutting frogs and cockroaches.

B.V. Swami: So modernization had started already, but still the people were worshiping God. Did the young boys ever want to join an *āśrama* or something?

Narmadā Swami: Very few. We heard of one relative who was like that. At first he went to Madras to study for his M.A., and there he came in contact with some sādhus.[51] He became attracted and then renounced everything, but he had already been married when he was about sixteen years old and the girl only nine. When she came of age they tried to fix her up with the man, but he had already renounced everything. Everybody said, "This is not good. You are married. Whatever you want to do you can do it at home." All the relatives brought him back, but he stayed for just one or two years and then went away again. After that they brought him again. Again he went away. In this way he was not in touch with his family. He became completely indifferent, and ultimately he gave up everything.

B.V. Swami: Did he have a child also?

Narmadā Swami: I think one daughter. But he was not in touch with family life. There were some cases like that. Sometimes we heard about people who left and became *sannyāsīs* and never returned.

---

51. *Madras* — Madras is now renamed Chennai.

B. V. Swami: I expect that most of the people would not be happy if one of their relatives took *sannyāsa*.

Narmadā Swami: Sometimes. But sometimes the relatives, and even the wives, would appreciate it: "Very good, he is becoming a devotee."

B. V. Swami: They respected. They also had some regard for the renounced order, unlike today when if a young man joins a religious organization generally the parents try to bring him back at any cost.

Narmadā Swami: But only when they were close to the person — like wife, mother, or father. They tested him at first maybe, but after that, nothing. Particularly when the wives were young.

B. V. Swami: It would be difficult for a young girl if her husband ran off to be a *sannyāsī*. She would have to live the austere life of a widow from an early age.

Narmadā Swami: Of course. At that time when something happened, if the parents were rich they would take care of them. If the girl was young and the husband died or something, they would bring her back to the house and maintain her, give her some share of the property, and take care of the children's education. Like in my mother's family: They were three sisters and two brothers. One sister was married locally, and the elder sister was married thirty or forty miles away, in the same district. She had one son and one daughter, and when she was about thirty her husband died. Somehow or other the circumstances were not good for them, so my uncles brought them back to their place. My mother's side was richer than my father's, so they gave her a house and some land and looked after her. They provided the son and daughter with an education and got them married.

B.V. Swami: That means that the wife had property separate from the husband.

Narmadā Swami: Yes, they are given that portion at the time of marriage; and when the boy grows up it goes to him. They continued to do everything the same, but the land became the son's land. Whatever they had received they would give him. In some families the women remain at their husband's place, because when the children are grown up they will not come out. When the girl went to the husband's house and they had married life and the children were grown up, there was no question of leaving the place. They became a part of the husband's family. But if there was any difficulty when they were young, the parents brought them back. Rich people are especially able to give them some property. If the girl and her children were young, and the circumstances were okay, they kept quiet. When the maintainer of the family died, if the circumstances were not good and they were not rich, the family would bring her back. They removed the burden from that family.

B.V. Swami: You were telling me that once you played *rāma-līlā* and you threw an arrow at Rāvaṇa.

Narmadā Swami: [laughs] Yes. That whole day we were playing *rāma-līlā* among ourselves. Another boy was playing the part of Rāvaṇa and I was Lord Rāma. When the climax came I took the bow and arrow — because we were children, you know. A conical metal ring was fixed to the arrow, and I did not realize that if it struck him it would hurt. Somehow or other I raised the bow to the sky and shot it. Because of the weight on the arrow it hit him near the eyes. Blood started gushing out near his eyes, but luckily there was no damage to the eyes [laughs]. I was confused, so I took the bow and arrow and ran away from there.

B.V. Swami: Your father must have chastised you.

Narmadā Swami: My father was there, just near our house, and his father was there. Everybody was there, so they all rushed.

B.V. Swami: Did your father beat you?

Narmadā Swami: He could not even see me. When I saw their temper I ran away. A postman was living just beside our house, and he was a very good man. He told them not to touch me.

B.V. Swami: The boy didn't mind afterward?

Narmadā Swami: No, he didn't mind. He was taken to hospital.

B.V. Swami: So your father sometimes beat you?

Narmadā Swami: Many times [laughs].

B.V. Swami: What naughty things did you do?

Narmadā Swami: Just like that — fighting with the boys, jumping here and there, going and eating fruits. Normally in the backyard of the houses there were so many nice fruit trees — papaya, *jambu, jamrud.* We used to jump in the backyards of the houses and clear them all out [laughs]. If somebody complained, then we got good beatings [laughs].

B.V. Swami: I recall a Mādhva *sampradāya brāhmaṇa* who told me how his father used to beat him to force him to learn *Viṣṇu-sahasra-nāma*. This *brāhmaṇa* was very appreciative, as he felt the chanting of *Viṣṇu-sahasra-nāma* as a great asset in his life. Anyway, you were telling me about your childhood pranks.

Narmadā Swami: There were very nice boys with me sometimes skipping school [laughs]. Although I was living in town, I couldn't wait for the holidays, to go on vacation.

B.V. Swami: Summer vacation.

Narmadā Swami: Yes. For summer vacation we used to go swimming, playing, and visiting temples like Chennakeśava. He is a most beautiful Deity. They celebrated a big festival every year, and there would be a big market for the pilgrims. They celebrated for ten days, each night with a different kind of celebration. The Śrī Vaiṣṇava groups in particular used to come with a lot of disciples, and they rode on horses and elephants. They came to a village and stayed for a week or fifteen days and held discourses, *Bhāgavata* classes. Everybody would go to take their *darśana*. Everybody came and gave charity. Somebody gave fruits, somebody gave milk, somebody gave curds ...

B.V. Swami: What did they do with so much? Did they make *prasādam*?

Narmadā Swami: Whatever they got they prepared and distributed to all who came there. They carried extra grains with them.

Sometimes the family would also go to Tirupati together.

B. V. Swami: During the school holidays?

Narmadā Swami: Yes, we used to spend three days there.

B. V. Swami: They had all facilities?

Narmadā Swami: Yes, right from the beginning. There were lodges for pilgrims, so we used to stay for three days and three nights. In one wedding hall there was a facility where you would give two hundred rupees and they would distribute *prasādam* to everyone in huge vessels.

B. V. Swami: At that time two hundred rupees was a huge amount.

Narmadā Swami: Yes, but big vessels, with three varieties of *prasādam*. Then they would distribute it to everyone in your precinct.

B. V. Swami: But now that facility is not there.

Narmadā Swami: No.

B. V. Swami: Please tell us more about the festivals.

Narmadā Swami: The biggest festivals were Makara-saṅkrānti and Vaikuṇṭha Ekādaśi. We would all go to the river by two-thirty a.m. — whole families, even little children and all — to take bath, and then go to the temple and wait for *darśana*. There was so much rush.

We had so many festivals, and they were celebrated so nicely, elaborately. Every festival had some special kind of food prepared for it, and certain rituals and customs. That's mostly forgotten now, or cut down to almost nothing. Festival meant people coming together, bolstering their goodwill and spirit of sharing, giving up any bad feelings that might have accumulated. And festival meant religious festival. Now it means firecrackers, intoxication, and noise.

Every temple had a huge *ratha* (chariot) for celebrating *Ratha-yātrā* — huge, all made of wood. Once a year they would take it out and paint it. During the festival everyone was cooperative. They would whitewash the temple and decorate it, and people would give donations. People from various districts would come. Many towns had temples and *Ratha-yātrās* just as big as in Tirupati.

In the morning they would take out the *ratha* and in the evening come back. In those days they would celebrate the festival for nine days, and every night the Lord would come out on different *vāhanas,* like Garuḍa, or the swan. The Lord rode on a *vāhana* decorated with gold, particularly in those days. Garuḍa *vāhana* is a very special day, when the Lord is carried on Garuḍa. Garlands used to come specially from Madras for that festival. The flowers were so fragrant. They carried garlands on the *vāhana,* which needed about twenty people to carry it. Hundreds of people were ready to carry it.

B. V. Swami: *Brāhmaṇas* used to carry.

Narmadā Swami: Mostly *brāhmaṇas.* And the smell of the flowers spread everywhere — big garlands, huge garlands. The rich people would donate for one *sevā,* like Garuḍa *sevā*. There would be traditions in each family. They also fed people with *prasādam*. The procession started around nine a.m. Outside every house they would wait for the Lord to come past. At each house the chariot stopped and the people would come out to offer something, perhaps some fruits. The procession would go on like this until about midday.

B. V. Swami: Did they offer *ārati*?

Narmadā Swami: Yes. They offered *ārati* with camphor and so many things. They offered *sevā* for a seven-day function, nine-day function, like that.

Some people were so enthusiastic to celebrate the festivals that they came from big towns to see, and people from the nearby villages also. There were so many villages nearby, within five or ten miles. Everyone used to come to their relatives' house and stay for two or three days for the festival, and everyone was so full of love and affection. Everyone from the surrounding area would attend.

B. V. Swami: Apart from festivals, did you used to go to the temple for *darśana*?

Narmadā Swami: Yes. Every evening, definitely, we used to go for *darśana*.

B. V. Swami: Why in the evening?

Narmadā Swami: *Ārati* time. The people would go regularly in the evening. Even though we used to go to school for playing, we would come home to take bath and then go to the temple. We used to play in the temple and take *darśana* and *prasādam* there. Even now, children play in the temple courtyards. The big open spaces make ideal playgrounds. Of course they are not meant for that, but we didn't know and no one stopped us. And we got the advantage of seeing the Lord and His devotees and taking *prasādam*. That has helped me throughout my life and is helping me now, although as a child I didn't realize the significance of what I was doing [laughs]. We spent nearly two or three hours in the temple every day.

B. V. Swami: Did the priests distribute *prasādam*?

Narmadā Swami: The priests had personal relationships with everybody in the villages, and they loved the children. They called the boys by name and gave them *prasādam*. In this way they developed a relationship. In a village everyone knows everyone: "He is So-and-so's son, and he is So-and-so's son ..."

B. V. Swami: The whole culture seems so attractive. In modern society it is horrible — *kāma, krodha, lobha.*[52]

Narmadā Swami: People were very peaceful. Now villages have become places of fighting, murders, and everything. Previously, we never heard these things.

B. V. Swami: There were no police.

Narmadā Swami: No. We never saw police unless there was a festival, some special arrangement. Otherwise the police were in their station. Now everything has changed. Everybody used to be so cooperative. In the festival season — November, December, and January — the new crops would be coming, so people would come back a little early in the evenings. At night they would be so loving, nice; they used to have *bhajanas, kīrtanas.*

B. V. Swami: In their houses?

Narmadā Swami: No, everywhere there were common nice places to meet: banyan trees, nice platforms. Forty or fifty people could assemble there every evening.

52. *Kāma* — lust; *krodha* — anger; *lobha* — greed.

Somebody would arrange *bhajana, kīrtana*. The *haridāsas* would play such nice music with *karatālas*. Youths used to play games until seven p.m. In the village there was generally no electricity, so after nightfall they would sing *bhajanas* and *kīrtanas*.

B.V. Swami: In what year were you born?

Narmadā Swami: I was born in 1929.

B.V. Swami: So in your childhood, by about 1940, the Indian independence movement had become strong. What was the attitude toward the British at that time?

Narmadā Swami: As the independence movement picked up, people gradually came to hate them. We did not understand. Many times I joined in the processions, shouting *Vande Mātaram*.[53] I saw all the police officers and district collectors there. But some people from the older generation had connections with the officers and other high-ups, and they respected the British for their discipline.

B.V. Swami: Prabhupāda said that in many ways India was better under the British.

Narmadā Swami: Yes. Many people say that. My father had a good friend from England, a Mr. Helding. He was a major in the Reserve Police.

B.V. Swami: Would your father bring him home also?

Narmadā Swami: Yes, many times, him and his wife and daughter. He had only one daughter. They used to come to our house and we would also visit them.

---

53. *Vande Mātaram* — "Hail Mother," the first words and title of a nationalistic song praising "Mother India."

B.V. Swami: But I thought the Hindus wouldn't bring such people home because they are meat eaters and so on.

Narmadā Swami: Well, in the beginning my father used to know all these people.

B.V. Swami: Your father spoke good English?

Narmadā Swami: Yes, he spoke English, Telugu, Hindi, and Kannada. My father did his B.E. in mechanical engineering, then became involved in the automobile business. He said he worked for some time in the Department of Engineering in Shiliguri.

B.V. Swami: And your grandfather?

Narmadā Swami: My grandfather was an agriculturist.

B.V. Swami: Your father built his own business. Did you have land also?

Narmadā Swami: Yes, we had so many crops, plenty of everything. We had wheat, rice, *dāl*, everything. It was fertile land [laughs]. We did not need to purchase anything in the market; it was all coming from the land. They never even purchased tamarind, because we had tamarind trees. Normally even the non-*brāhmaṇas* had the habit of never eating outside.

B.V. Swami: They were very particular about the purity of their food.

Narmadā Swami: Yes. That has changed, but what is especially missing now is the enthusiasm in celebrating the festivals. They were so enthusiastic. My father did some *pūjā*, although he was not particularly interested in religion.

B. V. Swami: It's interesting that your mother was more religious than your father.

Narmadā Swami: Yes, generally women are more religious. I got my religious feeling from my mother, for which I am now most grateful. It was not that my father was not religious. He would also go to the temple and take *prasādam,* but he never showed an interest in training us in religion. That is why, after some years when I was in high school, I forgot the village life, going here and there. I associated with the city kids — going to the playground to play cricket, playing tennis, going to the movies, eating outside. Although we were not following so strictly, we were religious in a way.

B. V. Swami: In those days the movies were mostly religious.

Narmadā Swami: Yes, but movies are movies [laughs]. Anyway, they were better than movies nowadays — a hundred times, one million times, one million million times better. They were all taken from *Bhāgavatam, Rāmāyaṇa* and *Mahābhārata*. They would take a particular theme — the story of Prahlāda, or Aniruddha, or Karṇa. Karṇa was the most popular. People used to go see it fifteen, twenty times. In many ways he was a good character — noble, generous, bold — but he was unlucky. He had bad association; a tragic life.

B. V. Swami: People must have cried like anything at those movies.

Narmadā Swami: [laughs] Some people would refuse to even go to the movies. They would say, "I can't sit and cry for three hours" — because the pictures would last at least three hours, four hours. The whole audience would simply be crying all the way through. Well, not all the time. There would be some funny scenes also. That crying was not devotional, maybe some sentiment.

B.V. Swami: Good sentiment, devotional sentiment. Did you live at home when you were going to high school?

Narmadā Swami: In the beginning I went to high school in Madras.

B.V. Swami: You were in a hostel?

Narmadā Swami: Yes, in a community hostel. After that, my mother fought with my father because she could not stay away from me. So then I remained in Nellore. There was a college there also.

B.V. Swami: Mother's love. That's nice. Your mother was very attached because you were the only son.

Narmadā Swami: Yes, that's why she fought with my father [laughs]. I stayed for only one and a half years in Madras.

B.V. Swami: But usually no woman wants to fight with her husband.

Narmadā Swami: Yes, she did not want that. I never saw my mother disagree with my father on any other point but this. She said, "Let him study here because there is a college here. Why should he go there?"

B.V. Swami: Your father wanted a better education for you.

Narmadā Swami: Yes.

B. V. Swami: What does it mean exactly, that your mother fought with your father?

Narmadā Swami: She would petition him saying, "You should bring him back." She used to tell him, "If you do not bring him then I will go to Madras and stay there." [Laughs] So eventually he agreed.

B. V. Swami: What did you do in Madras?

Narmadā Swami: In Madras there are so many temples. I used to live in Triplicane. In Nellore we lived on the main street. They had nice festivals. On the other side of Nellore there is a Veṇugopāla temple, and we would visit there occasionally. Once a year they had a big carnival. They had people who walked on fire [laughs].

B. V. Swami: I've seen fire-walking at Thaipūsam, a Tamil festival.

Narmadā Swami: Yes. It was a big fire, and they would run on it — this way, that way [laughs]. They also had a big hall there, mostly to perform marriages and other functions.

B. V. Swami: At the Raṅganātha temple?

Narmadā Swami: In Veṇugopāla temple. Everything was there.

B. V. Swami: That is also Śrī Vaiṣṇava.

Narmadā Swami: Yes. Actually my marriage was also done there. They have all arrangements for cooking, serving, everything. The marriages were so elaborate then. They lasted at least seven days filled with rituals and continuous feasting with so many different kinds of food. Everything was prepared at home — no catering companies. Now they are cutting it down gradually — four days, two days, now one day or even less than half a day. Probably eventually they won't even bother with that. They'll just live together like animals on the street. The heart has gone out of these ceremonies. People have no interest. They're too busy doing God-knows-what.

B.V. Swami: You used to go to the temple and pray to God?

Narmadā Swami: [laughs] I used to pray only for *prasādam* then. Although I was standing before the Deity, I used to pray for *prasādam* [laughs]. I would just go before the Deity and offer homage and think, "Oh, I must take *prasādam.*" And whenever I had an examination I used to pray, "Please let me pass." I prayed only for these things, nothing else. In the beginning I was just offering the *bhoga;* it was not a prayer. It was with some devotion, but I was always thinking of the *prasādam.* I remember nicely now. I used to think, "What *prasādam* will be there today?" That thinking is connected with Kṛṣṇa [laughs]. But when I became more mature I knew I should fast.

There were so many *brāhmaṇa* Śrī Vaiṣṇava boys that used to come to school nicely shaven with *śikhā* and big *tilaka.* I knew a boy, Krishnamachari, who was tall and never wore a shirt. He came to school with *tilaka* and no shirt, just an upper cloth and a dhotī [laughs]. Even in college we studied together. The principal called him and told him he had to come with a shirt. He said, "No, I will not wear a shirt." [laughs] He used to say it so boldly to the principal. He came to college without a shirt, clean shaven, with a nice *śikhā,* and decorated with *tilaka.*

B.V. Swami: Which subject was he studying?

Narmadā Swami: Mathematics, physics, and chemistry.

B.V. Swami: What about your studies?

Narmadā Swami: I was also studying science. It was tough. We hardly had time to think about anything else. In this way I became a bit estranged from our original culture — until I was saved by reading one of Śrīla Prabhupāda's books.

B.V. Swami: So Mahārāja, you've really seen two worlds within your lifetime. There's been so much change ...

Narmadā Swami: Not even in my lifetime; just in the past twenty years.

B.V. Swami: What are your thoughts about the progress of modern civilization?

Narmadā Swami: Progress? What progress? People are living like cats and dogs, all crushed together in these filthy, smelly cities. You see even the rich people here in Mumbai live in these tiny apartments. No room to move. A rat race. That is the exact description: rat race. They are all racing to become rats. No sense of decency. People don't even know how to talk to each other. Even for ordinary matters they talk harshly. No fresh air, no fresh food, no fresh water. And all this rubbish — everything made of plastic, this nasty loud music that shakes your bones ... How many things shall I say? And this women's liberation nonsense. Our daughters are being brought up as prostitutes. Beauty contest [laughs disdainfully]. This is progress? No, it is regress. We are regressing to become like dogs and cats and rats and monkeys. It's Darwin's theory in reverse. "Progress" is a politician's brainwash word.

B. V. Swami: Do you see anything good in modern life?

Narmadā Swami: Yes: the Hare Kṛṣṇa Movement. Śrīla Prabhupāda gave us this most wonderful process of chanting the holy names, by which we can cross over the ocean of Kali. This nasty Kali-yuga is full of faults, but the one redeeming factor is that just by chanting Kṛṣṇa's names everyone can become happy in this life and prepare to go back to the spiritual world. It's practical. It works. All over the world people are becoming happy by chanting Hare Kṛṣṇa. But we have to be careful to keep Kali out of our movement. We can't allow all kinds of cheating and hypocrisy to spoil it. The purity must be maintained. We have to be strong in our principles.

And along with our preaching we have to show this culture to the world. If we can recreate the same kind of simple village life, with Kṛṣṇa at the center, it will be a great step forward for our movement. We have to show people practically what we are talking about. Śrīla Prabhupāda wanted that, these farm communities. And we also want to give our devotees a better way of life. Why should they have to live like rats? And what to speak of the children. I'm quite dissatisfied with the way they're being brought up now. We must revive this old culture; then there will be hope for the world. Let the Golden Age come in. The way things are going now I see nothing auspicious ahead. Without Kṛṣṇa consciousness it's a very black future.

Brought up in Devotion

R. Raṅganāthan tells of his boyhood in Tamil Nadu. Among other things, he describes the schooling, festivals, and daily rites in the brāhmaṇa quarters around his village's Viṣṇu temple.

B.V. Swami: You are Mr. R. Raṅganāthan. What does the R stand for?

Raṅganāthan: "*R*" stands for Rāmānujam. That is my father's name. Among the Tamil people, we don't have surnames, but we keep the father's name as an initial. And among the Śrī Vaiṣṇavas, we always prefer to give boy children a name of God, such as Raṅganāthan, Śrīnivāsan, Gopāla Kṛṣṇan, Rāmānujam, and so on.

Previously, any respectable *brāhmaṇa* could remember his whole lineage going back so many generations — his father's name, his father's father's name, and so on — giving their family tree.

B.V. Swami: So they took great pride in the family.

Raṅganāthan: Yes. And family didn't just mean four or five people living in a rented apartment. It meant the whole extended family: aunts, uncles, and cousin-brothers all living together in the same house under the leadership of the eldest in the family. Our houses were big, because four generations of brothers, aunts, cousins, and so on used to live together in the same building. Every family would have at least five cows and a big piece of land for growing food. Each home would have a big well, a garden for growing vegetables and flowers, and a barn for storing big piles of straw for the cows.

We lived on the same land that our forefathers had lived on for more than a hundred years. Our forefathers were honorable, principled people, and lived a blissful life fully dedicated to God. They also expected us to maintain the Vaiṣṇava family traditions.

B.V. Swami: In which year were you born?

Raṅganāthan: I was born in 1946, in Serangulam, a village near Mannargudi town, in Thanjavur district, Tamil Nadu. In my family, altogether we are six brothers and two sisters. The sisters are the youngest.

B.V. Swami: You were born in a *brāhmaṇa* family?

Raṅganāthan: Yes. In Serangulam there is a temple of Lord Śrīnivāsan that is more than a thousand years old. In South India, *brāhmaṇas* engaged in the service of the Lord live in an area around the temple called the *agrahāram,* the *brāhmaṇa* housing quarters. The temple would have a high square wall around it, and on all four sides would be the *agrahāram.* In our village the *agrahāram* consisted of about 200 Vaiṣṇava houses, all big houses with big families. So there must have been at least 2,000 people living in the *agrahāram,* and together with other castes, a total of about 5,000 people in the village.

Behind the houses of the western street there was a rivulet called Pāmaṇi, a branch of the Kaveri. There was also a big tank just south of the temple walls. It was filled with water from the Pāmaṇi, to which it was connected by a short canal. Beyond the *agrahāram* there was a temple of Lord Śiva, facing the Śrīnivāsan temple.

B.V. Swami: Yes, the worship of Lord Śiva, and of course Murugan, is prominent in Tamil Nadu.[54] But Śrī Vaiṣṇavas keep themselves aloof from demigod worship and exclusively devote themselves to Lord Nārāyaṇa and Śrī (Lakṣmī), His eternal consort.

Raṅganāthan: In our village there was only one *smārta* family, which was the family of the *arcakar* of the Śiva temple. That temple was not very prominent. The Vaiṣṇavas in our village would never go to any temple other than Lord Śrīnivāsan's temple or Lord Rājagopālan's temple in Mannargudi, three miles away. The Śrī Vaiṣṇavas were very strict on this principle.

B.V. Swami: Did anyone follow any of these bogus incarnations or yogīs?

Raṅganāthan: We never heard of any of these rascals. We only knew the Supreme Lord Viṣṇu and His bona fide servants.

B.V. Swami: So tell me something about your early life. What was your father doing?

Raṅganāthan: He was mainly looking after land and properties. The annual income came from land, as it did for most of the *brāhmaṇas* at that time.

B.V. Swami: Didn't the *brāhmaṇas* in the *agrahāram* have duties in the temple?

54. Murugan — Tamil name for the powerful demigod Kārttikeya, a son of Lord Śiva.

Raṅganāthan: Yes, but most of them didn't have daily duties. That was only for certain families, who were called *arcakar*. Others would have duties only on festivals, and worshiped a *śālagrāma* at home.

B.V. Swami: But wouldn't they all visit the Śrīnivāsan temple daily?

Raṅganāthan: Of course. No one could think of conducting his daily affairs without first having *darśana* of the Lord. Everyone was eager to see Him who was the center of their lives. Their normal morning routine was to get up at four-thirty or five, go to the field for passing stool, and then take bath. They would always go to the river for taking bath. The family well was used only for house work, cooking, *pūjā*, and gardening, and the communal well was used only for drinking water and doing the *abhiśeka* of the *śālagrāma*.

After taking bath they would put on *tilaka*, perform their *sandhyā-vandanam*, and chant the sacred Gāyatrī mantra 108 times. *Sandhyā-vandanam*, if done fully, would take about 20 minutes. Many *brāhmaṇas* would perform these morning prayers on the bank of the river just at sunrise. Others would first come home to do it. They would go and come from the river chanting hymns from the *Sāma Veda* — beautiful, so sweet.

Around 6:30 the temple bell would ring loudly, resounding throughout the village, and everyone — men, women, and children — would at once hurry to the temple. That bell meant that the *bhoga* was being offered. After that the curtain would open and it would be time for *darśana*. The elder men would stand at the front, the younger men and boys behind them, and the ladies at the back.

Altogether the devotees would recite prayers from the *Divya Prabandham* for about fifteen minutes.[55]

B.V. Swami: Women would chant with the men?

Raṅganāthan: The women in restrained voices, not loudly.

B.V. Swami: Also, you mentioned how women stood at the back. Wouldn't they get the chance to come close to the Lord?

Raṅganāthan: They would. After the chanting, the group would disperse and everyone would come forward individually and take close *darśana*. They would be given in the hand three drops of water that had bathed the body of the Lord, and would drink that with great veneration and pleasure. They would have the helmet representing the Lord's lotus feet placed on their heads, and take His *prasādam* in their hands. So at that time the women would have close *darśana*.

Then everyone would go to their homes. The men would do the daily *pūjā* and rituals for the *śālagrāma* Deities.

B.V. Swami: Would all men in the house do *pūjā*, or just some of them?

Raṅganāthan: In our home mainly my father performed it, and we young boys would watch him every day. In this way we gradually learned what to do. We would also help in collecting flowers for offering to the Lord and in setting up the paraphernalia for *pūjā*. We were taught the mantras to chant in *pūjā* by the local priest, and we would practice chanting them along with our father.

---

55. *Divya Prabandham* — collection of four thousand hymns in high Tamil.

B.V. Swami: What about the ladies? What were their morning activities? Would they also bathe early in the morning?

Raṅganāthan: Yes. Everybody had to first take a bath. Only then could they enter the kitchen or perform *pūjā*. Cleanliness and purity were essential. They were very strict about that. Women were not allowed to cook during their monthly period. During that time they stayed in a separate place, away from everybody else. And when the women were cooking, the young children would be looked after by older children. Because children are always dirty, they could not enter the kitchen, nor could the women touch them at the time of cooking.

Anyway, the women would first boil the fresh milk and offer it to the Lord. Then after the offering, they would distribute the milk to everyone — except my father, who would not eat or even drink water until the morning *pūjā* was finished.

Then the ladies would clean the whole house inside and the yard outside with a mixture of cow dung and water. They would decorate the entrance to the home with various intricate designs made by sprinkling rice flour. Mostly they made symmetrical patterns with no particular meaning, but some resembled objects like a fish or the sun. They were pleasing to look at, and each house would attempt to present the most attractive figures. In the month of Mārgali,[56] pumpkin flowers standing in little patties of cow dung would be interspersed among the designs. At the front of each house at least three dozen flowers would

56. Mārgali — Tamil month corresponding to December-January.

be placed in this way. I don't know the significance of it but it looked very nice. From a young age the girls would be trained to very deftly make these designs.

They would quickly do all this to be ready in time to visit the temple. After coming back home the women would start cooking. In another part of the house the men would be doing *pūjā,* and just when it was coming to an end the women would have the preparations ready to offer to the Lord. The *pūjā* would take about half to one hour and the cooking would take about two hours. Including the time to prepare the *pūjā,* collect flowers and so on, the *pūjā* and the cooking would finish at about the same time.

The food was cooked in brass pots. All these big pots would be carried in before the Lord and everything would be offered to Him. In those days the real *brāhmaṇa* and Vaiṣṇava families had to offer everything before anyone could eat. At home no one would take any food cooked outside or not offered to the Lord. Some of them are still very strict about that.

The real orthodox Vaiṣṇavas would eat only in a temple or a house of another Vaiṣṇava *brāhmaṇa.* Some would only eat in the houses of relatives. I have heard of *brāhmaṇas* in some places who are so scrupulous that they do not drink even water from outside their own home, or eat their grown-up children's cooking, because they do not consider them strict enough.

Anyway, right after the food was brought for offering, the kitchen would be cleaned. And the ladies would clear off any *prasādam* that had been kept for more than three or four hours. They would not keep anything except rice, which was kept in water overnight. But they never wasted anything. Absolutely not. The ladies generally cooked just the right amount, and any extra *prasādam* would be given to the young boys in the afternoon.

The offering would take about fifteen minutes. Then the *prasādam* would be transferred from the cooking pots and we would have a sumptuous full breakfast between 9:30 and 10:00.

Taking food together was an important part of our life. It was not like in the West, where someone comes home and just fixes himself something from the fridge. For example, no lady would eat until after her husband had taken. Eating was a family event. There are still joint families where fifty or sixty people sit down at a certain time to eat together.

Eating brought us all together. It nourished not only our bodies, but our whole sense of being. In those days people used to take good food and plenty of it. They were strong, hale and healthy, and clear-minded. All the food was cooked, prepared, and served with love and care. It was so nice — not just the flavor, but everything about it. Everything was homemade. Even now, traditional families do everything at home as much as possible. They husk their own rice, make their own pickles and *pāpars,* and so on.

Nowadays you can go to the grocery store and buy something in a package already mixed up and you can serve it out very easily. But those days even everyday cooking was a whole art, with so many techniques, and a lot of labor and a lot of love went into it. It was certainly more pleasing in that way. The women would take the trouble to make it nice. After all, it was to be offered to the Lord. Then everyone would be satisfied to take tasty *prasādam* and would be happy to eat plenty. And that was the ladies' pleasure, cooking and seeing everyone happy by taking *prasādam.*

The head lady of the house would take charge of serving out *prasādam* to everybody, making sure that everyone got enough and that they were satisfied. Only on special days like *śrāddha,* when we invited many guests, were ladies not allowed to serve. Even on ordinary days, only ladies who were clean and who had been initiated would be allowed to work inside the kitchen, or to touch cooking pots.

B. V. Swami: So women were also initiated, but not into the Gāyatrī mantras, presumably.

Raṅganāthan: Immediately after marriage women would get initiation by the family *ācārya.* There would be a ceremony with a fire sacrifice, and the marks of Lord Viṣṇu's conch, mace, lotus, and disk would be impressed on their arms with hot stamps, the same as for men. They were accepted fully as devotees, but the tradition was that *Gāyatrī* mantras were to be chanted only by *brāhmaṇa* men.

B. V. Swami: What did the daily morning meal consist of?

Raṅganāthan: Water was served before anything else. Then a little fruit and sugar and a few drops of milk would be placed on plates of freshly-cut banana leaves — not the plastic and china rubbish they use today. Next came the vegetable preparations, usually one solid and one liquid, and cucumber mixed with curd.[57] After that they served

57. In Indian usage of English, curd means yogurt.

rice — the main item, a big pile on each plate — and they would pour a good amount of ghee on it. At this point we would all say various prayers and sprinkle water around our plates from our hands and drink a little water from the palms of our hands. Then *sāmbār* would be served and we would begin to honor *prasādam*.[58]

Everything they served was purely Vaiṣṇava-style food. People had not even heard about onion and garlic. No one in the whole *agrahāram* knew even the smell of onion.

B.V. Swami: What about coffee and tea?

Raṅganāthan: No one had ever heard of it. We had milk. We didn't want or need anything else. Plenty of milk was always there in the house. We never knew of shortages. Sometimes they also prepared milk with a mixture of a few powdered cereals, known as *dhānyak-kañji*. Coffee only started penetrating around thirty-five years ago, when I was thirteen. I had not even tasted coffee until I was seventeen.

B.V. Swami: But now coffee is everywhere in South India. Pretty much everyone takes it, including Śrī Vaiṣṇava priests.

Raṅganāthan: Yes.

B.V. Swami: Were there certain vegetables that people didn't use?

Raṅganāthan: They would not cook English vegetables like tomatoes, cauliflower, or potatoes.

B.V. Swami: Only the traditional vegetables.

---

58. *Prasādam* is honored by eating it respectfully.

Raṅganāthan: They were very particular about it. But so much variety was possible with the traditional vegetables alone. From just one vegetable they could make three preparations, having three different tastes. They would make one thick curry, one a little liquid, and another thin, like a soup.

Also, they would use only vegetables that were picked the same day. Every household had a garden, from which vegetables were plucked early in the morning and then cooked and offered. Even today, in Śrī Raṅgam the vegetables sold in the markets are freshly picked the same morning.

B.V. Swami: What would people do after the morning meal?

Raṅganāthan: Maybe look into some work, or relax for some time. And at midday they would do *madhyānnikam.*

B.V. Swami: Which means?

Raṅganāthan: The same as *sandhyā-vandanam,* but performed at midday (*madhyānam*). That would be finished around eleven or eleven thirty, a little early. Strictly speaking it should be done precisely when the sun is at its zenith. Then around one o'clock they might have a cup of milk, sometimes with some small tiffin, like *vaḍai.* But most people would not eat again until the evening, and then also only light food. The morning meal was solid, and pretty much sufficient for the whole day.

From about two o'clock till four-thirty they would read *Bhāgavatam* in every house. Or some people would go to the house of some local scholar, who would give a two- or three-hour lecture. And preaching would also be done in the temple hall. Everyday some *hari-kathā* would be held.[59] Sometimes people would come from outside of the village to hear, but mostly they were locals.

B. V. Swami: Didn't they take some rest in the heat of the afternoon? That's standard throughout India.

Raṅganāthan: No one would sleep in the afternoon. That is prohibited in Vaiṣṇavism. Day sleeping was allowed only if someone was sick. But we didn't get sick much. We all slept in the evening only, and on the floor. Nowadays they use thick pillows and velvet and all that, but previously we never used big pillows or mattresses. We would just sleep and then get up in the morning. We had no trouble getting to sleep. By the time night came we were so tired.

B. V. Swami: One thing I like about living in the tropics is getting to sleep outside in the fresh atmosphere. I would imagine that being from so far south in India, you probably slept outside most of the year.

Raṅganāthan: Yes. Every house had a veranda at the front facing the road. There was a wide tiled roof, so it was breezy and also protected from rain. There was a sort of elevated platform there for people to sit on during the day and sleep on at night. So in all four seasons people would sleep under the veranda.

B. V. Swami: Even in December? Wasn't it too cold to sleep outside?

Raṅganāthan: We would use a blanket. I never slept inside until I was sixteen, except on the rare occasions when I was sick.

---

59. *hari-kathā* — discussion of topics of Hari.

B.V. Swami: What about during the rains?

Raṅganāthan: Yes, in the rainy season also we would sleep there, as no water could seep through the tiled cover. We would only go indoors if there was too much wind blowing the rain in from the side. Otherwise none of the men normally slept inside, although the ladies often would. There were no separate bedrooms; everyone used the common area to take rest. So everyone had to get up early, as all the others would be up early.

The males would usually sleep outside with just a straw mat, or spread out cotton cloth, and in the winter they would use light blankets. After rising, the place used for sleeping was swept and mopped because it was considered to have become impure. No one would touch the bedding during the day, either. It would all be kept in one corner. At the time of waking they would fold it and put it in the loft. Once a week they cleaned the blankets. In some houses they even cleaned them daily.

B.V. Swami: You were talking about going to school. Please tell me more about that.

Raṅganāthan: The local school went up to elementary level only. That school started at 10:30. So before 10:00, the younger children would join their parents for a meal and then leave for school. The older children, who were attending the higher school, had to walk four miles to school. They would come back in the evening by 4:30 or 5:00. Upon returning from school, the children would immediately wash and change into dhotīs and *chaddars*.

B.V. Swami: What did you wear to school?

Raṅganāthan: Short pants and slack shirts. That was the uniform. After coming home from school our parents would insist that we take bath, change our clothes, put on *tilaka,* perform *sandhyā-vandanam,* and chant Gāyatrī. After evening *sandhyā-vandanam* we would recite the *Viṣṇu-sahasra-nāma,* which took about twenty-five minutes. Then only could we take *prasādam.*

B. V. Swami: What about wearing *tilaka* at school?

Raṅganāthan: Yes, putting on *tilaka* in the morning was a must. Even today you can hardly see my father without *tilaka.*

B. V. Swami: The Śrī Vaiṣṇava *tilaka* is very nice; thick white lines with red marks in the middle. It strongly proclaims the devotees' allegiance to Viṣṇu.

Raṅganāthan: My father used to say that a person without *tilaka* looks like a *brahma-hatti.*

B. V. Swami: A killer of a *brāhmaṇa.*

Raṅganāthan: Yes. If we did not have *tilaka* they would say, "What is this? Your forehead is empty?" Sometimes the elders would even hit us for it. We have this *tilaka* as a representation of Kṛṣṇa.

B. V. Swami: You were saying that the older children had to go some distance to school. At what time would they eat?

Raṅganāthan: In the morning they would eat with the rest of the family around nine-thirty, as I described before. Then they would take some curd-rice to school with them. That was made from rice cooked the previous day and soaked in water. The water was removed from the rice, then curd and a little salt were added. The boys would take that at school with some pickle. Or if the morning *prasādam* at home was late, they would take the same thing for breakfast also. After coming back in the evening, they would have a cup of milk, and then dinner at night. Dinner was light, not a heavy meal. The ladies would cook *sāmbār* and various types of vegetables and offer it to the Lord.

B.V. Swami: You were saying that they used to teach *Rāmāyaṇa* in the secondary school.

Raṅganāthan: Yes. That was in the Tamil class, taught by Vaiṣṇava *brāhmaṇas* — real *brāhmaṇas,* real scholars. Mostly they taught the Tamil versions of *Mahābhārata* and *Rāmāyaṇa,* scene by scene. And they didn't just teach them as academic subjects, but with real feeling. The teachers were absorbed in the description, as if they were living there in the forest with Sītā and Rāma. They would immerse the students in Tamil. It's difficult to explain if you don't know, but in the intricacies of the language there are all kinds of subtle expressions and poetic descriptions.

B.V. Swami: I have some idea from knowing Bengali.

Raṅganāthan: That was the one class we all liked best. We relished it and looked forward to it. They would tell us how Vālmīki described an episode in his *Rāmāyaṇa,* and would compare it with how Kamba dealt with the same in his *Rāmāyaṇa.*[60] At every stage they would explain the verses according to the commentaries of the previous *ācāryas.*

---

60. Vālmīki — compiler of the original *Rāmāyaṇa* in Sanskrit; Kamba — author of the Tamil version of *Rāmāyaṇa.*

And there was Sanskrit class, where we learned many verses. They used to teach us rhythmic chanting of the verses. Unfortunately, Sanskrit studies have now been stopped. So much valuable knowledge is practically lost to human society, due to the influence of politically motivated forces.

B.V. Swami: You said that after school you used to have a debating club.

Raṅganāthan: Yes. They invited the top students from various schools in the surrounding villages, and all local people would attend. They would hold debates on different topics, mainly from *Rāmāyaṇa, Mahābhārata,* and the history of the Ālvārs.[61] The topics would be like "Which character is the best, Rāma or Sītā?" or "'How do you like *Rāmāyaṇa*? Why do you like it?" Everybody would express his views and try to impress the audience and judges. Each debater would interpret the topic in various ways and try to establish the superiority of his arguments. For example, they might argue that even Rāvaṇa was good in some ways.

B.V. Swami: It seems that it was strongly oriented toward *bhakti*. Would Śaṅkara's *advaita* philosophy be presented at all?

Raṅganāthan: No, this was totally Vaiṣṇava. Only topics from the Vaiṣṇava scriptures were entertained. Gradually it started to deteriorate though, and other topics were introduced, including non-philosophical ones. They

61. Ālvārs — ancient saints of the Śrī Vaiṣṇava *sampradāya* who preceded the most prominent *ācārya* of that *sampradāya*, namely Śrīpād Rāmānujācārya.

picked those topics to attract people, but they lost the original beauty of the debates.

B. V. Swami: What else was taught at school?

Raṅganāthan: The traditional subjects were there — Tamil and Sanskrit and the scriptural stories. In the elementary school we were taught a few parts of the *Divya Prabandham* and the *Viṣṇu-sahasra-nāma,* and how to perform the *sandhyā-vandanam*. At secondary school there would also be modern science and English.

B. V. Swami: Did they teach Darwinian evolutionary theory?

Raṅganāthan: Generally they taught basic things like "H_2O means water," and that it contains hydrogen and oxygen. Evolutionary theory was also taught, but not in detail.

B. V. Swami: The idea that we descended from animals is completely against Vaiṣṇava philosophy.

Raṅganāthan: Definitely — against common sense even. The British set up the modern educational system to gradually inject Western philosophy and ideas. Thus everything started to decline and the original purity of Indian society was lost. Nowadays there is no more teaching of *Rāmāyaṇa* in the schools. Previously a person was considered educated if he was well versed in *Rāmāyaṇa* and *Mahābhārata,* but it is now forbidden to teach *śāstra* in the schools. Instead we are taught that our forefathers were monkeys.

B. V. Swami: How was the relationship between the teachers and the students?

Raṅganāthan: Teachers had command over the children and the power to punish them if necessary. The children had a lot of respect for them, and some fear also.

B. V. Swami: Teachers were much respected, weren't they? No one would expect a teacher to say or do anything wrong.

Raṅganāthan: Yes. Teachers were looked up to and trusted. The parents would not interfere in the dealings of the teachers with their children. The teachers were always considered to be right. They would call the parents and advise them as to how to correct their ward and get him to behave. If necessary, they would insist that the parents mend the life of the student at home.

The teachers took interest in the students and tried to improve them. Theirs were lives of selfless service, kindness, and discipline, without any hidden motives.

B. V. Swami: Were they mostly from the *brāhmaṇa* class?

Raṅganāthan: Ninety-nine percent were *brāhmaṇas*.

B. V. Swami: The teacher was respected like a guru.

Raṅganāthan: Definitely. The boys were afraid of him also. Naturally, as boys, we could be quite frivolous. But the teachers kept us in line. Discipline was strict. The boys were scared that a teacher would complain to their parents. That would be a disgrace.

B. V. Swami: What about education for the girls?

Raṅganāthan: Girls would go to primary school only, and learn to read and write. Everything else they needed to know they would learn at home.

B. V. Swami: In the Śrī Vaiṣṇava tradition there are many festivals. Could you tell us about some of them?

Raṅganāthan: Practically every month we had a festival. The yearly Brahmotsavam was one of the main ones.[62] At the Śrīnivāsan temple it lasted for ten days, but it took up the whole attention of the people of Serangulam and the surrounding villages for at least twenty days before also. We would all be engaged in cleaning the temple inside and out, whitewashing the walls, repairing and restoring the chariots, and so many other works.

The Brahmotsavam at the Rājagopālan temple would last for eighteen days. Actually, in other temples the Brahmotsavam lasts for just ten days. I believe that only for Lord Rājagopālan at Mannargudi is it celebrated for eighteen days. Mannargudi is also known as Dakṣiṇa Vṛndāvana, "Southern Vṛndāvana." The temple there is very big and the Deity of Rājagopālan is extraordinarily beautiful. He holds a flute and is accompanied by a cow and other paraphernalia.

Every morning the Deity would go out on procession on a palanquin in a very grand way. Different varieties of decorated palanquins would be used. There were the Puṣpa-ratham ("chariot decorated with flowers"), Sūrya-prabhā ("shining like the sun"), Ādi-śeṣan ("the divine snake-bed of the Lord"), Garuḍa, swan, elephant, horse, and others. Every day we would help in setting up the gorgeous decorations. We would all go along with the procession around the temple streets. At every house they

62. Brahmotsavam — the most important festival of the year, held on different dates in different temples.

would stop, and the members of each family would come and make offerings to the Deity.

The last day there would be a *Ratha-yātrā*. All the schools would declare a holiday to encourage and facilitate the participation of the students in pulling the chariot. In the evening the procession would go around all the streets adjoining the temple. It was a huge chariot. It was very difficult to move, even though thousands of people would come to pull it. The chariot would never be stationary except when an offering was being made. It would go on for long hours, throughout the day. Sometimes the chariot would not reach its destination by the end of the day and the festival would have to continue for one or even two days more. We never felt tired at the time, but afterward our bodies would be aching. Then on the tenth day of the festival there would be a big function called *annakuttu,* when the Lord would come to the beautiful green lawn near the temple well.

B. V. Swami: He had his own garden?

Raṅganāthan: Yes, inside the temple compound. They would spread plain white cotton cloth on the lawn, and put different rice preparations and other offerings on it in a lavish pattern. So in the evening the Lord would come there and a huge offering would be made to Him and then distributed to everybody. Several thousand people would participate.

B. V. Swami: And everyone was happy.

Raṅganāthan: Yes, everyone was very happy. They would enjoy this, and looked forward to it every year.

B.V. Swami: Would people come from all the adjoining villages?

Raṅganāthan: Yes. People would come in huge numbers from all the surrounding villages for several miles around.

B.V. Swami: Where would they all stay at night?

Raṅganāthan: Those from adjoining villages would go home and come back every morning. Others would sleep in the temple hall or on the verandas of people's houses.

Every day during the festival people would come to the temple in the early morning. After the morning *abhiśeka* and procession, *prasādam* was served in a very big dining hall. A few thousand people could dine there at the same time. During the biggest festivals, more than ten thousand people would take *prasādam* every morning. They would distribute first-class curd-rice and other dishes offered to the Lord.

Before *prasādam* was served, the area would first be purified by chanting the Gāyatrī mantra, and grass mats for sitting would be laid out on the floor. The *arcakar* would bring water that had been poured over the *śālagrāma*. Everyone would sip this water and then begin to honor *prasādam*.

Every day of the festival they served a first-class breakfast consisting of curd-rice and *sāmbār*. Then at midday there was a sumptuous lunch. For lunch there would be three varieties of vegetables, different types of liquid vegetables, sweets, *sāmbār, rasam* — which is a very light soup to be taken with rice — and different types of mixed rice preparations like tamarind-rice, coconut-rice, curd-rice, lemon-rice, sweet-rice, and mango-rice.

B. V. Swami: You were telling me that the boys used to help in the temple festivals.

Raṅganāthan: Yes, we assisted the cooks in bringing and cutting vegetables and firewood, placing plantain trees everywhere as decorations before festivals, serving *prasādam,* cleaning the area, and various other services. We had to learn to serve systematically. For serving we would transfer the *prasādam* from the cooking pots to smaller serving pots.

When everything was ready, we put samples of all the different preparations on the plantain leaves. The elders would give out *tīrtham* (sanctified water) and everyone would sip it. Then they started to take *prasādam,* while chanting the names of the Lord. Everybody would take to their capacity, and then return home.

In this way, one group after another would be served, often going up to six or seven groups. Generally everyone in each group would finish simultaneously. Then, after each batch, we would remove the leaves immediately, clean the hall with cow dung water, and mop the area for the next people — another 1500 or 2000 people.

We would serve *prasādam* to everyone without discrimination; but for cooking and serving, the person had to be clean and had to be initiated.

B. V. Swami: Would everyone wear dhotīs and top pieces and other traditional dresses?

Raṅganāthan: Of course. Everybody would come clean after a morning bath, with *tilaka,* and wearing the top piece around the waist, South Indian style. At that time Western dress was practically never seen. If anyone had dared to enter the temple in Western dress, they probably would have been slapped and told to leave.

B.V. Swami: On festival days would the women dress up with jewelry and everything?

Raṅganāthan: Yes. Naturally all the women had some ornaments that they would wear all the time: earrings, noserings, toerings, bangles. But on festival days the women would dress extra well, with silk and extra jewels, and go to the temple.

B.V. Swami: Only to the temple.

Raṅganāthan: And other places also. But everyone had to be dressed up nicely to go to the temple, especially on Dīpāvalī and Poṅgal day.

B.V. Swami: Would they dress up every day to go for *darśana*?

Raṅganāthan: Every day. They would put on good clothes and ornaments, to show themselves to the Lord. They would wear only nice clothes to the temple, then come back home and put on ordinary clothes. For everyday dress both men and women wore simple cotton clothes.

B.V. Swami: Would non-*brāhmaṇas* come to the temple also?

Raṅganāthan: Yes. They would come, participate in the *Ratha-yātrā* and other functions, and take *prasādam*. But certain areas were restricted. Non-*brāhmaṇas* were not allowed to enter the Deity room or the kitchen.

B.V. Swami: So in the *Ratha-yātrā* the *brāhmaṇas* didn't mind touching the bodies of non-*brāhmaṇas*?

Raṅganāthan: No. That way they wouldn't mind. The *Ratha-yātrā* was open to everybody. Everyone was allowed to pull the *ratha.*

B.V. Swami: But normally the *brāhmaṇas* wouldn't even touch the non-*brāhmaṇas.*

Raṅganāthan: No, it was not like that.

B.V. Swami: Not so strict.

Raṅganāthan: No. But only the *brāhmaṇas* could take the Deity around the streets. Although the others were always allowed to have *darśana,* they would not be allowed to go very near the Deity. Nowadays it is much different. Now they permit non-*brāhmaṇas* to take the Deity on procession too.

Festivals were also held on the birthdays of Rāmānuja, Nammālvār, and other big *ācāryas.* On these days they would prepare *prasādam* items which these *ācāryas* used to like, and distribute them to everyone.

In the winter during Mārgali, there was another grand function. Early every morning the people would perform *saṅkīrtana* on the streets surrounding the temple, and then the party would return to the temple.

B.V. Swami: What names were they chanting in the *saṅkīrtana?*

Raṅganāthan: The names of Lord Hari. It was known as *Govinda-nāma saṅkīrtana.* One person would sing, and everybody would follow, accompanied by *mṛdaṅgam* and *karatālas.* In the early morning some young boys would be sleeping on the granite floor outside the temple, and on hearing the *saṅkīrtana* they would suddenly come and join in, without even washing their faces. But the five or six elders who led the *kīrtana* would first take a bath, apply *tilaka,* and then start by four or four-thirty. Mostly it was all young men and boys, from ages five to thirty-five, who participated. It would go on for one and a half to two hours.

Later they would chant the thirty verses of the *Thiruppāvai*. *Thiruppāvai* is a work in Tamil in which Āṇḍāl sings in the mood of the *gopīs.*[63] One line goes: [sings in Tamil] "Birth after birth my only duty is to serve You. I have no other concern." It is very beautiful.

Then they offered hot *poṅgal* and distributed it to everyone in the morning. And by seven o'clock all the festivities would be over and everyone would disperse.

During festivals, many Vaiṣṇavas would come together in the temple to recite the *Vedas* and *Divya Prabandham.* A hundred people would recite together, divided into two groups chanting in turns. At the end of a verse chanted by one group, another group would start the next. They would chant very beautifully and feelingly. Then they would sing *maṅgalam* for the Lord.

B. V. Swami: What is that?

Raṅganāthan: *Maṅgalam* is a Sanskrit word that means "welfare," or "auspiciousness." These were prayers invoking auspiciousness for the Lord: "May Your fame be widely spread," "May You always be victorious and happy,"

63. Aṇḍāl — a partial incarnation of Lakṣmī, the eternal consort of Lord Viṣṇu. Her devotional songs form part of the *Divya Prabandham* and are much loved by Śrī Vaiṣṇavas.

and so on. Of course the Lord is Himself the source of all auspiciousness, so there is nothing we tiny beings can do to improve His condition. He is always automatically situated in the topmost happiness. But it is a tradition to pray like that. The prayers were concluded with a verse which means, "Everything is being done for the pleasure of the Lord. "

Then the temple *arcakar* would offer *tīrtham* to everyone and would place a kind of helmet, which represents the Lord's feet, on the heads of all the devotees. Then everyone would take *prasādam*.

Śrī Vaiṣṇavas also celebrate festivals for the appearance days of the great *ācāryas*. Just after my *upanayanam*, when I was seven years old, my father brought me to the birthplace of Rāmānujācārya at Śrīperambudūr. For days before he had collected rice, *dāl*, and other items from our village people. He sent these goods ahead of him by truck to Śrīperambudūr and brought me by train along with the cash he had collected. It was the time of a ten-day festival celebrating the appearance of Śrīpād Rāmānujācārya. When we got there my father presented everything to the *jīyar*. The *jīyar* knew my father very well. My father loved and respected the *jīyar*, and the *jīyar* was very affectionate and kind to him. The *jīyar* would engage my father in helping to oversee kitchen duties at the festival, making sure everyone got well fed and on time. There was a group of boys there from the *gurukula* — young, just my age — who would recite the whole *Divya Prabandham*, 4,000 verses, by heart, and so beautifully too.

We also held a grand festival in our village when an *ācārya* or *jīyar* would visit us. The entire village would come and offer respects to him. He would be accompanied by a huge retinue of followers, and also many cows and horses and five or six elephants all in a procession. He would look naturally majestic and very respectable. And the villagers would receive him with *pūrṇa-kumbha,* a traditional offering of rice and a coconut.

B. V. Swami: Can you explain more about the *ācāryas* and *jīyars*?

Raṅganāthan: In the Śrī Vaiṣṇava line, every disciple must have a guru, who is the link between the Lord and the devotee. The guru was called the *ācārya*, meaning one who teaches by his example. The functions of the *ācārya* were to lead daily prayers, give discourses on *śāstra,* and generally enlighten and inspire the devotees in the values of Vaiṣṇavism.

Every Vaiṣṇava family would be connected to a *paramparā-ācārya.* They were attached either to a family of *ācāryas* or to a *sannyāsī* head of a temple or monastery. The latter were called *jīyars.* In other words, generation after generation, members of a family would all be initiated by the descendants of the *ācārya* family they were connected to, or to the incumbent *jīyar* of a particular temple. Even the *ācāryas* who were married householders lived very simple, ideal lives, engaged fully in spiritual activities.[64]

---

64. Śrīla Prabhupāda comments: "Birth in a family of yogīs or transcendentalists — those with great wisdom — is praised because the child born in such a family receives a spiritual impetus from the very beginning of his life. It is especially the case in the *ācārya* or *gosvāmī* families. Such families are very learned and devoted by tradition and training, and thus they become spiritual masters. In India there are many such *ācārya* families, but they have now degenerated due to insufficient education and training. By the grace

B.V. Swami: Would the *ācāryas* and *jīyars* come on foot? They were very strict about the old traditions, one of which was that a saintly person or *sannyāsī* should not use any kind of vehicle.

Raṅganāthan: Yes, they would come by walking. And a big tent would be erected wherever they halted, for keeping the animals in. The *jīyar* and his party would stay in houses. One or two houses would be vacated for them to stay in, and the occupants would stay in someone else's house during that time.

B.V. Swami: Would the same *jīyar* come every time, or different ones?

Raṅganāthan: The same *jīyar* would come, as most of the residents in a given village would be from the same *paramparā*. The *jīyar* would normally stay for a month. During his visit a function was celebrated every morning, in a different house every day. Everybody would join together in the presence of the *jīyar* and recite many hymns in praise of the Lord. The *jīyar* would lecture on philosophical matters and pastimes of the Lord from scripture. At the end of the lecture the people would present him with offerings of fruits and money, and sometimes cows or land. The *jīyar* would distribute *akṣata prasādam* to everyone. Then full *prasādam* would be distributed to all.

And on one day during the *jīyar's* visit there would be a grand ceremony to felicitate the local scholars. All the

---

of the Lord, there are still families that foster transcendentalists generation after generation. It is certainly very fortunate to take birth in such families." (*Bhagavad-gītā As It Is* 6.42 Purport) local *brāhmaṇas* would come together, and the *jīyar* would honor those among them most reputed for devotional scholarship. He would accolade them by placing a symbolic cloth on their shoulders or wrapping it on their heads, and would praise their achievements. The scholars would give speeches, and the local people would take pride and pleasure in the erudition of their compatriots.

B.V. Swami: So learning was much looked up to.

Raṅganāthan: Oh yes, it was a great tradition. Scholarship was considered very important and was highly respected. Scholarship meant knowledge of *śāstra,* not this M.A., B.Sc. stuff. Even an ordinary *brāhmaṇa* was expected to be well versed in *śāstra* and the teachings of the *sampradāya.* And there were many real scholars who were extraordinarily learned, people you could ask any question to and they could give the answer. They had a great gift from God; otherwise they could not know so much. Of course they had to work for it also. Great scholars were said to have "crossed over to the other shore of scriptural knowledge, having spent long years studying from and serving the feet of self-realized souls."

Especially to be an *ācārya,* tremendous erudition was required. It wasn't just an honorific post. In those days there were many learned scholars of opposing schools also, so an *ācārya* had to have deep learning, and realization also, to defeat all challenges.

So by their scholarship they had to maintain the prestige of the *sampradāya.* They could also extract so many devotional meanings out of the verses of *Bhāgavatam,* to give pleasure and enlightenment to the other devotees.

Therefore such scholars were called *Bhāgavatās,* meaning, "those who know and personify the teachings of the *Bhāgavatam,*" and were treated with the highest respect.

But actually, every Vaiṣṇava was brought up to respect every other Vaiṣṇava, not only the most exalted devotees. Every Śrī Vaiṣṇava on meeting another devotee would immediately say, "I am a servant of the servants of the Lord," *nārāyaṇa dāsa dāsanudāsan.* Immediately both devotees would offer mutual obeisances. Neither of them would simply remain standing to receive respects. It was also customary for the ladies to offer respects to the elders in the family each evening. They would even go to the neighbors homes to offer obeisances to the elderly Vaiṣṇavas, who would be sitting outside.

B.V. Swami: Can you tell us about any other family traditions or functions? Among *brāhmaṇas* the *upanayanam* ceremony is an important family event.

Raṅganāthan: *Upanayanam* was normally done at the age of seven, or even earlier, to see to it that the children did *sandhyā-vandanam* properly. My father told my mother that unless I did my *sandhyā-vandanam,* she should not feed me: "You have to make him do *sandhyā-vandanam* before he leaves for school."

Another important festival was the thread-changing ceremony and Gāyatrī *japam* the next day. This came once a year, when all the *brāhmaṇas* ritually change their old sacred threads. So many ceremonies and festivals were there, all centered around worshiping the Lord, so that even in our family life we could never forget Him, nor forget that the goal of life is to serve Him.

There was also a big function for observing a person's death. As a person's end was nearing, the relatives would bring a cow with a calf, to give to some poor *brāhmaṇa*. Then at the stroke of death, they would give away the cow and calf. It was believed that the departed soul catches hold of the tail of the cow, which takes him to the spiritual world. Both on the day the person died and the twelfth day afterward, they would offer a cow and calf in donation to a *brāhmaṇa*. A very good cow, which provided like five liters of milk every day, would be offered.

B. V. Swami: What about observing Ekādaśi?

Raṅganāthan: Ekādaśi meant taking only *tulasī* water.[65] People wouldn't take anything else that day, and they performed more spiritual activity than usual. They would not use a mattress for sleeping — just the floor.

B. V. Swami: What about the night before?

Raṅganāthan: On the eve of Ekādaśi they would have very light food. They would not take heavy foodstuff, as they actually wanted to fast. The next morning they would break the fast by seven o'clock. They offered food to the *brahmacārīs* first, and then only would the others accept *prasādam*. They cooked many varieties of food on Dvādaśi, the day after Ekādaśi. The preparations were scientifically chosen so as to help soothe the stomach after the twenty-four hour fast. We took cooling foods that help soothe a burning, empty stomach. We didn't just fill the stomach indiscriminately after a day's fasting.

B. V. Swami: The most famous and important festival in Tamil Nadu is Poṅgal.

---

65. Water in which *tulasī* leaves have been soaked.

Raṅganāthan: Yes. We have another name for it. There is always some Vaiṣṇava name for every festival, and even every food. Mostly some name related to Hari was used for everything. That's why our Vaiṣṇava *brāhmaṇa* language is sometimes difficult for others to follow.

The day after Poṅgal was a festival for cows, known as Māṭṭu-poṅgal. On that day early in the morning, different varieties of *poṅgal prasādam* would be taken by the ladies to the riverside and spread out on turmeric leaves. Naturally so many birds would come and enjoy a feast. The ladies would pray that just as the birds live together and eat together, so they hoped for their families to stay together. This is the day also when brothers gave gifts to their sisters of ornaments, clothes, and cash, according to their means.

For Māṭṭu-poṅgal, the cows were bathed in the river and then decorated with *kumkum, tilaka,* and flowers. Later a congregation of a few thousand cows would be brought together in a big open area. And first-class *poṅgal* would be prepared for feeding the cows. The cows would enjoy *poṅgal* and plantains.

In the temple they used to keep thousands of cows. One would feel a difference in the atmosphere just by entering the temple. It was such a wholesome and sacred feeling to be among the cows. We used to always hear the mooing of the huge number of cows. The temple would also maintain two or three elephants, so we would hear them roaring from time to time.

In our house we had a cow named Lakṣmī. She was so sensible that my mother would put me on the floor next to her when I was a baby only one year old. Then my mother would just see to her household chores and Lakṣmī would oversee me. She wasn't even tied up. She would just come and go in and out of the house as she liked.

Even the ladies of the house would handle the cow without any fear. One of our family elders was 86, and still he would walk the cow in and out every day, guiding her by a rope tied to her nose. We would warn him not to take the risk, as he was so old and frail. The cow was big and strong, with long horns, but she was so tame that no one would expect her to misbehave. If the cow wanted, it could have lifted him off his legs effortlessly with its horns. But our relative would tell us, "This is my cow, and it is so nice and tame that it would never do such a thing. From a very young age we have been handling cows. It is our family tradition. The cow would not do us any harm."

B. V. Swami: When cows are treated well, they reciprocate. Nowadays cows are mostly mistreated and people are afraid to go near them.

Raṅganāthan: Some rich families would have a hundred cows. And of course bulls also, for plowing the fields. They would all be taken care of very nicely. There was a community known as *konār* in South India, whose main occupation was to take care of the cows of different households. The *brāhmaṇas* did not personally milk the cows. Every family had a *konār,* who would milk the cows, feed them, take care of their health, and churn the milk.

So this community would perform many of the functions on Māṭṭu-poṅgal, and on that day the members of their community would be honored. Every house would give their *konār* new clothes for his entire family, donations, various oils, and other gifts.

There were also hereditary barbers, serving specifically the *brāhmaṇa* families, who would shave their heads. And there were hereditary washermen, who would wash the women's and children's clothing. Normally the gents would wash their own clothes while bathing, but sometimes they would also use the services of the washermen to whiten their formal dresses.

B. V. Swami: Who looked after the home garden?

Raṅganāthan: Invariably there were at least a dozen people in the house, so maybe half a dozen of the boys would cultivate the garden in the evening. It was a hobby. Outside people also sold vegetables every day in the market place.

B. V. Swami: Did you also make your own oil at home?

Raṅganāthan: Sometimes, but there was also a place in the village where they used to produce oil. The bulls used to grind sesame oil seeds by walking round a mortar, to which they were attached by ropes. We used that oil to light lamps in the morning and evening.

B. V. Swami: Before, we were talking about religious rituals. In India the marriage function is still one of the most elaborate.

Raṅganāthan: But nothing like before. Now marriages are just hurriedly done in one or two days. Slip, slap — over and finished. Previously all the rituals were celebrated elaborately, keeping in mind their meaning and purpose.

Marriages were grandly celebrated — at least a five-day function. The whole village would attend. Even the bridegroom's family's invitation to the bride's people, and the reciprocation involved, was all done as a grand function. The marriage itself would consist of various rituals and rites, which often depicted the pastimes of Lord Kṛṣṇa and Rukmiṇī. Various indigenous instruments like the *nādasvuram* would provide background music.[66] The bride and the groom used to participate in games to test their physical and mental strength. And there was a song that depicted the pastimes of the Lord when he came to wed Aṇḍāl. There were so many aspects to the wedding. But nowadays very few people even know they exist, let alone appreciate their significance.

B. V. Swami: At what age would the boys get married?

Raṅganāthan: At 14 or 15. The age later became 22 or 23, and now it is around 30. As the boys were young, they did not know what marriage was. The elders would fix the marriage and make all the arrangements. There were also cases of people having a second wife, but they would be treated somewhat differently and looked down upon.

B. V. Swami: Who would be looked down upon, the second wife or those who took a second wife?

Raṅganāthan: Both.

B. V. Swami: But wasn't it common in Hindu culture to accept another wife, especially if the first wife was barren or produced only girl children?

---

66. *Nādasvaram* — wind instrument with a single-reed mouthpiece, similar to but less complex than a saxophone.

Raṅganāthan: Not among the people I knew. Only if someone's wife died young was remarriage considered acceptable.

B. V. Swami: Marriage partners were settled by the parents.

Raṅganāthan: Yes.

B. V. Swami: Before marriage, would the boys know who the girl would be? Were they from the same village, or would they be chosen from different villages?

Raṅganāthan: They would meet for the first time at marriage. Generally they selected the bride from another village, although in some cases she was from the same village. The main thing was to consult an astrologer. If their horoscopes matched, they would be sure that there would be compatibility between husband and wife.

B. V. Swami: Nowadays marriage seems to be so troublesome and burdensome that simply for there to be peace between husband and wife is considered a great achievement.

Raṅganāthan: We hardly knew or heard of such problems. People were very happy. Their simplicity and innocence kept them out of misunderstandings. Whatever the man preferred, the ladies would cooperate with and abide by. There was no question of differences. Very rarely would we see such cases.

B. V. Swami: So the women had to accept whatever the husband said.

Raṅganāthan: That was the custom, but at the same time, the women were treated very well. There was no question of fighting. You see, the whole way of thinking was that all saw themselves as servants of God, and their only aim was His service.

B.V. Swami: So after marriage they would continue to engage in the service of God.

Raṅganāthan: Yes. They would continue in the service of God under the instructions of the elders. There was no question of not abiding by the elders of the family. Some discipline was observed. What the elders said would not be transgressed.

B.V. Swami: They had great respect for the elders.

Raṅganāthan: Yes. Because very elderly people, of eighty or a hundred years, were present in the family, the youngsters had no chance to lead, and they had to listen to the elders. When the younger generation see themselves as the leaders, the problems start to come in.

B.V. Swami: There must have been at least some family quarrels.

Raṅganāthan: A few stray cases were there, but now gradually it has come down to the level of the husband and wife shouting and arguing in public. Previously it was not like that.

My father used to say that all of us from one *gotra* (dynasty) hail from the same ancestors, so even if we cannot relate to someone, we should remember that we are all from the same family and somehow or other keep the peace.

Even today that is our culture. I am living here in Dubai and my elder brother is in India, but still I have to respect him and follow what he says. Not that he tells me what to do in my day to day life, but if there is some family matter that involves us all, ultimately I have to do what he says. Sometimes I ask his advice also, even though I have grown-up children myself.

B. V. Swami: So if there was a quarrel, the elders would settle it.

Raṅganāthan: Yes. Most of the quarrels arose from differences regarding land and property. Another important factor was the selection of a girl for marriage. If the girl was good, there was no problem in the house. If not, then the problem would start. Once a quarrel started, if it couldn't be stopped in the early stages, then it would continue and be a permanent thing. Sometimes brothers of the same family would end up living separately. But that was rare — maybe two or three cases in the whole *agrahāram*.

But there was no discord in my family. I have never seen my father or mother fight, not even once. Sometimes there was a difference of opinion between them, but they would keep it to themselves so that we children would not be disturbed by it. Our parents went through some rough times, but they did not let us know about their problems. We only came to know about their difficulties many years later, when by the course of time things had anyway changed and the problems had passed over.

B. V. Swami: What type of problems did they have?

Raṅganāthan: Sometimes there was a lack of money, such as when the land was washed away by floods, or when there was no income from the land.

B. V. Swami: What about those who didn't even have land? Were there beggars?

Raṅganāthan: No professional beggars like today. Everyone had some occupation. They had at least enough self-respect not to live as professional parasites. If circumstantially the poorer people occasionally couldn't make ends meet, still no one was allowed to beg. Someone would at least give them *prasādam*. It would be considered a disgrace to the whole village if there was no one to help the poor. But now many people are begging on the road.

B. V. Swami: Would people always cook extra food?

Raṅganāthan: Yes, they cooked extra food and often fed the poor. When some hungry person happened to come, my mother would go and attend to him immediately.

B. V. Swami: What about police, and law and order?

Raṅganāthan: We had never seen any policemen, or even heard of them. The atmosphere was peaceful. The houses were left open but there was no fear. The houses were not locked, but still no one would touch anything.

B. V. Swami: What about the government?

Raṅganāthan: We knew very little about it.

B. V. Swami: So how was the temple being funded and managed?

Raṅganāthan: The temple had huge lands and there was a group of trustees who managed it. They were highly respected people, chosen from among the Vaiṣṇavas only.

B. V. Swami: They cared for God and the temple properties.

Raṅganāthan: They took care of the Lord's properties, income, and everything. The people were happy that by the Lord's grace they had such a nice Deity and temple.

B.V. Swami: So the government did not levy any tax there?

Raṅganāthan: No, nothing. The Vaiṣṇavas managed the temple and its affairs.

B.V. Swami: It seems that for people born in the original culture of India, it wasn't a struggle to be Kṛṣṇa conscious. It was most natural for them. They didn't know anything else. Their minds weren't cluttered with so many doubts or nonsense ideas, or dreams or schemes for sense gratification. They had their home and family lives, but it was all centered around Kṛṣṇa. There must have been hundreds of thousands of people leading normal, ordinary lives who were saintly devotees. It was easy for people to remember Kṛṣṇa and go back to Godhead. Bhārata-bhūmi was so blessed.

Raṅganāthan: But look at her condition today.

B.V. Swami: Still the culture is alive. In Jaipur there are always a few hundred devotees for *maṅgala-ārati* at the Rādhā-Govinda temple.[67] Even during the winter, when the temperature drops to zero, there are regulars who won't miss. And during Kārttika, the temple is packed all around throughout the whole day. And throughout India there are still some learned saintly people and scholars.

Raṅganāthan: Still, the general spiritual condition of the country is not good.

---

67. *Maṅgala-ārati* — first worship ceremony of the day, performed before dawn.

B. V. Swami: That I have to admit. How has this come about? How did such a great culture become degraded in such a short time?

Raṅganāthan: I was just telling you about the temple administration. Now the government has taken away the temple's lands. The original trustees were replaced with government officers, and then all this corruption started. Things just degraded overnight. They instituted policies like "Land to the tiller," which meant that all of a sudden the land owned by the *brāhmaṇas* did not belong to them any more. If someone was engaged in plowing your land, he would take the bulk of the crop. So the land owners ended up being at the mercy of the tillers. The owner could not even sell or control his own land. The *brāhmaṇas* were badly hit, as the land was their only source of income.

So the younger generation were forced to take up jobs elsewhere. Basically the *brāhmaṇas* are intelligent people, so wherever they went they did well. Many South Indian *brāhmaṇas* are highly placed government officers, or hold other responsible posts in India and around the world. Even in my company in Dubai, the top positions are mostly held by South Indian *brāhmaṇas*.

Many became envious by seeing the *brāhmaṇas* at the top, and they brought in job quotas to deny them most options in the government. So today these jobs are often given to some idiot who does not know anything. And see the nasty situation now: government in India means bribery, corruption, and inefficiency.

B. V. Swami: You were telling me that when you returned to your village after a long absence, you were very disappointed.

Raṅganāthan: Oh, terrible! Even now I feel like crying when I talk of the situation in these ancient temples. The last time I went to Mannargudi temple, the priest asked me for ten rupees. I literally wept. I have seen with my own eyes how respectably the priests used to live. Seeing their position now, I just want to cry.

The temples are filthy and run down. No one seems to care. The same temple that was filled with bliss, that was so joyous and vibrant, is now gloomy, almost deserted. I doubt whether they are even doing the proper daily *pūjā*. The *gośālā* has been converted into a warehouse, full of rice bags — hardly any cows left, and those not properly looked after. Things have come to such a bad condition. I become really mad when I think how these temples are being managed. The spirit of participation has been broken; we have to revive it.

That is why I would like to suggest that the Hare Kṛṣṇa people acquire these Vaiṣṇava holy places and bring them back to their past glory, instead of constructing new temples. At least the main 108 Vaiṣṇava *divya-deśam* temples have to be renovated, decorated, and reinstated to their past glory.[68] We should ensure that the ceremonies are observed in time, the priests are honored, and that there is some arrangement for their sustenance.

I fear that constructing new temples in this atheistic period might only leave more temples neglected in course of time. The way Kali-yuga is going on, constructing new temples seems very risky. If you build some temples

68. *Divya-deśam* — one of the 108 holy places of foremost importance in Śrī Vaiṣṇavism.

today, you may not be able to manage and maintain them over a long period of time.

B. V. Swami: The government has a program to restore noteworthy old buildings.

Raṅganāthan: That's all right, but what about the culture that inspired people to make such buildings? What about using them for what they were built for: worshiping the Lord? They may repair a temple as an archeological exhibit or tourist attraction, but they destroy the culture that was its life. A temple isn't just a building to come and look at. A person visiting a temple should get involved and be swept away by the atmosphere of devotion. "Archeological Department" means the temple is already dead. Therefore this work has to be taken up by devotees, those who feel for the Lord, not bureaucrats.[69]

I still remember very well the surcharged atmosphere that prevailed in my youth. I still relish the memories of those festivals, and of listening to the *Divya Prabandham*. There are many things regarding the specific practices that I have forgotten, or may be inaccurate about, but I remember how gloriously those people lived.

We were very happy in our daily lives. In the morning we used to go pick flowers to offer to the Lord, singing His glories as we went. Throughout the day we would be engaged in various spiritual activities, directly or indirectly. We didn't feel the need for anything else. We had no ambition to go anywhere or do anything else. We didn't need more money or material possessions.

---

69. Since this interview was conducted, local Śrī Vaiṣṇavas have taken up the work of restoring the temple at Serangulam.

Nor did we hanker for modern ways. Modern life just happened to us without our realizing it. I never even saw a car in my childhood. I never rode in one till I was twenty years old. Now driving to work, driving to see friends, driving everywhere for everything, is intrinsically part of my life. Even to get food we have to drive. And food comes wrapped in plastic bags, stored in a refrigerator.

I never knew any of these things before. I never imagined that I would live in an apartment, perched in the sky like a bird, crammed in a building with so many people who do not even know my name. But here I am today, living in the Gulf, with a good job, a car, enough money, and all comforts of life. But these things have not made me happy.

By Kṛṣṇa's mercy I have no more material aspirations. But do you know what I want? I want to go back to that simple village life centered around the Lord. That's why we Indians here participate in these *kīrtanas* and festivals, cooking and sharing *prasādam* together. This is only due to Śrīla Prabhupāda's mercy. These things have brought us life again. Otherwise, we were in *māyā*.

Respiritualize or Perish

While recalling his early life, Rāsarāja Dāsa suggests that the spiritual and philosophical foundations of Hindu society are missing and that only vestiges of the true Vedic culture remain. He says that we must bring back this spiritual dimension, based on Śrīla Prabhupāda's books and instructions, which are the prime source of spiritual knowledge in modern times. Otherwise, Indian people will not have the strength to maintain their culture under the onslaught of the modern, materialistic way of life.

This interview took place in 1994.

B. V. Swami: Please tell us about yourself — when you were born, your family background, and what India was like when you grew up.

Rasarāja: I was born in 1951 in Madras. We're basically from a Śrī Vaiṣṇava Iyengar family.[70] Our ancestors' home is near the Pārtha-sārathi temple in Madras.

B. V. Swami: So you're real Madras people.

Rasarāja: Well, my grandfather lived there, and his father moved to Madras, I believe from a place near Coimbatore.[71] I don't know what my great-grandfather did, but my grandfather was a mathematics teacher in a school in Triplicane, where most of the *brāhmaṇa* boys

70. Iyengar — generic family title for Śrī Vaiṣṇava *brāhmaṇas.*

71. Coimbatore — a large city in Tamil Nadu.

went to study.[72] My mother used to tell me that my father became the first person of our community to do business in that locality. That shows you how rare it was in those days, in the 1930s, for *brāhmaṇas* to enter business. In the '40s my father was doing pharmaceutical business, importing medicines. When the Second World War came, there was a great demand for imported medicines, and he made good money. To give a rough idea, a plot of land called a "ground," about a quarter of an acre, used to cost about 100 rupees — and Mylapore was supposed to be a really posh area of Madras in those days. And I have heard from my mother that my father was earning a couple thousand rupees a month.

B.V. Swami: That is a huge amount.

Rasarāja: Well, even today that's a decent salary, right? I don't think we can even know what that amount was capable of purchasing in those days. I can only recall the prices of some commodities, to give you an idea. My mother used to say that her father, who was a customs inspector, earned twenty-seven rupees a month. But when he got my mother married, he gave her seventy-five gold sovereigns.

Even when I was a child we would purchase rice in big jute sacks called *gonis*. One *goni* would contain about fifty kilos. Even middle-class people never bought less than a *goni* at a time. And that cost only thirteen rupees. First-class rice.

Even in 1957 or '58, when I was seven or eight years old, I remember eating two *idlis* for half an anna. That is three

72. Triplicane — a ward in Madras.

paisa by today's calculation. In those days there used to be vegetarian restaurants called "*brāhmaṇa* hotels."[73] Ideally that meant the food there was nicely prepared and first offered to the Lord before being served. By that time *brāhmaṇas* had started working outside for a living, so these hotels were catering to them. However, as I was growing up I noticed that although the name "*brāhmaṇa* hotel" remained, the practice of offering the food to the Lord was gradually being given up.

B.V. Swami: Madras is even now known as a very traditional place, and must have been even more so then. Please tell us something about your growing up there.

Rasarāja: Madras, like most cities in India, is an ancient city. It has many temples, many of which are famous Viṣṇu temples, thousands of years old. There is also the Kapālīśvara temple, for Lord Śiva. About 2,000 years ago Mother Pārvatī took the form of a peacock and worshiped Lord Śiva there. Around the same time the poet-saint Tiruvalluvar lived in Mylapore and wrote a famous book called *Tirukkural*.

The most famous temple in the city is the Pārtha-sārathi Perumāl Kovil (*Perumāl* means the Supreme Lord Viṣṇu, or Kṛṣṇa, and *kovil* means temple). It is one of the 108 important temples for the Śrī Vaiṣṇavas. The temple is at least 5,091 years old, since Lord Kṛṣṇa personally came there after the Kurukṣetra war. He stayed at the temple for a few days and then remained there in His Deity form. That was just before the start of the present Kali-yuga. Even today if you go to the temple, you will see that the

73. In Indian parlance, hotel commonly means a restaurant.

utsava-mūrti has unlimited arrow marks on His face — what you would expect after the Lord had driven Arjuna's chariot on the battlefield.[74]

The temple already had the Narasiṁha Perumāl Deity when Lord Pārtha-sārathi visited the temple, so the temple is really ancient. There are also other ancient Kṛṣṇa temples in other parts of the city. The Ādi-keśava Perumāl Kovil has existed from a previous Satya-yuga.[75] So Madras is really an ancient city. Recently it got its older name, Chennai, back.

I grew up playing daily in the courtyards of two old temples: the Keśava Perumāl Kovil and the Mādhava Perumāl Kovil. Every day around six p.m. there would be an *ārati,* and right after, the priest would bring out nice *prasādam* freshly offered to the Lord. They would distribute hot *ven poṅgal, sarkkarai poṅgal,* and sometimes even nice *suṇḍal.*[76] He would give everyone a little ball of each item, rolled in his hand. After eating it, we children would put our hands out again and ask the priest, "*Māmā* (uncle), *māmā,* please give some more *prasādam!*" and he would give us some more. Of course in those days I hardly had any idea about the transcendental nature of *perumāl-prasādam,* so I say we ate it. Properly speaking, I should say we would honor it.

---

74. *Utsava-mūrti* — small Deity who comes outside the temple in festivals.

75. In other words, from several million years ago.

76. *Ven poṅgal* — white *poṅgal; sarkkarai poṅgal* — sweet *poṅgal* cooked with brown sugar; *suṇḍal* — dry preparation made from chickpeas.

Years later, when I grew up and went to work in America due to my bad karma, I could have become degraded. I was saved by Śrīla Prabhupāda's books, Śrī Śrī Rādhā-Kuñjabihārī [the Deities at Detroit ISKCON temple], and the devotees there. They made me once again conscious of Lord Kṛṣṇa and my eternal position as His servant. I was earning plenty of money but I was still suffering, because I had forgotten my relationship with Kṛṣṇa. My childhood experiences started making philosophical sense only after I read Śrīla Prabhupāda's books and started practicing the principles in my own life.

At the ISKCON temple I would hear American devotees say, "Let us go honor *prasādam.*" I would then recall that in our younger days, orthodox Vaiṣṇava elders would not say "Let us eat *prasādam.*" They would say, "Let us do *prasādam sevai.*"[77]

In any case, I recall that the *prasādam* was most delicious, with ghee and many other nice things, such as cardamom, cloves, camphor, and rock candy. After getting the *prasādam,* we would run and play. In this way we grew up, little knowing the importance of the great culture we were born in.

There was one elderly lady who stayed opposite our house. She would call the neighborhood children to her home in the evenings to teach us *Viṣṇu-sahasra-nāma.* Every evening we would sit with her and recite the Lord's thousand names.

We were Śrī Vaiṣṇavas, so in our house we didn't take any food without first offering it to Viṣṇu. When we kids went

---

77. *Prasādam sevai* — "service to *prasādam.*"

inside the kitchen, my grandmother would say, "Don't touch the food yet. It's not offered to Perumāl." We would offer everything to a big picture of Viṣṇu.

B.V. Swami: A picture of which Deity? Śrī Raṅganātha?

Rasarāja: It was a picture of Govindarāja Perumāl of Chidambaram.[78] We also had a *śālagrāma-śilā*. He was not so properly worshiped, but at least everybody's consciousness was on the Lord in His picture form. We would offer our respects to the picture every morning.

B.V. Swami: Was it a print or a painted picture?

Rasarāja: A large painted picture, about five feet by six. In those days there were no prints. It was old, a family heirloom.

B.V. Swami: How many brothers and sisters do you have?

Rasarāja: Seven brothers and four sisters. We are a big family.

B.V. Swami: Those days most families were big. Tell us something about your family life.

Rasarāja: There are so many things. When we were children, the husbands and wives never spoke in public to each other. Among all my uncles and aunts, their interactions in public were minimal. When my eldest sister got married, it was an occasion for much mirth for the younger ones if we could catch the new couple talking together in public. In Indian culture, even within my own memory, a husband and wife were expected to maintain distance in public. They would speak with each other

78. Chidambaram — a well-known "temple town" in Tamil Nadu.

only in private. If someone was seen speaking to his wife in public too often, he would be called *asat*. *Sat* means "eternal," so *asat* means one who is on the temporary platform, attracted and attached to his material relations.

B.V. Swami: The joint family system helped maintain demureness and respectability.

Rasarāja: Yes. Another aspect of the joint family was that the grandfather and grandmother were the chiefs. In our house there was just father and mother. But in joint families, the grandmother and grandfather always had higher status than the father and mother. As people got older, they were given more respect. They were taken care of and respected. When I lived in the West I saw how the elderly people practically have no place to live. Now it is also happening in India.

B.V. Swami: Terrible — neglected, miserable.

Rasarāja: They are sent to senior citizen homes.

B.V. Swami: So unhappy. So unhappy.

Rasarāja: Their last years are spent just waiting to die, unhappy and alone. In America, the older you get the more you are neglected, whereas previously in India, the older you got the more you were respected. In the joint family system, the grandfather and grandmother were always the bosses of the family, no matter how much the father was earning.

B.V. Swami: I've seen that myself. You can't go against the elders. A man may be fifty years old, with grandchildren, but as long as his father is alive, he is subservient to him.

Rasarāja: It is not difficult to figure out why there is such a difference between India and the West in treating elders. In the West the goal of life is to enjoy the senses. So the older you get, the less you are able to enjoy the senses. Then you are not able to achieve what they consider to be the goal of life.

And nobody wants to be with these people and take care of them, because by seeing them one is reminded of one's impending fate. The elders are just removed from mainstream life, so everything looks idyllic for the young people, until they themselves get old. Then the cycle repeats itself.

B.V. Swami: Yes. Some even desperately try to become young again, by face-lifts and all kinds of crazy things.

Rasarāja: In India, on the other hand, at least in previous generations, advancement in spiritual life and the acquisition of wisdom were considered the goals of life. Control of the senses was considered paramount. Thus the older one got, the more one was able to exclusively focus on spiritual life. Sense control also became easier. Therefore the older ones were considered better equipped than the youngsters. Their wisdom and experience was sought and accepted by the younger ones.

B.V. Swami: Right. It makes sense. Because you learn from the mistakes you make in your youth.

Rasarāja: Exactly. But since people in modern society don't have the proper goal of life, such social anomalies as disrespecting older people exist now in India too. Indians in modern times don't seem to understand that without going back to the spiritual goal of life, they cannot correct these things.

B.V. Swami: The Western society is a complete disaster, and Indians are blindly following them due to propaganda from the West.

Rasarāja: A main part of that propaganda is the idea that women in India are treated improperly. Some years ago I was giving a lecture in India. In the audience were many educated, cultured, middle-aged women who felt they were being oppressed. I asked them, "Suppose you go into the bazaar in the evening to buy vegetables. Can any man who doesn't know you come and say hello to you?"

They said, "No."

I asked, "Do you think a man you do not know can ask you, 'What's your name?'"

They said, "No! He cannot ask!"

"Do you think he could ask you, 'Would you like to go for dinner someday?'"

They said, "Impossible! No stranger can behave like this with us. If anyone tried to talk to us like that, the public would beat him up."

"But in the West," I told them, "men will approach even women that they have never met and speak to them like that. So, where would you say women are given more respect, in India or in the West?"

They all replied, "In India."

Then I said, "So this idea that women in India are not

respected is a big propaganda myth. Actually India is a place where women are treated very nicely."

In India, the women's need for chastity is respected. If a society does not respect that need of a woman, and in fact encourages her to shed it at every opportunity, what kind of freedom is that? Freedom to degrade? What kind of respect can they claim to have for women?

Economically also, the women were protected in traditional India, yet they had a lot of say, a lot of control. The father would not usually do anything without consulting the mother. That's a very high-grade life.

B.V. Swami: Definitely. Even two generations ago in the West they used to have the same ideas, respect for women and so on. Women wouldn't even go out to shop alone.

Rasarāja: That's right. You are exactly right. Even in the mid-seventies, when I worked for General Motors, I had a colleague, who was about forty-five. I was only twenty-six then. He told me that when he was in college, boys and girls did not go out freely and mix together. He said, "All this is new. We have never seen such things."

It was only in the '60s that all this so-called liberalism came in. Or maybe we should call it animalism. Before that, many of the adults were having illicit sex life, especially rich people. But that was all kept behind closed doors.

B.V. Swami: Yes, in the '60s they philosophized it.

Rasarāja: That's right. The youngsters lost faith in the parents, because the parents were cheating on each other and then fighting and separating. So for such young people, any instructions about sense control or respect for elders appeared hypocritical. That spawned the hippie generation. The children of the '60s threw out the culture they grew up in.

Now the present generation of parents in India are doing the same thing. They are imitating the West. Even Indian movies and TV serials treat such themes with approval. For example, a working married woman having an affair with another man. Still, they think at home they can make their children grow up with moral values. These parents don't realize how the next generations will cast everything away, thinking it is all hypocrisy.

Someone might ask, "But aren't there many evils in contemporary Indian society? How can you deny that?" Our answer would be, "Yes, there are problems. But we have to be sure of how to solve them. Suppose there is an expert musician who has gotten old, and there is a young man who has never learned any music. Neither may be able to sing well, but their situation is not the same.

Similarly, there may be social problems both in the West and in India, but the West — in particular America, the country that tries to force its culture on everyone else — is like a young man who has never learned any music. It has never had a sound spiritual or cultural system. India is like the great old musical expert. It has a great spiritual and cultural tradition. So the solutions have to be different. We should try to solve our problems by going back to the best in our spiritual tradition — not by ignoring it completely and imitating the West.

B.V. Swami: India still has very good things to offer to human society. Restriction between the sexes makes civilized life possible. Without it, everything becomes hell.

Rasarāja: Another thing we should talk about is dowry. Officially it's now illegal, although it is still as much a part of Indian life as it ever was. There's a lot of propaganda against it nowadays, and it is certainly clear from newspaper reports that the system has degenerated into an evil. But Śrīla Prabhupāda explained that dowry in ancient India was not a compulsory thing. It was a voluntary expression of the parents' love for their daughter. The proper word for dowry in Sanskrit is *vara-dakṣiṇā*. *Vara* here means wife, and *dakṣiṇā* means that which is voluntarily given as a mark of respect and love. Quantity was not important.

Whatever the girl brought as dowry was hers, and the women would never sell it. Generally they would just pass it down to their daughters, and it went on like that. Jewelry, gold pots, gold vessels, and all that. Of course in the olden days everyone in India was rich enough to give such *dakṣiṇā*. Even in my memory, the system served as some kind of an economic insurance and stability for many families. If the husband got into some trouble, the wife would pledge her possessions, and then it would be the duty of the husband to redeem them later on and give them back to her.

In olden days, people had good karma and therefore some wealth to pass on to their sons and daughters. Nowadays there is not even that kind of love of parents toward children.

B.V. Swami: No responsibility.

Rasarāja: No dharma.[79] As a result, there's no wealth.

B. V. Swami: Horrible, horrible, horrible.

Rasarāja: Oh, I was saying that in the joint family system all the men, meaning the grown-ups and the older boys, would always go to the temples in the morning — and only then, go to the school, office, or whatever. And when we returned in the evening we would wash our feet and go first to the Perumāl room in our house. Then we would pray or recite some verses from *śāstra*. Otherwise mother would not give us anything to eat. Then after eating, we would read, do our homework, and so on.

B. V. Swami: Even in the West, my mother, who was Irish and a staunch Catholic, insisted on taking me to church every morning and getting all the family to say prayers together.

Rasarāja: Yes, religion was all over the world. The unique thing India had and still has, if we want it, is the Vedic culture, which is the best.

B. V. Swami: Far advanced, far advanced.

Rasarāja: It is the best of all cultures. And the *ajñāta-sukṛti* in India is far higher than what you can get in other countries.[80]

B. V. Swami: Oh yes, of course.

---

79. Dharma here refers to compulsory rules of conduct given in scripture and the sense of duty underlying them. In a higher, transcendental sense, dharma connotes the inherent nature of each individual living being.

80. *Ajñāta-sukṛti* — unknowingly acquired pious credit.

Rasarāja: People in general are spiritually foolish, whether they are Indians or Westerners. But the *ajñāta-sukṛti* you get in India is high, because basically life is in accordance with the regulative principles. But in the West people are generally not following even what little the priests gave them. And in India Viṣṇu is there. They're eating *viṣṇu-prasādam* so often. It's practically a way of life, even for non-Vaiṣṇavas. That is a very great thing.

B.V. Swami: You're saying that even non-Vaiṣṇavas would take *kṛṣṇa-prasādam*?

Rasarāja: Always! Everybody used to go to the big Viṣṇu temples, and they always got *viṣṇu-prasādam*. No one ever went to the Perumāl Kovil without getting *prasādam*.

B.V. Swami: *Smārtas* also?

Rasarāja: Everybody. Everyone went to Viṣṇu temples. Viṣṇu temples were considered the best. Even the *smārtas* had high regard for Viṣṇu.

B.V. Swami: But the Vaiṣṇavas wouldn't go to Śiva temples.

Rasarāja: Well, that depended on the individual family. But by and large the Vaiṣṇavas limited themselves to the worship of the Supreme Lord, although they did not disrespect the demigods. The main point is that everyone would go to the Viṣṇu temples, and Viṣṇu temple *prasādam* was always the best.

For the women of the house — my mother, aunts, and so on — life revolved around the almanac, which listed the important festival days for practically every temple in Tamil Nadu. The ladies would look at the calendar and discuss the festivals. Often I would get up in the morning and go into the kitchen and my mother and grandmother would be discussing how on that day there was Garuḍa *sevā* in such and such a temple. I would ask them, "Is it very famous?" and my grandmother would tell me some wonderful pastime of the Lord in that temple.

At Nācchiyār kovil, a temple in Tamil Nadu, twice a year the Lord is placed on a Garuḍa *vāhana* and brought out in procession. My mother told me that the wonderful thing about the festival is that inside the Deity sanctum just five *pūjārīs* can lift the Garuḍa *vāhana.* But by the time they bring the *vāhana* with the Lord seated on it to the inner courtyard, at least fifteen people would be required. Then by the time the *vāhana* with the Lord reached the outer courtyard, forty to fifty people would have to join to lift the Lord on Garuḍa. And by the time the Lord came outside the temple walls, at least 100 people would struggle to carry the Lord mounted on the Garuḍa *vāhana.* It would have become incredibly heavy. After the procession, when the Lord re-entered the temple, the whole thing would happen in reverse. The hundred people would not be needed once He entered the outer courtyard, fifteen people would be sufficient in the inner courtyard, and eventually just five people would again carry Garuḍa and the Lord inside the sanctum. This festival goes on even now and the same thing happens.

So, like this, every day the women would consult the almanac and come to know of a major festival or two in some major temple around the state, and we would get to hear a new story every day. The cooking in the houses was also arranged according to the festivals in distant temples. So the ladies were always busy making things for the different festivals. For Dīpāvalī, my father would buy dresses not only for all the children and family members, but he would also buy one nice silk dhotī and one silk sārī to offer to Pārtha-sārathi and Lakṣmīji. On Dīpāvalī day the *utsava-mūrti* would come out in procession and the ladies would throw flowers from the balcony. The men and children would receive the Lord on the street and offer dhotīs and other clothes. By the time They went back to the temple, the Deities would be covered with gifts.

B. V. Swami: What would they do with it all? They'd keep it in stock?

Rasarāja: Yes. The Deities were dressed every day. So these offered clothes were used.

B. V. Swami: Would the *brāhmaṇa pūjārīs* also get some of the clothes after they were offered to the Lord?

Rasarāja: I have no idea. I remember my mother would always first offer any new clothes to Lakṣmīji.

B. V. Swami: It would have to be offered in the temple?

Rasarāja: In the house. Whatever sārī she bought, she would place on the altar and leave it there for two or three days. Then only she would take and wear it. That principle was recognized, *īśāvāsyam idaṁ sarvam:* "everything belongs to God."[81] In other words, nothing was used without offering it.

B. V. Swami: God-centered life.

Rasarāja: Even though people did not know the philosophy that well, their lifestyle reflected that philosophy.

---

81. Quoted from *Īśopaniṣad.*

B. V. Swami: Śrīla Prabhupāda said modern-day Hinduism is Vedic culture without philosophy. Knowledge of philosophy is necessary. Unless *ācāryas,* powerful spiritual leaders, continue to teach proper philosophy, it gradually becomes lost and everything becomes spoiled.

Rasarāja: You're right. I'll tell you how culture not based on good philosophical understanding can get easily spoiled. Many Indians are vegetarians, but due to training, not philosophy. When they go to the West, they become non-vegetarians by imitating the Westerners. They don't know why they were vegetarians in the first place, so they see it as just adjusting to a new social situation. They go to some office parties or some such social occasions and see everyone eating meat, so they also eat meat, thinking it is just a social convention. They don't realize how terribly wrong it is.

Some manage to remain vegetarian, but that does not make them spiritual. Śrīla Prabhupāda said that even monkeys are vegetarians. It is a necessary, but not sufficient, condition for spiritual life. When you become a devotee, you learn from Śrīla Prabhupāda's books the philosophical and spiritual basis why one should not eat meat. The word for meat in Sanskrit and most Indian languages is *māṁsa*. It is a conjunction of two words *mām* (me) and *saḥ* (he). So the word *mām-saḥ* means: "Just as I kill and eat you (the animal), you will get a chance to kill and eat me in another life." The meat eater is effectively acknowledging that he is collecting karma. So if you eat chicken, you must be born as a chicken and get eaten. What to speak of the meat eater, Manu explains that one who kills the animal, one who transports it to the market, one who sells, one who cooks, one who eats, all get the karma. But the reason the devotees don't eat meat is because they don't eat anything that is not first offered to Lord Kṛṣṇa. And we can offer Lord Kṛṣṇa only vegetarian products. That is stated in the *Bhagavad-gītā* itself.

Recently I was flying from Mumbai to Delhi, and the person next to me saw that I was not taking the food being served on the plane. So he looked at me and said, "I know, ISKCON devotees eat only food offered to Lord Kṛṣṇa, right?" I said, "No." He was really confused. I then explained, "We don't eat any food that is not first cooked for Lord Kṛṣṇa!" Offering comes next. Then we eat.

If one understands the philosophy and the spiritual reasons, what to speak of not taking meat, there is no question of even eating vegetarian food if it is not first lovingly prepared and offered to the Lord.

Yet when one is a vegetarian simply by childhood practice, then he can easily change: "The people I associate with eat it, so I will also eat it."

B. V. Swami: *saṅgāt sañjāyate kāmaḥ.*[82]

Rasarāja: Yes. You can get drawn away and not even know why what you are doing is wrong. So without philosophy, culture can be very rapidly lost. All cultures are based on some kind of philosophy. Even modern materialism developed from the philosophical ideas of atheists like Freud, Hume, and Russell. But a culture of real value can exist only if it is based on positive knowledge of God.

---

82. From *Bhagavad-gītā* (2.62): "Desire develops by association."

That knowledge was developed as a great science in India, to a superlative level, not approached even to a slight degree anywhere else in the world. This tremendous culture, which can do so much good for the world, is being supplanted by this ridiculous Mickey Mouse, indulge-your-senses antithesis of culture from the West. It is the greatest disaster, and it is our job to reverse this rush for insanity. We have to give real philosophy and show people the goal of life. That is the importance of ISKCON. It's the Vedic philosophy that we can contribute to whatever remnants of Vedic culture are still left.

B.V. Swami: There were so many traditional elements in your upbringing. Later you went to America and had some position there but eventually came around full circle to Kṛṣṇa consciousness.

Rasarāja: Well, I think by *ajñāta-sukṛti* I got to take birth in a Śrī Vaiṣṇava family, but because of my sinful nature I was not able to take full advantage of it from the beginning.

B.V. Swami: But also because of lack of training within the *sampradāya*.

Rasarāja: Yes, but I take that also as due to my own sinful life.

B.V. Swami: The previous *sukṛti* got you that far, but not far enough.

Rasarāja: You are absolutely right. People nowadays don't even understand what a great boon it is to be born in India. They are neglecting this rare and valuable opportunity. Many young men who have gone to the USA and become Westernized, they just lose all morals. But once they come around, when they learn this philosophy given in Śrīla Prabhupāda's books, then they'll understand how by their own sinful nature they have wasted a fantastic opportunity to obtain spiritual perfection. Of course it is fashionable to say, "God is everywhere." But then we have to ask, "Who is that God you say is everywhere?" Positive knowledge is required.

That knowledge is relevant to all places and circumstances. For instance, Cāṇakya Paṇḍita says that if someone has to leave the place of his birth and settle down in another village, that is due to his sins. If that is so, then what to speak of going to another country? This may sound like some quaint, outdated notion, but it is not. There is no doubt that all the Indians who go to the West experience that they become second-class citizens. When Indians go to the West they think they will get the best of India and the best of the West. But in fact they end up getting the worst of both.

Some of the most successful Indians in the USA. have told me that because they are Indians they can't go further. I have also seen many retired Indian gentlemen who go to the US and settle down because their son or daughter is there. Soon they realize they are just a nobody in America, whereas back home they would have been socially important, with so many friends and relatives. And that is nothing unique to the USA. It is the same everywhere. There are many foreigners who come to India and learn Indian music or some such thing, but they can never become as famous or venerated as an Indian musician.

Prabhupāda once said, with reference to Indians who go to the West, that Kṛṣṇa allowed only the biggest pigs to cross the ocean.

B. V. Swami: Prabhupāda said that?

Rasarāja: Yes, one devotee told me that. In my own case that is certainly true. There are still pious people who refuse to go abroad. I remember reading that Kamalapati Tripathi, the president of the Congress party, never left India because he had a Deity of Gopāla and had to worship Him every day. So even though he was a big leader and got many invitations to go abroad, he never went. He said, "I may not be able to get proper paraphernalia with which to worship my Gopāla. I can't leave Him behind. So I won't go." He was the president of the Congress party, a lifelong politician, but he never went abroad.

I am not saying that nobody should go abroad. But we must at least try to understand and appreciate the platform on which those who followed Vedic culture stood. Then even if we can't follow them, we can appreciate them, and even if we can't appreciate them, at least we can try to understand them.

B. V. Swami: One king of Jaipur went to England, in the eighteenth century, I think. He took upon the ship two huge silver urns filled with Gaṅgā water. He didn't want to drink any other water when he was in England. Those urns are still in the palace museum in Jaipur.

Rasarāja: Isn't that amazing? Nowadays when foreigners come to India, the first thing they watch out for is drinking the water, and here is a king, 200 years back, who didn't want to drink the water in the West. It shows how far we have become degraded by giving up our culture and tradition.

Sometimes I used to go and chat with Sumati Morarji.[83] She's from an old rich family. These old families used to maintain the culture. She told me that the "Quit India" movement was launched from her house. Motilal Nehru, Gandhi, and all the leaders would visit her home. So she was quite used to dealing with leaders in society. She told me once that the King of Travancore and his eight wives stayed with her. Of course her house is a big mansion, with big gardens. The king was no longer ruling, but she said she could still understand what royal life was by watching him.

The first morning, the queens cooked for the king. One queen went out into the garden and took leaves, and made all the eating plates and all the bowls out of leaves. Another queen went and got flowers and made all the flower decorations. In this way, each queen did something by her own hand, and in the end they served the morning meal to the king. Sumati Morarji said she understood that day what is meant by "a meal fit for a king." The atmosphere was perfect. He had beautiful clean plates with nice cups and everything — attractive flowers, fragrances, everything nicely arranged. She said she also understood what it means to be a queen. They were highly trained. They were not people who didn't know what to do. They had servants, but they were personally serving the king, and they knew how to take care of him. She said that when she saw their level of culture she was stunned. And Sumati Morarji herself was no stranger to tradition.

Looking back, I can say I have seen Vedic culture wasting away in front of my own eyes. I am in one of the last

83. The well-known business magnate of Mumbai (now expired).

generations which has one foot in tradition and the other in the modern way of spoiling life. I grew up in an environment with all the external trappings of the Vedic culture. I learned Sanskrit for six years in school, but I didn't even know that I'm not the body but a spirit soul. So it appears that in learning Sanskrit I was having a traditional upbringing, but in actuality I didn't know the real purpose of studying Sanskrit. Therefore, when our generation went to college, we all got Westernized very quickly. So unless we Indians take up this message of *Bhagavad-gītā* seriously, we might become betrayers of our own tradition without even realizing it.

Nowadays it is quite normal for a husband and wife, even if they are on good terms, to live and work separately in two different cities just for the sake of earning a living. And it seems that every second family in India has a failed marriage. When I was a kid there was a newspaper item reporting a divorce that took place in Pune. Can you imagine that? It was a newspaper item, because divorce was so unheard of in India, even in my childhood, and that was only the '50s.

To "justify" divorce, people say, "What is the use of staying together in a forced way if we are not happy?" That only shows that we have forgotten that the real goal of life is to make spiritual progress. Previously, Indians accepted each situation in the context of the larger goal. You may have a bad set of cards dealt to you, but you are not allowed to try to change the cards directly by reaching into the deck. You just have to play with the cards you have been dealt.

B. V. Swami: Accept your lot.

Rasarāja: That's it. They had a sense of dharma. People judged and molded all aspects of their lives according to the principle, "I'm where I'm at now because of what I did in previous lives, and I should act so as to make my future better." They understood life in a context far broader than the immediate here and now. They knew their present lives to be following on from many, many in the past.

B.V. Swami: But this doctrine of reincarnation is sometimes cited as an excuse to restrict peoples' freedom of choice. Weren't their lives more or less chalked out for them from birth? Wouldn't they have to adopt such a way of thinking because they had no other option? Doesn't modern society give much more independence to move around and choose what you want to do?

Rasarāja: Yes, I know that argument: "In the olden days there was no alternative, so people lived together. If you had given them choice, then how many of them would have stayed together?" This is a pretty silly, if not an outright wrong, claim. Let us say, for the sake of argument, that in olden times marriages held together because there was social compulsion. So what alternative is modern society giving us? Look at the result. In the West the divorce rate is over 70%. When I was in Germany I heard that the divorce rate there is even 85%. So they may say whatever they want, but the figures speak for themselves. Practically 100% of the marriages were successful in the olden days. Now it is exactly the other way.

So which system is more successful, and why? If you are in a town on a short business visit, then you try to get the best hotel. If you cannot, then you stay in some place, do your job, and get out. People in the past lived controlled lives and strove primarily for spiritual progress, not material progress. Therefore they could tolerate materially less-than-ideal situations. Today, when the goal of life is to create a materially perfect situation, why should people tolerate a materially imperfect situation?

Even on the grossest plane, the modern idea that we should freely experiment until we find an ideal partner has failed. In the '60s and '70s it was common in the West to say, "I am looking for Mr. Right, or Ms. Right," and in the meanwhile one lived with anyone one wanted. If it didn't turn out to be the right person, no problem — another person, another experiment.

I was recently looking at an Indian newspaper article in the weekend magazine section, although in general I don't even look at newspapers. One thirty-year-old woman was quoted as saying, "I live in my own apartment alone. I don't know my neighbors and I don't care to. I go out with any man I want. My mother has known no man other than her husband, and is shocked by my lifestyle, but I don't care. She is just a village woman." She considers that now that she is a city girl she is more cultured, but her actions don't reflect any higher culture.

This kind of uncivilized life is spreading everywhere. Now with the AIDS threat, doctors are advising people to stay with one partner only. Isn't that what they were trying to get away from? Either you follow the laws of God voluntarily, or you will be forced to by nature. Śrīla Prabhupāda gave the example that a citizen can voluntarily follow the rules of the state and be a free citizen, or be forced to follow the rules of the state in a prison.

No one should blindly accept propaganda like "Oh, there are so many problems with the traditional society, so we must find alternatives." It may be true that we have an ailment and need a cure, but are you qualified to cure it? If not, you will make it worse. So they may perceive something as an evil and try to cure it, but they succeed only in bringing back the same principle in a worse form. Like I said before, they said we don't want arranged marriages in which you must stay with one man all your life, and they started experimenting, but now they have AIDS and are being forced to come back to a totally material version of the "one person, one partner" principle of marriage. What kind of bogus experimentation with people's lives is this?

I will give you another example that gets right to the nerve of the matter. When I was living in the States, someone asked me, "Is it true that in India they have child marriages?"

I said, "Yes. My mother got married when she was eleven."

He said, "Isn't that barbaric?"

Now, this would put most Indians on the defensive. If you are a pseudo-intellectual following one of these shallow Westernized Indian writers, you may even vigorously agree! However, by this time I had just started reading Śrīla Prabhupāda's books, so could thus come up with a good response. Already in the late '70s they had separate resting rooms in the high schools of Detroit for pregnant schoolgirls.

So I asked him in turn, "Is it true that in America even young girls, eleven or thirteen years old, get pregnant?"

He said, "Yes."

Then I asked him, "So which is more barbaric, child marriage or child pregnancy?" The answer was obvious to him.

Indians busy imitating the West want to give up child marriage, but now they will have to accept extramarital child pregnancies. That is already happening. What else can we expect when we let boys and girls mingle unrestrictedly?

And in India, even though marriages were performed early, the girl moved into the in-laws' house only when she was sixteen or older. Anyway, the point is — as much as every Tom, Dick, and Harry is ready to criticize Vedic tradition — let them also try to comprehend its deep spiritual dimension. Whether it should be adopted in all its details is another question. The first thing is to understand and follow the underlying spiritual principles. In this case the underlying principle is chastity. Exactly how that principle is adhered to can be adjusted according to the changed circumstances in modern times. But the principle itself should not be abandoned.

There is no doubt that many traditional practices of Indian or Vedic society, shorn of their deeper spiritual context, have in modern times degenerated into abominable caricatures. The modern caste system based on birth alone, child marriage, and dowry are examples of that. But in their own context the deep underlying principles are not only not abominable but positively holy, being meant to further the spiritual aim of life, namely, developing love of God.

So I am not arguing that we should go back and conduct our lives exactly as people did in the olden times. Realistically speaking, that is not possible. However, we cannot afford to renounce the basic theme of our tradition, namely, that the purpose of human life is to achieve spiritual perfection. That is my point in comparing the old way of living life with the modern way of wasting life.

We should know how to fix the problems, not just "throw out the baby with the bath water." Śrīla Prabhupāda knew how to introduce ancient spiritual practices in a form that is completely relevant and practical for the modern age. He told us to follow the four regulative principles — no meat, fish, or eggs; no intoxicants, including tea and coffee; no illicit sex; and no gambling — chant the *mahā-mantra:* Hare Kṛṣṇa, Hare Kṛṣṇa, Kṛṣṇa Kṛṣṇa, Hare Hare/ Hare Rāma, Hare Rāma, Rāma Rāma, Hare Hare, and read *Bhagavad-gītā As It Is,* a little every day. Whatever other activities you are obliged to perform in modern times you may go on doing. You will make spiritual progress.

So this is our challenge to the modern civilization, and to Hindus in particular: What is your objection to adopting this essential form of spiritual life — chanting Hare Kṛṣṇa, following the four regulative principles, and reading *Bhagavad-gītā As It Is*? What is the difficulty? So we say stop criticizing the old Indian tradition you don't understand, and stop blindly imitating the Western civilization, which you also don't understand. Just add this basic program, which even by common sense is reasonable. What can be the objection?

B. V. Swami: What you are getting at is that Indians have lost their philosophical understanding. Whatever of the culture they still follow is done blindly or out of habit, and at the slightest distraction is given up. So they must at least read the books of Śrīla Prabhupāda and take up the process of chanting and following regulative principles.

Rasarāja: Yes. In newly independent India we were mesmerized by the promise of technological development, and Nehru's slogan was, "Industrialize or perish." Now that we have industrialized and perished spiritually and culturally, we recommend a different slogan: "Respiritualize — or perish!"

B.V. Swami: Not only for India; for the West too.

Rasarāja: Another motto of newly independent India was, "First let us develop economically. Only then will the poor masses be able to practice dharma." But the Vedic prescription is first dharma, then *artha,* not the other way around.[84] If we have dharma, *artha* will come, but if we go for *artha* first, only *adharma* (irreligion) will follow.

So they're cheating themselves by thinking that after we develop economically, we'll once again be religious. One time in a college one student challenged me, "So many people are starving in India. Isn't it better to give them food rather than offer so many nice things to God in the temple?"

I said, "OK, but then you must also agree that many other activities should also be stopped: movie making, manufacture of cigarettes and liquor, horse racing, cricket, and so on. Use the millions spent on all these to feed the starving. Why don't you campaign to stop all these things? Besides, Kṛṣṇa does not even keep what you offer. He

84. *Artha* — economic development.

kindly gives it back, fully intact and spiritualized. Why do you complain only about offering something to God?" He could not give a single word in reply. He just sat down.

It is all propaganda. Helping the starving millions is not their real concern, if such a concern is at all there. If it were, they would be running the government far more efficiently and honestly. Actually they use the situation of starvation, which they have created, as a way of arguing against the worship of God. They may contend, "We didn't create these problems. The damage religion has done to society is so deep that it will take time to undo." Such statements are simply mischievous nonsense. For anyone who has eyes to see, it is plain that under their management the country has become increasingly worse over the last fifty years.

So gradually even the most basic understanding of our spiritual tradition and its real greatness is being lost, and the culture is set to completely collapse. This is because despite all the appearances of tradition, children grow up without any real spiritual knowledge. My own case may be a bit extreme, but for all my good Śrī Vaiṣṇava background, I did not know about karma or reincarnation until I read a book about them in America.

B. V. Swami: [Amazed] You had never heard about karma or reincarnation before going to the States?

Rasarāja: Of course I had heard the word *karma*. People would say things like, "It was his karma." I remember when I was a young child, if any of us did some extreme mischief my mother would put her hand to her forehead and say, *"Prārabdham."* At the time I thought it was a

Sanskrit word for children's mischief. Now I know that there are several stages of fructification of karma, and that *prārabdham* is one of them. Evidently she meant to say, in a jocular way, that she got such a mischievous child due to her past misdeeds. In the same way, I must have heard and understood the words *punar janma* (repeated birth), and practically every story dealing with it that we learned as we grew up. But I had not the slightest idea of how karma and reincarnation personally affected me. I learned about them as philosophical and spiritual concepts that vitally relate to my own existence only in that book I read in the USA. Can you imagine that?

B. V. Swami: I'm shocked.

Rasarāja: Well, don't be. After I became a devotee one of my brothers who lives in England called me up in the Detroit temple and inquired, "What happened? Why have you joined the Hare Kṛṣṇas?"

I told him frankly, "Well, I have learned that there is a next life and if I don't lead this life properly but develop only animalistic propensities, I will be born as an animal or even lower in my next life. On the other hand, if I develop my spiritual inclinations I will progress on the path back home to Vaikuṇṭha, where Lord Kṛṣṇa eternally resides with an unlimited number of souls like me. I am trying to attain a better destination in my next life. That is why I joined the Hare Kṛṣṇa movement."

He said, "What is all this nonsense about 'next life'? When you die it is all over. That's it." I was shocked. Before I had been ignorant, but my brother spoke as if he had thought about it all and come to a definite conclusion on his own.

B.V. Swami: See how much they're divorced from this philosophy.

Rasarāja: Yes. I myself was amazed when I learned about the principle of reincarnation, that I could go into a lower species if I didn't watch out. I said to myself, "Wow! I never knew about this cycle of birth and death. Why did no one tell me about this?" Can you imagine that?

B.V. Swami: It's very difficult for me to imagine how you could be brought up in a traditional Śrī Vaiṣṇava family yet not have the slightest idea about what karma and reincarnation actually mean.

Rasarāja: Many Indians think that they know about reincarnation. But actually they don't believe in it. They don't know they can go down into animal life. It is just like a thief who thinks he won't get caught, even though he knows that so many thieves have been caught before. Similarly, so many so-called pious Hindus will surely go down to animal life, or lower, if they don't watch out. But they won't accept that. It takes real spiritual knowledge to realize that all these stories are meant for each one of us.

Instead, they think that simply hearing all these scriptural stories about karma and reincarnation is a pious activity that will take them to heaven in the next life. They imagine that is enough, just to hear these stories. They don't realize they are supposed to act on them. Most Hindus don't seem to consider that it in any way applies to them.

I was even more naive. I heard all the religious stories when I was a kid. My mother would serve dinner from a big pot, maybe *sāmbār*-rice, giving one handful to each of us children in turn, and would go round and round until the whole pot was finished. Then she would serve the next course — maybe *rasam*-rice — then curd-rice, and so on. And all the time she would tell us stories from *Rāmāyaṇa* and *Mahābhārata*.

So there was no dearth of the so-called great Indian tradition. It all seemed very idyllic. I remember my mother used to say, "Don't waste any food. If you waste even one grain, that grain will go to Viṣṇu in Vaikuṇṭha and cry to Him, "I was not eaten." Today, looking back, I guess that should have conveyed to us the idea that we must honor all the *prasādam* properly, but philosophically speaking, our training in the Indian tradition was zero. It is like someone repeating a sentence in Chinese without knowing any Chinese.

B. V. Swami: You are from a Vaiṣṇava family. You knew and heard about Viṣṇu from the beginning of your life. Yet you say you didn't really understand Viṣṇu.

Rasarāja: That's right. In my childhood I went every day to the Viṣṇu temple, but only to play. Of course I was getting *prasādam* every day, and that was benefiting me, even though I didn't know it. Later, when I was in Chidambaram studying engineering at Annamalai University, I would go every Friday to the famous Govindarāja temple for *darśana*. I always made a point to buy some *prasādam*, but only because it tasted so superb. But I never thought about God or my own relationship with Him. I guess I felt somewhere deep in my consciousness that God is a person, but I had never applied my thinking capacity to the subject of that Person, nor had anyone stimulated me to do so. I knew Viṣṇu was there in our house. He was always there, and I'd always go into His room. But I did not have scientific knowledge of God.

That knowledge is easily obtainable when someone who knows teaches us that Viṣṇu is the source of everything and that everything is meant for His pleasure. I even remember my father used to say, "As soon as He breathes, so many universes come into being. When He inhales, all the millions of universes are withdrawn." No doubt, that is true.

My father had a big book entitled *Viṣṇu Purāṇa,* written by one Wilson, that was perhaps his source of knowledge. Much later, after I became a devotee, I could understand that the book was complete nonsense. I remember flipping through it in our Bhaktivedanta Institute library and seeing a description of Śvetadvīpa, the island abode of Lord Viṣṇu in the Milk Ocean of this universe. Literally translated, the name means "the white island." But this fellow Wilson wrote a footnote that ran something like this: "After much consideration and consultation, I have come to the conclusion that this must refer to the British Isles." Can you imagine that? I mean, even if he had to think that it referred to some island where Caucasians lived, what about all of continental Europe and the whites who live there? What conceit! What arrogance! Of course my own father might not have accepted that part of Wilson's book, but the fact is that most academically approved writings on our scriptures are quite bogus. Yet most modern Hindus don't know this.

When you tell most Indian people about God, they are likely to respond, "Oh, I know Kṛṣṇa and Rāma." But most of them either know nothing or have some weird distorted ideas. Without proper philosophy, it all adds up to nothing. That is proved by the way we are becoming degraded in India today, despite all the tradition. Actually, the Hindus seem to be throwing their tradition out more readily than the Muslims and Christians. Hindus don't seem to realize that much of the impressions they receive about their tradition is from those who are intent to devalue it at any cost.

I am not calling for a mindless adherence to rituals. Hinduism is plagued with rituals followed without any understanding, which naturally turns off most scientifically minded people. My point is that we must go back to understand the supreme science of theism. That is the contribution of Vedic society to all of mankind. That philosophy in its perfect form is available today only in Śrīla Prabhupāda's books — nowhere else. In one sense ISKCON is just a growing movement that has to build its own tradition. But the movement has a solid philosophical foundation. Present-day India has just barely kept its cultural tradition alive — and all credit to the Hindus for that. Now the true philosophy of Vedic tradition, as presented by Śrīla Prabhupāda, should be added to the ancient culture, and in that way India and the whole world will benefit. Both culture and true philosophy are required for Vedic tradition to survive.

B.V. Swami: I definitely have to agree with you on that. The real benefit of being religious cannot be attained unless there is genuine philosophical understanding — just like the story you told of the grain of rice complaining to Viṣṇu. Such stories are fine for children, but unless a child develops genuine understanding there is every chance of him abandoning his training when he becomes an adult, as was the case with you; whereas if someone actually understands what *kṛṣṇa-prasādam* is, he will never throw it away or let it go to waste.

So it seems that your cultural training was good inasmuch as you were taught to do all the right things. You were taught to honor Lord Viṣṇu, not waste His *prasādam,* and not mix freely with girls — and all these things are good for spiritual upliftment and social sanity — but your tutelage was incomplete, because you were not sufficiently taught the basic reasons why you were doing it all.

Rasarāja: Yes. The purpose of driving on the road is to go somewhere. The purpose is not to follow the traffic rules. Of course, to go somewhere you have to follow the traffic rules, but that is not the main purpose of driving. If one has no place to go but simply goes round and round driving nicely, following all the traffic rules, what use is that? One is bound to get tired sooner or later and stop following the rules.

Similarly, Śrīla Prabhupāda taught that the purpose of human life is not to be merely religious. We have to know the goal of life and follow religious principles, because following religious principles will help us to attain the goal of life. The real goal of life is to attain love of God, and to do every activity directly in relation to Him. Unless one understands and is convinced of this spiritual goal of life, one is bound to give up the religious rules sooner or later. And that is precisely what is happening.

B.V. Swami: By caste your father was considered a *brāhmaṇa,* but he took up the profession of a businessman, or a *vaiśya*. Nowadays many caste *brāhmaṇas* do service for others, which in the *Śrīmad-Bhāgavatam* is forbidden for *brāhmaṇas*. Nevertheless most caste *brāhmaṇas* maintain much of their culture, even though they are not engaged in brahminical duties. Still many are vegetarian, rise early to perform *pūjā* and recite Sanskrit prayers, and so on. So even though in one sense they are fallen, in another sense they were culturally so high before that even in their fallen state they are still quite elevated. What do you think?

Rasarāja: It is true that the modern Hindu society has a higher culture than the rest of the world. But it is very much like a ladder inside a well. You can use the ladder either to go further into the well or to come out. We can either regain our spiritual culture or use it to become further entangled in material existence. This is a decision we have to make individually and collectively.

Śrīla Prabhupāda gave the example that however many zeroes you put together, they will have no value, but if there's a one in front of them they become valuable. Similarly, we may have many material qualities but if we do not understand and serve the Supreme One, Kṛṣṇa, then they are useless. Indeed the *Bhāgavatam* says, "How can a person have good qualities if he is not a devotee of Kṛṣṇa?"

So your question reinforces the main point I've been trying to make throughout our discussion: although Indians still have parts of their ancient culture, because they are out of touch with its spiritual basis, they are losing the essence and are left with externals only. That old high culture set the *brāhmaṇa* apart, but now the old traditions are rapidly being lost — not only amongst *brāhmaṇas,* but amongst everyone. So it is essential to understand that the good qualities that culture breeds are of little or no value without the spiritual context which they are meant for.

Shortly after joining the ISKCON temple in Detroit I met an elderly Indian gentleman there. He was going around the temple with a bit of a smug attitude, as if he already knew everything and was ahead of everyone else. When he saw me he was surprised to see another Indian there, because the others were mostly American devotees. So we chatted for a while, and at one point he said, "In my life I never ate meat and never drank."

I could understand that he was implying that the others, before they became devotees, may have done such things.

I asked him, "In Detroit is it legal or illegal to pick pockets?" He was surprised and replied that of course it was illegal.

"Is it legal or illegal to commit murder?"

"Illegal."

So I told him, "We're not supposed to commit murder or to pick pockets. But if you go around telling everyone, 'I've never committed a murder or picked a pocket,' people will say, 'That's fine, but what positive activities do you perform?' Not doing wrong is not sufficient. You have to do some proper activity. Similarly, in spiritual life it is not sufficient to simply refrain from breaking the regulative principles."

Similarly, simply to have a remnant of Indian culture is not sufficient in itself. We must do something for Kṛṣṇa, in an attitude of loving service.

B.V. Swami: You are from a *brāhmaṇa* family, and *brāhmaṇas* are supposed to teach others about religion. The Śrī Vaiṣṇava *brāhmaṇas* had a strong philosophical tradition, but despite being brought up in a Śrī Vaiṣṇava *brāhmaṇa* home, you didn't even get the ABCs of spiritual knowledge in your childhood. So would you agree that the downfall of religion in India was because *brāhmaṇas* in particular became ignorant of philosophy? *Brāhmaṇas* are expected to be rigidly fixed in religious observances based on scriptural understanding. Others, non-*brāhmaṇas,* have to learn from them how to lead a religious life. So when the *brāhmaṇas* did not maintain their exemplary behavior and fell down, they took everyone with them.

Rasarāja: I agree with that. But the term *brāhmaṇa,* as you know, must be properly understood. The original and actual usage of the word does not refer to someone born in a *brāhmaṇa* family. Śrīla Prabhupāda has explained that the son of an engineer cannot be called an engineer. He has to himself become a qualified engineer — otherwise he will remain just the son of an engineer. Similarly, the son of a *brāhmaṇa* has to become a *brāhmaṇa* by his own qualification. So whenever someone today says, "I am a *brāhmaṇa,*" it could only mean that in his family, maybe 5,000 years ago, before the Kali-yuga started, one of his forefathers was a real *brāhmaṇa.* So practically all of the modern-day *brāhmaṇas* must understand that they are *brāhmaṇas* in name only.

A real *brāhmaṇa* is one who knows the goal of life. *Brahma jānātīti brāhmaṇa:* "A *brāhmaṇa* is one who knows *brahma,* or the Supreme." Such a person will not worry about the so-called necessities of life, just as a person who knows why he boards a bus will not worry about whether the driver knows how to drive, whether there is enough gasoline in the tank, whether the driver knows the route, and so on. He presumes these are already taken care of by the bus company. In the same way, a person who knows that the goal of life is to understand God is convinced that if he dedicates himself to that purpose, then God, the supreme organizer of the universe, will surely take care of his basic bodily necessities. Therefore any person born in any family can become a *brāhmaṇa* simply by having this understanding.

Śrīla Prabhupāda practically showed how to establish brahminical culture in its purest form. In ISKCON, any person, be he Indian or American, Hindu or Muslim, *brāhmaṇa* or from the so-called lower caste, can become a *pūjārī* and act as a *brāhmaṇa,* provided he follows all the principles of brahminical living. No doubt a son of a *brāhmaṇa* may have a good chance to become a *brāhmaṇa* himself if he so chooses. Even in modern times the son of an educated person automatically has good chances of getting educated himself.

A *brāhmaṇa* means an intellectual who studies *śāstra* and controls his senses to achieve devotion to Kṛṣṇa. *Kṣatriya* means the administrative class, which gives protection to the citizens. *Vaiśya* means the mercantile class, which moves goods within society, and *śūdra* means the laborer class, those who have little control of the senses but are willing to serve those who are sense controlled.

So ultimately the divisions of human society were based on qualification, not on birth. Lord Kṛṣṇa says in the

Bhagavad-gītā that this system of four social divisions is created by Him. What He creates cannot be undone by anyone. Śrīla Prabhupāda often pointed out that the four-fold division of intellectuals, administrators, business community, and laborers are found everywhere in modern times, even in the communist countries, which claim to have set up a state of equality. The difference is that the *"brāhmaṇa"* of today is the material scientist, who instead of enabling everyone to lead a life of controlled senses, claims credit for providing better facilities for sense enjoyment. The modern-day administrator, instead of protecting the people, exploits them, or rather, loots them. Too many members of the business community are more interested in moving shares and stealing money from the innocent public, rather than moving goods and facilitating the economy. And the sufferers are the laborers, who are thus forced to work for the most abominable class of leaders.

And this all goes on in the name of ridding society of its evils! What cheating! If our old tradition is all evil, then why is it that no one respects India for anything other than our culture and spirituality? In fact, these modern-day leaders who claim to be improving the nation and ridding it of social evils, have made India one of the most corrupt nations in the world and a laughing stock in general, as far as efficiency is concerned. We have fallen into an oblivion in which India has neither spiritual focus nor material progress. India is today ruled by a class of people whose moral standards are so low that most Indians wouldn't like to invite them into their house as guests. They are mostly plunderers. Forget inviting them into their homes

— people wouldn't even employ them as servants, because they are potential thieves. Yet these people are allowed to rule the nation!

The average Indian must seriously reflect on his inability to understand even the present situation we are in, what to speak of protesting or correcting it.

B. V. Swami: I see culture like this: when a man is walking on a tightrope he has a net underneath. So spiritual life is like walking a tightrope; it means strictly following everything. But if you can't follow and you fall, at least the culture saves you from breaking your head. If you have culture, then even if you can't come to the highest standard at least you won't break your head and be killed.

Rasarāja: Yes, that is why we should emphasize that ISKCON needs to incorporate the culture that we call Hinduism. Even though a lot of what goes on in the name of Hinduism is absurd or abominable, the true and ancient culture on which it is based is most valuable for human society. We should not dismiss it entirely. I sometimes feel that even some non-devotional Hindu organizations have better culture than ISKCON does, even though their philosophical basis is flawed.

B. V. Swami: Could you elaborate on that? Isn't it supposed to be that culture needs ISKCON? We have chanting, dancing, feasting, regulative principles, Deity worship, festivals — what more culture is needed? *Śāstra* states that a person develops all good qualities by becoming a devotee. So what is the need to consider culture separately? Is not much of Hindu culture extraneous and unnecessary for devotees?

Rasarāja: I'll give an example. In a big feast, everyone needs to sit down peacefully and be served sumptuous *prasādam*. Similarly, proper Vedic culture centered on Kṛṣṇa will feature both perfect philosophy and perfect culture. In ISKCON the philosophy is there, but we are culturally in our nascent stage. It's as if at a feast the *prasādam* is there but no one is serving it properly — everyone just sort of runs and makes a plate for himself. In modern Hindu society we have a long tradition of culture still intact, but it has lost its philosophical substance. It's as if everyone has sat down nicely to take *prasādam* and people are ready to serve it, but there is no *prasādam*.

Hindus need to become spiritual in the real sense. Real religion goes far deeper than rituals, praying for material benefits, and a shallow, sentimental semblance of devotion. Without proper understanding of the spiritual and philosophical basis of their culture, Hindus will not be able to survive the onslaught of modern materialism. Gradually more and more Hindus are coming to realize that ISKCON is the only real antidote to materialism, because it offers the substance that modern Hinduism lacks.

On the other hand, Hindu society is still far more advanced than others in the world today, because even the dying semblance of Vedic culture is so valuable. And members of ISKCON cannot function in or survive the onslaught of materialism without absorbing the culture and values of the Vedic or Hindu society. Vedic philosophy is indeed flawless and transcendental. It cannot be touched by the vagaries of the material world. But as followers of that philosophy aiming to achieve perfection, we need very much to incorporate the culture and tradition steeped in and growing out of that philosophy.

B. V. Swami: That's a good point. We have hardly even thought about it, yet we should.

In talking about Vedic culture, one of the things we're demonstrating is the importance of family life. Society is built on family life. The principle of renunciation is meant for everybody, but renunciation as a way of life (*sannyāsa*) is for only a very few.

Rasarāja: I like that distinction. Yes, even family life has the principle of renunciation in it. That is why it is also called *gṛhastha-āśrama*.

B. V. Swami: Maybe we can't completely give up the modern way of life because we're so much integrated with it, but the closer we move to the Vedic culture, the more that will help us.

Rasarāja: For spreading Kṛṣṇa consciousness in the world, the two streams of philosophy and culture have to meet and reintegrate. That is an important part of Śrīla Prabhupāda's plan to respiritualize the world.

B. V. Swami: It will take time for Westerners to pick up the fine points of Vedic culture.

Rasarāja: But it need not take much time for Hindus to understand and adopt the actual philosophy of Kṛṣṇa consciousness. And when the two streams of philosophical understanding and ideal culture meet and integrate, Kṛṣṇa consciousness will effectively spread throughout the world. Śrīla Prabhupāda says in the *Bhāgavatam* that this movement is a cultural presentation meant for the respiritualization of human society.

B.V. Swami: Sometimes the word culture is used to indicate "that which catalyzes a change, a medium in which something develops," like adding yogurt culture to milk. So philosophy is the real milk, and culture is the ingredient we need to add to let the spiritual society develop.

Rasarāja: That's a good example. It also triggers another recollection: In India yogurt is made fresh every day. At the end of the day the womenfolk in the house ensure that some yogurt is saved and mixed with milk to make the yogurt for the next day. So the first day's yogurt made in the family continues throughout. The yogurt gets sweeter and sweeter by the day. Now when I was young, I had to pass through a slum area to go to school. Once I passed two ladies there who were having an argument. I recall one of the ladies telling the other, "Do you know that even the yogurt in our house is five generations old?" So in those days even the so-called slum people had a sense of tradition and its importance in their lives.

B.V. Swami: It could well take a few generations to get this culture established throughout the world. We have to be patient. Vaiṣṇavism has just started in the West and India is now confused. It may take time before things settle into place. But because Śrīla Prabhupāda told us, we can be sure that this culture will eventually reshape human society.

Modern civilization has no sublime purpose. People are working hard and making all kinds of technological discoveries, but they are not happy. Thoughtful people all over the world are looking for something better. Śrīla Prabhupāda talked of "cultural conquest" of the Western civilization. By that he meant a lot more than dancing troupes. If we actually show people that we have a better way of life, why shouldn't they take it up?

Rasarāja: So this is the challenge: to show that this Vedic philosophy is perfect and that the way of life based on it is also perfect. We have a great task ahead of us, but if we persevere with faith in Kṛṣṇa, He will surely help us.

The Procession: A Reminiscence

by Rasarāja Dāsa

[The following story, lightly edited herein, originally appeared as an article in *Back to Godhead* magazine, Nov/Dec 1991.]

In Madras the reigning Deity of Kṛṣṇa is known as Pārtha-sārathi. And as in many Kṛṣṇa temples, on festive days the Lord goes out on procession. The main Deity stays in the temple, and the pūjārīs bring the Lord out touring in a smaller form, known as the utsava-mūrti, or festival Deity.

"*Ammā*," I shouted, throwing down my school bag, "give me tiffin."[85] I'd just returned from school and wanted to go quickly out for play.

"Wash your hands and feet first," my mother responded from the kitchen. I ran into the bathroom, splashed water everywhere, and ran back into the kitchen.

"I saw a procession of Lord Pārtha-sārathi going somewhere," I volunteered as I sat waiting for the tiffin to appear.

My mother, reaching into the *upmā* pot, suddenly stopped, turned around, and fired a volley of questions: "Lord Pārtha-sārathi? Where did you see Him? Why is He going out today, and at four in the afternoon?"

85. *Ammā* — Tamil for "mother."

"I saw Him being carried on a palanquin near Luz, that's all. I don't know why or where He was going. Just please give me my tiffin now. It's getting late," I urged, sensing the imminent delay.

My grandmother, who always sat in one corner of the kitchen silently observing all proceedings, was now intently peering at the calendar." Today is the harvest tax collection day," she announced. "The palanquin will be passing through Eldams Road."

My mother began to calculate how long it would take for the Lord's procession to pass Eldams Road, one block from our street. "When exactly did you see the procession near Luz?" she demanded.

"At three-forty," I said, "just before I caught the bus."

"That means He'll be here in twenty minutes," my mother said, her voice now full of anxiety. "What can I make for the Lord in twenty minutes?"

"*Ravā-kesari.*[86] That's the easiest," my grandmother replied, cool and alert.

By now my mother was already putting the steel wok on the stove and pouring a cup of farina into it, simultaneously setting a pot of water to boil.

"Just what is harvest tax collection day?" I asked, resigned to a delayed tiffin.

"Once a year Lord Pārtha-sārathi visits the fields He owns just outside Madras city," my mother explained. "The farmers

86. *Ravā-kesari* — sweet preparation made from farina.

bring the harvested grain in front of the Lord, measure it, and then pay a portion of it as tax to the Lord. The grains are used to make offerings at the temple throughout the year."

"Why does the Lord have to go?" I asked. "Can't the *pūjārīs* collect it?"

"Well, the *pūjārīs* feel that when the Lord is in the field there's less chance of the farmers trying to reduce the tax by hiding the harvest. But just as important, people who live far away from the temple get to see the Lord."

"This also gives the Lord a chance to get out of the temple," my grandmother sagely added.

By now my mother's cooking was nearing the end. "Five more minutes and the Lord will be here," she calculated, looking up at the clock. "Now go to the corner and stand there till you sight the procession. When it nears our street, wave to the *pūjārī* to stop. Go right now! Run!"

I reached the corner in no time. Shielding my eyes against the late afternoon sun, I peered across the street. "What if the Lord has already passed by?" I worried.

Suddenly, there was the procession turning onto Eldams Road! A Śrī Vaiṣṇava *pūjārī* walked in front of the stately but small procession of four palanquin carriers bearing the *utsava-mūrti* of the Lord. I was surprised to see the procession moving so quickly, the palanquin carriers almost trotting. I waved frantically, afraid I would go unnoticed, since the procession showed no sign of slowing down for me. As it neared, I looked over my shoulder and was relieved to see my mother appearing out of the house, practically running. Grandmother was behind her, making slower progress.

My mother was carrying the pot of *ravā-kesari,* covered by a fresh banana leaf.

"Please! Stop!" I shouted to the *pūjārī*, "My mother has brought an offering!"

The procession halted, and the carriers set down the palanquin. By now my mother had arrived. Handing me the pot she said, "Give it to the *bhaṭṭar*."[87]

As I struggled with the weight of the pot, the *pūjārī* reached over and took it. "*Namaskāram,*" he brightly greeted my mother.

By now my grandmother had joined us. She pulled some camphor from the corner of her *sārī* and gave it to the *pūjārī*. He placed the pot of *ravā-kesari* in front of the Lord and removed the banana leaf. He put the camphor in a brass holder, lit it, and then offered it to the Lord, sonorously chanting Vedic hymns, all the time ringing a bell. The three of us folded our palms and fell before the Lord to offer our respects.

As the *pūjārī* returned half of the offering to my mother, he said, "In this Kali-yuga not many people know how to receive the Lord when He comes in procession. May the Lord bless you and your family for your loving devotion."

My mother responded, "May He always remain glorious and keep us as His servants."

My grandmother offered advice as usual. "Don't go too fast," she told the *pūjārīs*. "On a hot day like this, you should make sure He's comfortable."

---

87. *Bhaṭṭar* — synonym for *priest*.

Soon we were back in the kitchen and I was busy eating my tiffin, now supplemented by the *kesari prasādam* freshly offered to the Lord.

"Delicious!" I exclaimed. "I don't mind a late tiffin every day if you can make a sweet like this."

Appendix 1

Relevant Quotes from Śrīla Prabhupāda

Real Civilization

Civilization means to push the man forward for perfection. The society and economic condition, everything, should be so arranged that the human child is gradually pushed for the perfection of life: to go back home, back to Godhead. This is civilization. (Conversation, 2 August 1976)

Civilization means calmness, peace, prosperity. In peace and prosperity one should be Kṛṣṇa conscious always. (Lecture, 13 April 1973)

The Glory of Traditional Indian Culture

In India, because they are still inclined to the system of *varṇa* and *āśrama,* there are so many benefits for the Indians. I have traveled all over the world so many times. Because there is no *varṇāśrama-dharma*, how loose they are. (Lecture, 19 October 1972)

India's position is now chaos and confusion because we have lost this Vedic civilization, we have lost Kṛṣṇa consciousness, we have lost God consciousness. We are being directed by whims. That is the very lamentable condition of India. This Kṛṣṇa consciousness is India's original culture, Kṛṣṇa culture. Kṛṣṇa appeared on this land. Although Kṛṣṇa is not for any particular land, still Kṛṣṇa appeared in Mathurā, in this holy land of Bhārata-varṣa. So it is the duty of Indians to understand Kṛṣṇa culture, the Kṛṣṇa consciousness cultural movement, and take part in it seriously. (Lecture, 26 September 1973)

In India we have got the ideal purified family, *brāhmaṇas.* Of course nowadays, due to material advancement of civilization, everything is polluted. Still there are some families who are very purified. If you go to their house at once you will feel, "Oh, it is a fully purified place." (Lecture, 28 July, 1966)

Formerly India was very advanced in devotion. (Conversation, 24 April, 1977)

Modern Society vs. Simple Living

Advancement of civilization is estimated not on the growth of mills and factories to deteriorate the finer instincts of the human being, but on developing the potent spiritual instincts of human beings and giving them a chance to go back to Godhead. Development of factories and mills is called *ugra-karma,* or pungent activities, and such activities deteriorate the finer sentiments of the human being and society to form a dungeon of demons. (*Śrīmad-Bhāgavatam* 1.11.12 Purport)

I don't find in the *Bhāgavatam* big factories and slaughterhouses, no. Nothing. Now the whole atmosphere is surcharged with sinful life. How will people be happy? Now they are coming to crimes and hippies, problems, diplomacy, CIA. And what else? So much unnecessary waste of energy, time, and money. Vicious condition. Better give up the city. Make Vṛndāvana. City life is abominable. If you don't live in the city, you don't require petrol, motor car. It is no use. You can use a bullock cart. What is the difficulty? Suppose you are coming in one hour, and by bullock cart it takes one day. And if you are satisfied, in such life there is no question of moving. Maybe local moving, from this village to that village. That is sufficient, bullock carts. Why motor car? Drive here and parking problem. Not only parking problem, there are so many things. There are three thousand parts in a motor car. You have to produce them in a big factory. (Conversation, 1 August 1975)

Human prosperity flourishes by natural gifts and not by gigantic industrial enterprises. The gigantic industrial enterprises are products of a godless civilization, and they cause the destruction of the noble aims of human life. The more we go on increasing such troublesome industries to squeeze out the vital energy of the human being, the more there will be unrest and dissatisfaction of the people in general, although a few only can live lavishly by exploitation... The natural gifts such as grains and vegetables, fruits, rivers, the hills of jewels and minerals, and the seas full of pearls are supplied by the order of the Supreme, and as He desires, material nature produces them in abundance or restricts them at times. The natural law is that the human being may take advantage of these godly gifts by nature and satisfactorily flourish on them without being captivated by the exploitative motive of lording it over material nature... .The more we attempt to exploit material nature according to our whims of enjoyment, the more we shall become entrapped by the reaction of such exploitative attempts. If we have sufficient grains, fruits, vegetables and herbs, then what is the necessity of running a slaughterhouse and killing poor animals? A man need not kill an animal if he has sufficient grains and vegetables to eat. The flow of river waters fertilizes the fields, and there is more than what we need. Minerals are produced in the hills, and the jewels in the ocean. If the human civilization has sufficient grains, minerals, jewels, water, milk, etc., then why should it hanker after terrible industrial enterprises at the cost of the labor of some unfortunate men? But all these natural gifts are dependent on the mercy of the Lord. (*Śrīmad-Bhāgavatam* 1.8.40 Purport)

My father, say forty years before, at most, used to stock at our house in Calcutta a cartload of rice (fifteen mounds), ten *seers* of pure ghee, a bag of potatoes, and a cartload of soft coke, always ready for use. Our family was not a rich family, and my father's income was within 250 rupees per month. And it was within his easy reach to stock household provisions in the above manner. But at the present moment, no house in the cities and towns generally stocks more than fifteen *seers* of rice. Formerly they used to enquire rates of commodities in the terms of mounds, and now they ask for it in terms of *seers* or *cataks* — although we are able to keep more glittering cars than cows at the present moment.[88] (*Back to Godhead* vol. 3, no. 12, 1956)

Grains and vegetables can sumptuously feed a man and animals, and a fatty cow delivers enough milk to supply a man sumptuously with vigor and vitality. If there is enough milk, enough grains, enough fruit, enough cotton, enough silk, and enough jewels, then why do the people need cinemas, houses of prostitution, slaughterhouses, etc.? What is the need of an artificial, luxurious life of cinema,

88. Traditional Bengali measurements for weight: *seer* — approximately one kilogram; *catak* — one sixteenth of a *seer*.

cars, radio, flesh, and hotels? Has this civilization produced anything but quarreling individually and nationally? Has this civilization enhanced the cause of equality and fraternity by sending thousands of men into a hellish factory and the war fields at the whims of a particular man?... It is said here that the cows used to moisten the pasturing land with milk because their milk bags were fatty and the animals were joyful. Do they not require, therefore, proper protection for a joyful life by being fed with a sufficient quantity of grass in the field? Why should men kill cows for their selfish purposes? Why should man not be satisfied with grains, fruits, and milk, which combined together, can produce hundreds and thousands of palatable dishes? Why are there slaughterhouses all over the world to kill innocent animals?... Mahārāja Parīkṣit, grandson of Mahārāja Yudhiṣṭhira, while touring his vast kingdom, saw a black man attempting to kill a cow. The king at once arrested the butcher and chastised him sufficiently. Should not a king or executive head protect the lives of the poor animals who are unable to defend themselves? Is this humanity? Are not the animals of a country citizens also? Then why are they allowed to be butchered in organized slaughterhouses? Are these the signs of equality, fraternity, and nonviolence? (*Śrīmad-Bhāgavatam* 1.10.4 Purport)

There is no need of machines and tools or huge steel plants for artificially creating comforts of life. Life is never made comfortable by artificial needs, but by plain living and high thinking. The highest perfectional thinking for human society is suggested here by Śukadeva Gosvāmī, namely, sufficiently hearing *Śrīmad-Bhāgavatam*. (*Śrīmad-Bhāgavatam* 2.2.37 Purport)

India is not meant for machines. These rascals, they do not know. India's culture is plain living, high thinking. You require some food. Produce food, and take it, and chant Hare Kṛṣṇa. But they'll not accept: "Oh, this is primitive. We must have the motor car, motor tire." (Conversation, 6 March 1974)

India is originally village life — city life, very limited. Perhaps there was only one big city, New Delhi now — in those days, Hastināpur — and next to that was Dvārakā. So very big cities, they were only, two, or three. Mostly people used to live in villages. Still ninety percent of the population of India is in the villages. (Lecture, 6 December 1968)

Satisfaction

That is Vedic civilization. They were not very much anxious to improve their material position. Even now, the innocent villagers are satisfied with the position Kṛṣṇa has given them, but they are anxious to improve their spiritual life. (Lecture, 15 October 1973)

This is the Indian attitude. They do not care for the modern, civilized way of life, wasting time reading some nonsense books or going to the bars, the cinema, talking unnecessarily. Those who are old style, they do not like. (Conversation, 3 January 1977)

Varṇāśrama Society

Devotee: Which way is India headed toward, the capitalists or the communists?

Prabhupāda: India has had no such ideas. They are borrowing ideas. India's idea is self-realization. Live a very simple life — *brāhmaṇa, kṣatriya, vaiśya, śūdra.* The *brāhmaṇas,* they are living simple lives, becoming very learned scholars, pure in character, advanced in spiritual life — one class, ideal. And *kṣatriyas,* they are supposed to be the kings; they distribute the land on nominal taxation. And the *vaiśyas* utilize the land for cultivation and cow keeping. And the *śūdras* are engaged as weavers, blacksmiths, goldsmiths, and supplying other necessities of life. In this way the whole society is simplified and the central point is how to become advanced in Kṛṣṇa consciousness by cooperation. This is India's civilization. There is no question of industry, *ugra-karma.* It has been condemned in the *Bhagavad-gītā* as *ugra-karma:* "laboring very hard for livelihood." (Conversation, 9 April 1976)

Every state is supposed to be a welfare state. Every citizen of that state should be happy, prosperous. There should be no anxiety. I do not know if every state is taking care of the citizens in that way. People are always full of anxieties. They are creating a situation where everyone is full of anxiety. This material world is made so that it is full of anxiety. Even the bird, you will see, when he is taking some grains he is also full of anxiety. He is looking like this and that: "Oh, somebody is coming or killing me." So this is the nature. So human society should be so arranged that its members should be free from all anxiety. Therefore we require good citizens, good father and mother, good system of government, and pious, virtuous, people for cooperation between God and nature. Everything will be helpful for my spiritual realization. If I am full of anxiety, how can I make progress in spiritual realization? It is not possible. Therefore it is the duty of the state, the father, the teacher, the spiritual master, to give the chance to the small children to develop in such a way that they become fully realized spiritual souls at the end, and so that their miserable life in the material existence is over. That is the responsibility. (Lecture, 29 July 1966)

So this is the system of *varṇāśrama-dharma*. The whole idea is that everyone should be given the chance of being liberated in this very life. (Lecture, 29 July 1966)

Still in India, although it is fallen so much, in the interior village you'll find the social divisions are maintained and they live very peacefully. (Lecture, 13 September 1973)

1. The protection of the *brāhmaṇas* maintains the institution of *varṇa* and *āśrama*, the most scientific culture for attainment of spiritual life.

2. The protection of cows maintains the most miraculous form of food, i.e. milk, for maintaining the finer tissues of the brain for understanding higher aims of life.

3. The protection of women maintains the chastity of society, by which we can get a good generation for peace, tranquility, and progress of life.

4. The protection of children gives the human form of life its best chance to prepare the way of liberty from material bondage. Such protection of children begins from the very day of begetting a child by the purificatory process of *garbhādhāna-saṁskāra*, the beginning of pure life.

5. The protection of the old men gives them a chance to prepare themselves for better life after death.

This complete outlook is based on factors leading to successful humanity, as against the civilization of polished cats and dogs. (*Śrīmad-Bhāgavatam* 1.8.5 Purport)

Brāhmaṇas

The *brāhmaṇas* especially were known as *sajjana,* or respectable gentlemen who guided the entire society. If there were disputes in the village, people would approach these respectable *brāhmaṇas* to settle them. Now it is very difficult to find such *brāhmaṇas* and *sajjanas,* and thus every village and town is so disrupted that there is no peace and happiness anywhere. To revive a fully cultured civilization, the scientific division of society into *brāhmaṇas, kṣatriyas, vaiśyas,* and *śūdras* must be introduced all over the world. Unless some people are trained as *brāhmaṇas,* there cannot be peace in human society. (*Caitanya-caritāmṛta, Ādi-līlā* 17.42 Purport)

Human life should be blissful and should have as its goal spiritual advancement. At one time that was India's principle of life, and there was a class of people, the *brāhmaṇas,* who engaged themselves exclusively in spiritual culture. (*Elevation to Kṛṣṇa Consciousness,* Ch. 6)

Formerly, even fifty year or sixty years ago, in India a *brāhmaṇa* would not accept anyone's service. Because whoever had knowledge, he would sit down anywhere, underneath a tree or in somebody's corridor, and would invite the village small children and teach them a little grammar, little mathematics, gradually. And the children would bring presents from their father and mother. Somebody would bring rice; somebody would bring *dāl.* So he had no necessity of making any contract, that "You give me so many dollars, then I shall teach you." No. Free education. (Lecture, 6 July 1975)

Men and Women

The Vedic civilization, being based on spiritual understanding, arranges association with women very cautiously. Out of the four social divisions, the members of the first order (namely *brahmacarya*), the third order (*vānaprastha*), and the fourth order (*sannyāsa*) are strictly prohibited from female association. Only in one order, the householder, is there license to mix with women under restricted conditions. (*Śrīmad-Bhāgavatam* 3.31.35 Purport)

There are so many things in Indian culture for becoming happy and advancing toward the goal of life. Now I am appreciating more and more, seeing the whole world, what is India's culture. Formerly I was thinking, "It is a custom. To become a faithful wife, this is a custom." But when I come outside I see what is a faithful wife. In India still, in the village, even if there is a fight between husband and wife the wife is faithful — still — completely dependent on the husband. The husband also, in spite of fighting, is always careful that the wife does not get any inconvenience. It was the culture. Now it is breaking. (Conversation, 2 August 1976)

Children

This is the Indian way of raising children. When the mother was young, she became pregnant. There were three or four ceremonies within the first three years of the child's life. One is called *svāda-bhakṣaṇa*. The idea is that at the time of delivery the woman is in danger. There may be so many dangers. Therefore twice *svāda-bhakṣaṇa,* at the period of seven months and perhaps at nine months. Whatever the mother likes, she should eat. For that ceremony she should be very nicely dressed in new cloth, having taken bath, with all the children — not only her children but other children also. Very nice foodstuff is made and they sit together, and with the children the mother will eat. And the *brāhmaṇas* should be given some charity. They will chant Vedic hymns... So much care is taken for the children. (Conversation, 17 June 1977)

Hearing Śrīmad-Bhāgavatam

In our childhood we saw in every village, every town, transcendental knowledge. Any common man could speak about *Rāmāyaṇa, Mahābhārata,* Lord Kṛṣṇa. And the system was — still there are some, but they are practically closed now — that in the evening in the village, everyone should assemble in a place to hear messages from *Mahābhārata* and *Rāmāyaṇa* especially, because these two books can be understood by the common man. Vedānta philosophy was also discussed. My maternal uncles were in a suburb of Calcutta, about ten miles from our house. So sometimes when we used to go there, in the evening after taking their meals, by eight o'clock, they would go to a place, assemble, and hear about *Rāmāyaṇa, Mahābhārata, Bhāgavatam.* And they would discuss while coming home, and they would go to bed remembering that. So they would sleep also *Rāmāyaṇa* and *Mahābhārata*, and dream also *Rāmāyaṇa* and *Mahābhārata.* (Lecture, 31 May 1972)

In India the principles of this science were followed strictly. Even fifty years ago I saw in the villages of Bengal and the suburbs of Calcutta, people engaged in hearing *Śrīmad-Bhāgavatam* daily when all their activities ended, or at least in the evening before going to bed. Everyone would hear the *Bhāgavatam*. *Bhāgavatam* classes were held in every village and thus people had the advantage of hearing *Śrīmad-Bhāgavatam,* which describes everything about the aim of life: liberation, or salvation. (*Śrīmad-Bhāgavatam* 7.14.2)

Temples

In India, especially in Viṣṇu temples, the system is that apart from the big Deity, who is permanently situated in the main area of the temple, there is a set of smaller Deities which are taken in procession in the evening. In some temples it is the custom to hold a big procession in the evening with a band playing and a nice big umbrella over the Deities, who sit on decorated thrones on the cart or palanquin, which is carried by devotees. The Deities come out onto the street and travel in the neighborhood while the people of the neighborhood come out to offer *prasāda*. The residents of the neighborhood all follow the procession, so it is a very nice scene... .When the Deity is coming out, the servitors in the temple put forward the daily accounts before Them: so much was the collection, so much was the expenditure. The whole idea is that the Deity is considered to be the proprietor of the whole establishment, and all the priests and other people taking care of the temple are considered to be the servants of the Deity. (*Nectar of Devotion,* Ch. 6)

Drama

Even one hundred years ago in India, all dramatic performances were centered around the superhuman activities of the Supreme Lord. The common people would be verily entertained by the performances of dramas, and *yātrā* parties [drama troupes] played wonderfully on the superhuman activities of the Lord, and thus even the illiterate agriculturist would be a participant in the knowledge of Vedic literature, despite a considerable lack of academic qualifications. (*Śrīmad-Bhāgavatam* 1.11.20 Purport)

Rituals

Vermilion, *khai* (fused rice), bananas, coconuts, and turmeric mixed with oil are all auspicious gifts for such a ceremony (of honoring a newborn child). As there is puffed rice, so there is another preparation of rice called *khai,* or fused rice, which along with bananas, is taken as a very auspicious presentation. Also, turmeric mixed with oil and vermilion makes an auspicious ointment that is smeared over the body of a newly born baby, or a person who is going to marry. These are all auspicious activities in family affairs... .We see that five hundred years ago, at the birth of Lord Caitanya Mahāprabhu, all these ceremonies were performed rigidly, but at present such ritualistic performances hardly ever take place. Generally a pregnant mother is sent to the hospital, and as soon as her child is born he is washed with an antiseptic, and this concludes everything. (*Caitanya-caritāmṛta, Ādi-līlā* 13.110 Purport)

Cleanliness

You can see from this poor class of men how their utensils are cleansed. In our school days there were sweepers who cleaned the toilets; they lived in a different quarter. But when you come to his living quarter, it is so clean that you would like to sit down there — the bed, the room, the utensils. And they also will take twice, thrice bath, then they will eat. That is Hindu culture. Even the sweeper class, lowest class. And I have seen one sweeper class, who were in Allahabad, regularly worshiping the Deity — very nice worship. They took initiation from the Vṛndāvana Goswami and followed strictly the rules and regulations. (Conversation, 24 August 1976)

Śrīla Prabhupāda remarked that even if Indians only have one piece of cloth, they will not fail to wash it every day. That is Vedic culture. (*Transcendental Diary,* by Hari Śauri Dāsa, vol. 1, p. 259)

In India the rivers are very clean and people take pleasure in taking bath in rivers. If there is a river nobody will take bath at home. They will all go to the river. And it is very refreshing. (Lecture, 24 April 1975)

He told us that in India the utensils used for cooking must be very, very clean. If a black portion remains, a *brāhmaṇa* cook will not touch them. "Even on the bottom, on the outside?" Puṣṭa asked. "Yes. They'll not touch: 'Oh, it is still dirty.' But in our temples it is going on. What can be done?" Prabhupāda told us our mentality considers it sufficient to rub dirty things with a little soap. But that is not cleanliness, he said. (*Transcendental Diary,* vol. 2 pp. 23–4)

Seeing the inability of some of his disciples' to imbibe even simple principles of cleanliness understood by village children in India, Śrīla Prabhupāda commented that, "For a Westerner to be clean is somehow a very artificial condition." (*Transcendental Diary*, vol. 1, p. 331)

[Prabhupāda said that] Western people have no sense of cleanliness. We do not bathe regularly, whereas in India *brāhmaṇas* bathe not once, but three times daily, changing their clothes each time. (*Transcendental Diary*, vol. 2, pp 23–4)

In India, even in the poorest man's house in the village, you'll find everything neat and clean; at least the kitchen and eating place is very neat. The climatic condition is also nice. Almost all the year there is sunshine. (Conversation, 13 July 1976)

Cows

If one is trained to honor and worship the cows and *brāhmaṇas*, he is actually civilized. (*Śrīmad-Bhāgavatam* 6.18.52 Purport)

The Supreme Personality of Godhead generally appears in various types of incarnations to give protection to the cows and *brāhmaṇas*. The Lord is described as *go-brāhmaṇa-hitāya ca;* in other words, He is always eager to benefit the cows and *brāhmaṇas*. When Lord Kṛṣṇa appeared, He purposefully became a cowherd boy and showed personally how to give protection to the cows and calves. Similarly, He showed respect to Sudāmā Vipra, a real *brāhmaṇa*. From the Lord's personal activities, human society should learn how to give protection specifically to the *brāhmaṇas* and cows. Then the protection of religious principles, fulfillment of the aim of life and protection of Vedic knowledge can be achieved. Without protection of cows, brahminical culture cannot be maintained; and without brahminical culture, the aim of life cannot be fulfilled. The Lord, therefore, is described as *go-brāhmaṇa-hitāya* because His incarnation is only for the protection of the cows and *brāhmaṇas*. Unfortunately, because in Kali-yuga there is no protection of the cows and brahminical culture, everything is in a precarious position. If human society wants to be exalted, the leaders of society must follow the instructions of *Bhagavad-gītā* and give protection to the cows, the *brāhmaṇas* and brahminical culture. (*Śrīmad-Bhāgavatam* 8.24.5 Purport)

Kṛṣṇa practically demonstrated how to protect cows. At least people who are in Kṛṣṇa consciousness should follow in His footsteps and give all protection to the cows. Cows are worshiped not only by the demigods. Kṛṣṇa Himself worshiped the cows on several occasions, especially on the days of Gopāṣṭamī and Govardhana-pūjā. (From *Nectar of Devotion*)

In India, of course, a cow is protected and the cowherdsmen derive sufficient profit by such protection. Cow dung is used as fuel. Cow dung dried in the sunshine is kept in stock for utilizing as fuel in the villages. They get wheat and other cereals produced from the field. There is milk and vegetables and the fuel is cow dung, and thus, they are self-sufficient in every village. There are hand weavers for the cloth. And the country oil-mill (consisting of a bull walking in circle round two big grinding stones, attached with yoke) grinds the oil seeds into oil. (Letter, 14 June 1968)

Appendix 2

A Letter to Time Magazine

This letter to the European edition of Time, *published on 1 September 1997, was in response to a lead article on American economic, military, and cultural hegemony, in which accompanying photos showed the McDonald's arch in Beijing and Coca-cola on sale in rural Pakistan.*

McDonald's and Coca-cola symbolize a grossly materialistic civilization centered on profit making and mindless enjoyment. That America is foisting this type of anti-culture on other countries is nothing to be proud of. Traditional religious, family, and social values are being crushed by the relentless steamroller of Western culture. Aestheticism and finer sentiments are subjugated to lust, violence, and endless passion for material things. America, take another look at yourself, lest you go down in history as the most exploitive and intellectually decrepit civilization ever.

Bhakti Vikāsa Swami

Baroda, India

Appendix 3

World Happiness Survey

The following article appeared in the Deccan Herald, *an Indian newspaper, on 9 December 1998*

Would you believe it, Bangladesh is the happiest nation in the world! The United States, on the other hand, is a sad story: it ranks only forty-sixth in the World Happiness Survey.

That's way behind India, the fifth happiest place in the world, and others including Ghana and Latvia, Croatia and Estonia. Research led by London School of Economics professors into the link between personal spending power and the perceived quality of life has conclusively proved that money can buy everything but happiness.

The study revealed that people in Bangladesh, one of the poorest countries in the world, derive far more happiness from their small incomes than, for example, the British (32nd on the list) do from their relatively large bank balances.

In fact, people in most rich countries including Austria, Netherlands, Switzerland, Canada, Japan and others are much unhappier than their poorer counterparts in countries like the Dominican Republic and Armenia.

Most unfortunate, however, are Russians and people in some other parts of the former Soviet Union. They are neither rich nor happy, indicates the World Happiness Survey.

Slovenia, Lithuania, Slovakia, Russia, Ukraine, Belarus, Bulgaria and Moldova follow the United States in the list to bring up the rear. The study shows that although the British have twice as much money to spend in real terms compared with 40 years ago, their perceived quality of life has not improved.

Earlier surveys revealed that many Britons thought money could bring happiness. The new study shows that such a link still exists in poor countries because a small increase in income can mean large improvements in lifestyle.

However, beyond a certain income-level that direct relationship breaks down. According to the research, happiness in rich countries now is far more dependent on close personal relationships, good health and job satisfaction.

People in Britain are generally less happy than they were ten years ago. Two-thirds would rather see the environment improved than have more economic growth and personal spending money, said Robert Worcester, visiting professor of government at the LSE and co-author of the study.

The researchers have concluded that although Britons are rich compared with most other countries, many suffer from an emotional poverty caused by consumerism and the breakdown of family life.

We are being seduced by an economic juggernaut and our personal needs are not being met, said Nic Marks, a social sciences researcher at Surrey University who also worked on the report.

Glossary

Words explained herein may also have other meanings. The definitions given are as apply to usage within this book and are thus not comprehensive.

Abhiśeka — ritual bathing of a Deity or exalted person.

Ācārya — one who teaches by example; a guru. It may refer to any spiritual master but especially denotes (a) a head of a religious institution or (b) an exceptionally prominent and influential spiritual leader.

Advaita philosophy — *See* Māyāvāda.

Ajāmila — a sinful person who was saved from hell by chanting the holy name of Nārāyaṇa. His story is told in the *Śrīmad-Bhāgavatam*.

Akṣata — unbroken, uncooked rice. Considered auspicious, it is often mixed with turmeric and/or *kumkum* powders and thrown by exalted persons upon the heads of those approaching for blessings, as a benediction.

Ārati — formal ceremony of worship, in which a Deity or venerable spiritual personage is offered various paraphernalia (particularly a ghee lamp, and often also incense, water, and other items).

Arcakar — temple priest; in South India, commonly used as the equivalent of *pūjārī* in North India.

Āśrama — any of the four spiritual orders in the Vedic social system: *brahmacarya, gṛhastha, vānaprastha,* and *sannyāsa.*

Bhāgavata, Bhāgavatam — *see* Śrīmad-Bhāgavatam.

Bhajana — religious song.

Bhakta — devotee, especially of Kṛṣṇa, the Supreme Personality of Godhead, or His direct *avatāras* or expansions.

Bhakti — devotion to Kṛṣṇa, the Supreme Personality of Godhead, or His direct *avatāras* or expansions.

Bhārata-bhūmi, Bhārata-varṣa — India.

Bhoga — items such as food or flowers meant to be offered for the Lord's enjoyment.

Bori — small edible ball usually made of dried ground *dāl.*

Brahmacārī — member of the first *(brahmacarya)* order of Vedic spiritual life, i.e., a celibate student of a spiritual master.

Brāhmaṇa — (1) a first-class man dedicated to fulfilling the transcendental purpose of human life; (2) a priest, teacher, or intellectual; (3) the first occupational division of the Vedic social system. (Nowadays brahminical status is wrongly generally determined by birth alone, although relatively few descendants of *brāhmaṇa* families are engaged in their traditional duties.) *See also* Varṇa; Varṇāśrama-dharma.

Brahmanical — of or relating to *brāhmaṇas.*

(Śrī) Caitanya-bhāgavata, (Śrī) Caitanya-caritāmṛta — the two principal biographies of Śrī Caitanya Mahāprabhu.

(Śrī) Caitanya Mahāprabhu — (1486–1534) the Supreme Lord who appeared as His own devotee to teach love of Himself, especially by the process of congregational chanting of His holy names. Also known as Lord Caitanya.

Caturmāsya — the four month period of the rainy season.

Chaddar — shawl; piece of cloth worn on the upper body.

Dāl — dahl.

Darśana — "seeing;" audience given by Deities or spiritually advanced persons.

Dīpāvalī — festival of lights, on the evening of which buildings are covered with small lamps.

Ekādaśī — eleventh day of the lunar month, on which at least partial fasting is observed by devotees. (Most Gauḍīya Vaiṣṇavas fast at least from grains and beans.)

Gāmcha — light bathing wrapper. Bengali *gāmchas* are usually bright and multi-colored.

Gaṇeśa — a demigod with an elephant head, whose worship is especially popular in Maharashtra.

Garuḍa — the eagle carrier of Lord Viṣṇu.

Gaura-Nitāi — Gaura is another name for Caitanya Mahāprabhu and Nitāi is another name for His divine brother Nityānanda Prabhu.

Gāyatrī — a mantra chanted silently at morning, noon, and night by those initiated into it.

Gopīs — Kṛṣṇa's transcendental cowherd girl friends, who are His most surrendered and confidential devotees.

The *gopīs* of Vṛndāvana are central figures in the esoteric pastimes of Lord Kṛṣṇa.

Gośālā — cowshed.

Gura — partially processed sugar, made by boiling sugar cane juice, or the sap of date or palmyra trees, into a thick liquid or solid, and ranging from pale yellow to dark brown in color.

Gurukula — literally, "place of the guru;" a traditional school for training boys in Vedic literature, celibacy, and good character.

Hari — another name for Kṛṣṇa.

Harināma party — a group of people chanting the Hare Kṛṣṇa mantra in a public place, to the accompaniment of music.

Jagannātha — literally "Lord of the universe;" wooden Deity form of Lord Kṛṣṇa worshiped with similar forms of His brother, Baladeva, and sister, Subhadrā, at Puri, Orissa; and in many other parts of India, especially in Bengal and Orissa, and now throughout the world. There is a vast and ancient culture surrounding the worship of Jagannātha.

Jīyar — Śrī Vaiṣṇava guru.

Karatālas — small hand cymbals played primarily in *kīrtana*.

Kali-yuga — the present age of degradation and quarrel, which began approximately 5,000 years ago.

Karma-kāṇḍīya — relating to *karma-kāṇḍa,* the Vedic religious system meant for material elevation.

Kārtika — the lunar month from mid-October to mid-November, sacred to Vaiṣṇavas, during which they engage in increased austerities and spiritual practices.

Kīrtana — chanting of Kṛṣṇa's glories; usually refers to the chanting of Kṛṣṇa's names with musical accompaniment.

Kṛṣṇa — the Supreme Personality of Godhead.

Kṛṣṇa consciousness — absorption in devotional thoughts of or activities for the satisfaction of Kṛṣṇa.

Kṣatriya — member of the second of the four Vedic social divisions; an administrator and warrior.

Kumkum — red powder used mainly for making auspicious marks on the head by pious persons.

Lakṣmī — the eternal consort of Lord Nārāyaṇa.

Līlā — transcendental activities of the Lord and His devotees.

Lota — rimmed cup or mug without a handle.

Mādhva sampradāya — A Vaiṣṇava sect prominent in parts of South India.

Mahābhārata — epic compiled 5,000 years ago describing the history of greater India. It includes many teachings on morality and spiritual knowledge.

Mahā-mantra — the most important of the innumerable mantras in the Vedic literatures is the Hare Kṛṣṇa mantra; thus it is known as the *mahā-mantra.* (*Mahā* — great.)

Mārgali — Tamil month corresponding to December-January.

Māyā — the state of being in illusion, i.e. without knowledge of Kṛṣṇa.

Māyāvāda — the philosophy which holds that the Absolute Truth is an undifferentiated entity, and that any perception of difference or form is ultimately illusory.

Mleccha — Meat-eater; a person not following Vedic principles; a person considered low class, unclean, and uncivilized.

Mokṣa — liberation from material existence.

Mṛdaṅga, Mṛdaṅgam — certain type of two-headed drum.

Namaskāra(m) — a respectful greeting.

Nārāyaṇa — another form of Kṛṣṇa.

Oriya — (1) of or pertaining to Orissa; (2) the language or people of Orissa.

Pan — (1) a betel leaf; (2) a masticatory of betel nut, lime, betel leaf, and often spices also. Usually pan shops are small and also dispense cigarettes and other trivia.

Paṇḍita — a scholar, particularly of Vedic knowledge.

Pāpar — (popadum) lentil-flour wafer.

Paramparā — the chain of succession from guru to disciple to granddisciple, and so on, through which transcendental knowledge is conveyed.

Piṇḍa — oblations of food to forefathers.

Poṅgal — (not to be confused with the festival of the same name) a genre of rice preparation popular in South India, where it is standard at Hindu festivals.

Prabhupāda, Śrīla Prabhupāda — His Divine Grace A.C. Bhaktivedanta Swami Prabhupāda, the founder-*ācārya* of ISKCON, and the most prominent devotee of the modern age. He departed from this world in 1977.

Prasāda, Prasādam — "mercy;" food or other items spiritualized by being first offered to the Supreme Lord or His topmost devotees.

Pūja — a ceremony of worship.

Pūjārī — priest engaged in Deity worship.

Purāṇa — "ancient history;" a category of Vedic scripture.

Rādhā — Lord Kṛṣṇa's most intimate consort; the personification of His internal spiritual potency.

Rākṣasa — man-eating demon.

Rāma — another manifestation of Kṛṣṇa.

Rāmāyaṇa — ancient epic and religious classic describing the pastimes of Lord Rāma.

Ratha-yātrā — religious procession in which a deity is mounted on a chariot and pulled through the streets (*ratha* — chariot; *yātrā* — journey). In Orissa, *Ratha-yātrā* means that of Lord Jagannātha.

Śākta — worshipper of Durgā, the female personification of the material energy.

Śālagrāma-śilā — a particular type of stone worshiped as nondifferent from Lord Viṣṇu.

Sāmbār — thin vegetable soup cooked with *dāl* and soured with tamarind.

Sampradāya — lineage of spiritual practitioners, maintained by the principle of disciplic succession and distinguished by a unique philosophical position.

Sandhyā-vandanam — prayers and rituals conducted three times daily by *brāhmaṇas.*

Saṅkīrtana — "congregational *kīrtana;*" often used interchangeably with the term *kīrtana.*

Sannyāsa — celibate renounced order of life.

Śāstra — the *Vedas* and literatures that represent Vedic tradition and are approved by traditional Vedic authorities.

Sevā — service, particularly a particular formal service offered to a deity.

Śikhā — tuft of hair kept on the back of the head by Vaiṣṇavas and adherents of some other sects within Vedic society.

Smārta — adherent of *karma-kāṇḍīya* regulations.

Smārta-brāhmaṇa — hereditary priest of *karma-kāṇḍīya* rituals, and generally a worshiper of Lord Śiva.

Śrāddha — a rite meant to benefit departed forefathers.

Śrīmad-Bhāgavatam — the most important literature of the Vaiṣṇavas, composed in 18,000 Sanskrit verses.

Śrī Raṅgam — the main center of the Śrī Vaiṣṇava *sampradāya.*

Śūdra — (1) laborer or artisan; (2) the fourth occupational division of the Vedic social system. *See also* Varṇa; Varṇāśrama-dharma.

Telugu — the language of Andhra Pradesh and Telangana.

Tilaka — symbolic marks designating religious affiliation of a Vaiṣṇava or other Hindu sect.

Tirupati — the most popular place of pilgrimage in India, situated in Andhra Pradesh, near the state border with Tamil Nadu.

Tulasī — a sacred plant worshiped as a great devotee of Kṛṣṇa.

Ulu-ulu — auspicious sound made by women.

Upmā — savory preparation made from farina.

Upanayanam — initiation ceremony that entitles a young boy to study the *Vedas* (nowadays generally performed simply as a formality).

Vaḍai — spicy fried patty made from a paste of *dāl.*

Vāhana — float for carrying a deity in procession.

Vaikuṇṭha — "devoid of anxiety;" the spiritual world.

Vaiṣṇava — devotee of Viṣṇu (Kṛṣṇa).

Vaiśya — member of the third of the four Vedic social divisions; merchants or agriculturists.

Varṇa — any of the four occupational divisions in the Vedic social system: *brāhmaṇa, kṣatriya, vaiśya,* and *śūdra.*

Varṇāśrama-dharma — the Vedic social system of four occupational divisions and four spiritual orders. *See also* Āśrama.

Viṣṇu — another form of Kṛṣṇa.

Viṣṇu-sahasra-nāma — recital of a thousand names of Viṣṇu, as recorded in the epic *Mahābhārata* and other scriptures.

Vṛndāvana — (1) the topmost transcendental abode of the Supreme Lord, Kṛṣṇa; (2) the same abode descended to the town of Vrindaban, India, situated about ninety miles southeast of Delhi, in which He enacted childhood pastimes five thousand years ago.

Sanskrit/Bengali Pronunciation Guide

Used within this book is a standard transliteration system accepted by scholars that approximates Sanskrit sounds. Most Bengali words transliterated herein are also rendered according to this system (employed in the publications of His Divine Grace A. C. Bhaktivedanta Swami Prabhupāda), even though the pronunciation of some Bengali letters differs significantly from their Sanskrit equivalents. Some Bengali words have been rendered approximately phonetically, without diactrical marks.

In both Sanskrit and Bengali, long vowels are indicated by a line above the letter representing it.

In Sanskrit, the short vowel **a** is pronounced like the **u** in *trust,* long **ā** as in *sari.* Short **i** is pronounced as in *bliss,* long **ī** as in *unique;* short **u** as in *flute,* long **ū** like the *oo* in *moo.*

The vowel **ṛ** is pronounced like the *ri* in *Krishna;* **e** as in *whey* or sometimes as in *pen;* **ai** as in *parfait;* **o** and **au** as in *glow* and *beau.*

The *anusvāra* (**ṁ**), a pure nasal sound, is pronounced as in the French word *bon;* the *visarga* ( ), a strong aspirate, like a final **h** sound. At the end of a couplet, **a** is pronounced *aha,* **i** pronounced *ihi,* etc.

The guttural consonants **k**, **kh**, **g**, **gh**, and **ṅ** are pronounced from the throat in much the same manner as in English — **k** as in *kind,* **kh** as in *pack-horse,* **g** as in *god,* **gh** as in *bighearted,* and **ṅ** as in *sing.*

The palatal consonants **c**, **ch**, **j**, **jh**, and **ñ** are pronounced: **c** as in *chant,* **ch** as in *thatch hut,* **j** as in *joy,* **jh** as in *bridgehead,* and **ñ** as in *banyan.*

The retroflex consonants **ṭ**, **ṭh**, **ḍ**, **ḍh**, and **ṇ** are pronounced with the tip of the tongue turned up and drawn back against the dome of the palate — **ṭ** as in *temple,* **ṭh** as in *light-hearted,* **ḍ** as in *devotee,* **ḍh** as in *Godhead,* and **ṇ** as in *nectar.*

The dental consonants **t**, **th**, **d**, **dh** and **n** are pronounced in the same manner as the celebrals, but with the tip of the tongue against the inside of the upper teeth.

The labial consonants **p**, **ph**, **b**, **bh**, and **m** are pronounced with the lips — **p** as in *perfect,* **ph** as in *uphold,* **b** as in *boon,* **bh** as in *subhead,* and **m** as in *mantra.*

The semivowels **y**, **r**, **l**, and **v** are pronounced as in *yoga, respect, love,* and *vow.*

The sibilants **s**, **ṣ**, and **ś** are pronounced: **s** as in *soul,* **ṣ** as in *shine* but with the tip of the tongue turned up and drawn back against the dome of the palate, and **ś** as in *shine* but the tip of the tongue against the inside of the upper teeth.

Bengali and Oriya sounds that are pronounced differently from Sanskrit are:

Short **a** is pronounced like the *o* in the Southern British pronunciation of *hot;* **ai** like the *oy* in *boy*. In Bengali, the final **a** of many words is silent.

When between two vowels, **ḍ** is pronounced similarly to the **r** in *red;* **ph** is pronounced as *f;* **v** is pronounced as *b,* except after ś, ṣ, or *s,* when it becomes almost silent.

M is pronounced as in *mantra,* except after ś, ṣ, s, and *kṣ,* in which cases it becomes almost silent, and after *ṭ, ṭh, ḍ, ḍh, t, th, d, dha,* when it becomes almost silent and doubles the consonant it follows (e.g., *padma* is pronounced approximately *padda*).

When at the beginning of a word, and after *l* and *r, y* is pronounced as *j*. After other consonants, it becomes almost silent and doubles the consonant it follows (e.g., *anya* is approximately pronounced *anna*). After vowels it is pronounced as in *prayer.*

Ś, **ṣ**, and **s** are each pronounced as in *she;* **kṣa** as *kha.*

Bhakti Vikas Trust

Books by Bhakti Vikāsa Swami

A Beginner's Guide to Kṛṣṇa Consciousness

Read this book and improve your life!

All you need to know to get started in Kṛṣṇa consciousness. Easy-to-understand guidance on daily practices that bring us closer to Kṛṣṇa. Packed with practical information. Suitable both for devotees living in an ashram or at home.

A Message to the Youth of India

Youth of India, Awake!

Your country is destined to lead the world by spiritual strength. Understand the power of your own culture, which is attracting millions from all over the world.

Arise, come forward, be enlightened!

Brahmacarya in Kṛṣṇa Consciousness

A "user's guide" to *brahmacārī* life. The first part consists of elaborate discussions and practical guidance regarding many aspects of *brahmacarya.* The second portion is a compilation of quotations on *brahmacarya* from Śrīla Prabhupāda's books, letters, and recordings.

Rāmāyaṇa

Countless eons ago, when men and animals could converse together and powerful brāhmaṇas would effect miracles, the uncontrollable demon Rāvaṇa was terrorizing the universe. The Rāmāyaṇa records the adventures of Rāma, the Lord of righteousness, as He struggles to overcome the forces of Rāvaṇa. This absorbing narration has delighted and enlightened countless generations in India, and its timeless spiritual insights are compellingly relevant in today's confused world.

My Memories of Śrīla Prabhupāda

An ISKCON *sannyāsī* recalls his few but precious memories of the most significant personality to have graced the earth in recent times.

Also includes:

• On Serving Śrīla Prabhupāda in Separation
• Vyasa-pūjā Offerings

On Speaking Strongly in Śrīla Prabhupāda's Service

Why followers of Śrīla Prabhupāda should speak strongly, as he did. A comprehensive analysis of how to present Kṛṣṇa consciousness straightforwardly, intelligently, and effectively. Features many anecdotes and more than five hundred powerful quotes.

Mothers and Masters

Mothers and Masters presents traditionalist arguments for the direction of the Kṛṣṇa consciousness movement, proposing that we should take up Śrīla Prabhupāda's mandate to establish *varṇāśrama-dharma* rather than capitulate to the norms and ideologies of secular culture.

Śrī Bhaktisiddhānta Vaibhava

Śrīla Bhaktisiddhānta Sarasvatī Ṭhākura altered the course of religious history by reviving and forcefully propagating pure Kṛṣṇa consciousness. His boldness in combating cheating religion earned him the appellation "lion guru"—yet his heart was soft with divine love for Kṛṣṇa.

Śrī Bhaktisiddhānta Vaibhava is presented in three volumes

Śrī Caitanya Mahāprabhu

Hundreds of thousands of people throughout the world now follow the spotless path of Kṛṣṇa consciousness as given by Lord Caitanya. Chanting the holy names of Kṛṣṇa and dancing in ecstasy, they desire only love of Kṛṣṇa and consider material enjoyment to be insignificant. This book gives an overview of the life and teachings of Śrī Caitanya Mahāprabhu, the most munificent avatar ever to grace this planet.

Jaya Śrīla Prabhupāda!

There is no limit to Śrīla Prabhupāda's transcendental attributes, nor do we wish to ever stop describing them. His qualities, combined with his achievements, undoubtedly establish Śrīla Prabhupāda as an extraordinarily great transcendental personality.

On Pilgrimage in Holy India

Travel with an ISKCON *sannyāsī*, including to some of India's less-known but most charming holy places.

Śrī Vaṁśīdāsa Bābājī

Śrīla Vaṁsīdāsa Bābājī was a great Vaiṣṇava who although physically present in this world, had little communication with it. This book introduces us to a personality of such extraordinary, inscrutable character that we simply offer him obeisance and beg for his mercy.

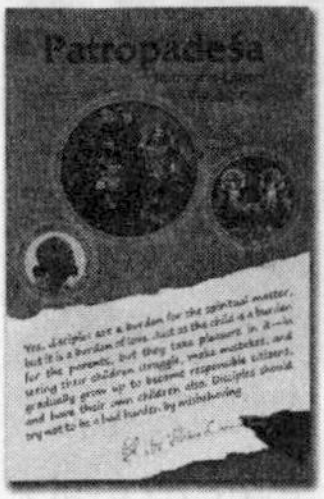

Patropadeśa Vol. 1&2

An anthology of selected correspondence with disciples and other devotees. Packed with realistic advice on how to practice Kṛṣṇa consciousness in a complex world.

Books by Other Authors

Śrī Cāṇakya-nīti (by Patita Pāvana Dāsa)

Practically every recorded statement that His Divine Grace Śrīla Prabhupāda ever made about the great Cāṇakya can be found here in this definitive edition. For the modern reader, the wisdom of Cāṇakya is nothing less than the key to a life that is in every way successful, happy and fulfilled.

Rethinking Darwin (by Lalitānātha Dāsa)

In Rethinking Darwin, Danish science writer Leif A. Jensen, in collaboration with leading Intelligent Design proponents such as Dr. Michael Behe, Dr. William Dembski, and Dr. Jonathan Wells, points out flaws in the Darwinian paradigm and examines the case for intelligent design.

Who is Supreme? (by Gokula Candra Dāsa)

Who, if any, among the plethora of gods and goddesses in the 'Hindu pantheon' is supreme? *Who Is Supreme?* tackles this riddle—not with the pablum and word jugglery characteristic of many of today's popular gurus, but with a straightforward and lucid analysis of the seminal sources of Vedic knowledge.

Bhakti Vikasa Swami Mobile App

(For Android, iOS, and iPad OS)

Bvksdigital Webapp

(https://web.bvksdigital.com/)

(for desktop and laptop computers)

To order books in print
and digital formats visit:

books.bvks.com